KOMPANY
THE MAKING OF THE MAN

Published by
Legends Publishing

E-mail david@legendspublishing.net
Website www.legendspublishing.net

Copyright 2024

Edited and updated by Edward Couzens-Lake

Front cover photo: Vincent Kompany pictured during a Belgian national training session in September 2012. Taken by Bruno Fahy (Belga Photo / Alamy).

CONTENTS

INTRODUCTION
FIGHT FOR
YOUR RIGHT

'The more I travel, the more I consider the world my home. Why shouldn't I be welcome somewhere, provided I respect the local traditions? Then that country can be as much mine as much as that of the people born there.'

Vincent Kompany in the weekly *Sport-Voetbalmagazine,* December 5th 2007.

GET UP, STAND UP.

STAND UP FOR YOUR RIGHT.

GET UP, STAND UP.

DON'T GIVE UP THE FIGHT.

Yes, he'd done it. He'd done it again.

Of *course*, he'd done it again; we'd said he would in Belgium, a great smile forming on our collective faces as we did so. It was a knowing but satisfying contentment that had come about when Burnley Football Club confirmed what we'd seen as inevitable and achieved their new status as winners of the English League Championship, long renowned as one of Europe's most competitive and challenging leagues.

Burnley's triumph had come as no surprise to us at all. Getting hired as the head coach at Bayern Munich in the summer of 2024 after getting relegated at Turf Moor, well, pehaps a little more so!

It had all come about because of the revolutionary playing style their newly appointed 36-year-old Belgian manager had introduced to the club, one which was previously associated with a more parochial approach on the pitch.

Not any more. Vincent Kompany is a man who never stops amazing the footballing world. After all, he'd already got his statue outside the Etihad Stadium in Manchester.

He is a man who only ever wants to win and is 100% committed to the cause until the last second. If he has to speak his mind to ensure the best possible chance of getting what he wants, then speak it he will, no matter who might be aggrieved at his plain speaking. He does so because he does not doubt what he says, not even for one second.

This is the way that Kompany will connect with people, convincing them, in the process, to want to head in the same direction as him. But don't mistake this single-mindedness for anything else but wanting to help others to improve themselves.

Kompany believes in those long-championed qualities of truth and justice for all. More than anything else, he is a man who looks to build bridges, not destroy them. For Vincent Kompany, it is borders rather than bridges that are there to be demolished. It is not how you look or your origin that counts, but your actions and work ethic.

Kompany is free-thinking, liberal and progressive in his outlook and easily able to convey his points. As his mother and father did before him, he advocates equality of opportunity, social justice, solidarity and other progressive themes, such as the importance of education for all, especially the underprivileged. This is why he has long committed to the *SOS Children's Villages* project and his social organisations, such as *V4K Limited* and the football club BX Brussels.

Kompany wants to make the world a better place. And he practices what he preaches, regularly taking a very public platform on his social media, tweeting about how important it is to take a stand on issues you strongly believe in, pleading for tolerance and condemning racism in all its vile forms, handing out either kudos or criticism to world leaders in the process.

'That's all very well', some will say. 'If you have a lot of money, then you are free of worry and can do whatever you want.'

And this is, of course, true. But you still have to do it.

His upbringing was positive in spirit, and eclectic. Kompany grew up in a multilingual city, played his early football at a bilingual club and spoke French as his mother tongue whilst attending Dutch-speaking schools and in touch with, regularly, both Dutch and German-speaking football coaches and scouts. In an interview with *The Guardian* newspaper in 2019, he described himself as "100% Congolese, 100% Belgian, 100% Manc", a sure sign of his confidence in his identity.

Working in England, or now in Germany, he uses his masterful command of those languages, a man with an identity that isn't restricted to borders, a contemporary citizen of the modern world.

Not that his upbringing wasn't without its problems: this wasn't a childhood spent in Utopia. And, whilst it was hardly comparable to New York's notoriously violent Bronx district of the 1970s and 80s, the population of Brussels' North Quarter at that time did not live in ideal conditions. Much of the neighbourhood had, by the 1960s, been deemed 'unhealthy' and large parts of it were razed to the ground as part of a scheme rather ostentatiously referred to as the Manhattan Project.

This included the demolition of 130 acres of the old working-class district and the creation of a new central business district in its place, a policy decision that, unsurprisingly, caused no little controversy at the time as it meant over 15,000 residents were forced out of their homes. Kompany's parents would most certainly have spoken out against and acted in defiance of the plans and planners, not in their interests but for all of those displaced residents. They were campaigners for truth and justice, a personal philosophy that soon attached itself to the young Vincent Kompany, as he went on to explain in that same *The Guardian* newspaper article.

'My mum and dad instilled this in me. My mum was a Union leader fighting for the rights of the deprived. Justice was crucial to her. And when we talk about justice, we need to remember my dad fought the regime of Mobutu*. My dad protested in the streets of Kinshasa, which saw him lose lots of his fellow students. He had to go to a labour camp for fighting for what he believed in'.

Inspired by his parents, Kompany has argued for tolerance, co-operation, solidarity and self-reliance ever since, indicative of his standing of a generation of people with diverse origins who talk forcibly of a bright future for all, just as his parents had done and without taking up the position of victim in the process.

Kompany stood up for his rights, walking the walk Bob Marley and Peter Tosh practised and sang about and whose lyrics were used at the start of this chapter. Get up, stand up, stand up for your rights. It has become Vincent Kompany's mission statement.

The more I looked into Vincent Kompany's upbringing and background, the more compelling the story became, not just his, but that and the influence of the people he grew up with. I talked, at length, to his father, Pierre Kompany, who, to my delight, agreed that no topic should be regarded as 'off limits', especially concerning the turbulent history of the Kompany family.

We talked for hour after hour, and I found I could ask him anything. He never held back with his answers, some of which nearly made me fall from my chair, such was his honesty in recalling some of the traumatic events that have marked his life. Yet, even when reflecting on another persecution that affected him and his peers, Pierre Kompany remained calm, considered and thoughtful, never prone to outbreaks of rage or self-pity. A remarkable man.

These conversations, on a more informal note, also gave me a great insight into Vincent's burgeoning life and career as a footballer, something that Pierre could relate to as he played football in what was the Belgian Congo, which then became Zaire, and is now the Democratic Republic of the Congo, a country that made its impact on the sport for the first time by qualifying for the 1974 World Cup that was held in the then West Germany.

*Joseph-Désiré Mobutu, the Congolese politician and military officer who was the President of Zaire from 1965 to 1997.

My meetings with Pierre increasingly fascinated me, to the point where I wanted to do nothing more than write a book about Vincent. But not the Vincent you know, the one who represented Belgium at two World Cup tournaments, or who won Premier League and FA Cup winners' medals with Manchester City, not even the Vincent who capped a successful start to his coaching career by transforming Burnley FC and leading them back into England's Premier League at the first attempt in 2023. Nor the Vincent who has just been handed one of the biggest jobs in European football with Bayern Munich.

No, this is a book primarily about the younger and much less well-known Vincent Kompany, one that details the first two decades of his life and his move to Hamburger SV of the German Bundesliga in 2006. A book that attempts to trace the development of both the man *and* the footballer Vincent Kompany.

To help me do this and to try to understand the man more, I have spoken to more than forty people who have contributed to his life. This includes coaches from all age groups as well as individuals who played alongside Vincent at Anderlecht and the Belgian national team.

But, going further back than that, I also wanted to bring to your attention Vincent Kompany as a toddler, a child, an adolescent and a young adult. So I also spoke to teachers in Vincent's schools who have painted a rare and occasionally funny portrait that offers a razor-sharp and hitherto unknown insight into how Vincent thought and acted as a child, which has yielded some surprising insights.

There are, of course, some darker issues regarding the young Vincent's life that are revealed here, such as, ultimately, his parents' broken relationship and his expulsion from school, the spark that compelled Vincent to change his life, a period that eventually led to him making his debuts for both Anderlecht and the Belgian national team. His new challenge was to polish himself up on the pitch as well as he had done off it and transform himself from an excellent Belgian footballer into a world-class one capable of performing on the biggest stages. He succeeded in doing just that.

One particular conversation I had comes to mind at this point. It was with Michel Verschueren, the general manager of Anderlecht from 1981 through to 2003, who told me, 'Vincent broke through at Anderlecht, and then the big adventure started: to Hamburg, to Manchester City, where he became a world-class player. As a footballer, he also gained the charisma of a person concerned about society and those struggling. He has also become an ambassador of the *SOS Children's Villages*'.

'Vincent obviously cannot give a speech and cut a ribbon every day. He is wise by nature, but probably also because of the schools and life he has been through. He has something that many men do not and never will have: he belongs to an elite. Not only as a footballer but also as a human being and intellectual. And he plays that out very exemplarily, with an eye for the social problems in society. In that, I see him going far.'

A touching portrait from 'Mister Michel'.

The latest, unexpected, development in Vincent Kompany's outstanding career, both as a player and now as a head coach, made newspaper headlines all over the world and had social media in meltdown at certain stages of the negotiations. Some championed Vincent's many positive atributes, although they were undoubtedly counterballanced by those questioning the decision to hand him the Bayern Munich top job and whether he deserved such a prestigious role based on his record last season with Burnley.

BBC Sports writer Shamoon Hafez wrote an article ironically titled 'Can "eighth choice punt" Kompany restore Bayern glories'? Of course the Belgian wasn't Bayern's first choice. Is he too young? Is he too inexperienced? Who cares?

Kompany has become a wonderful icon for second generation migrants, characterises brilliant intelligence and underlines what is possible if you aim for the top in a chosen profession and 'don't give up the fight'. So there he was. In his white t-shirt. Where he was one day, sooner of later, destined to be.

But now the real work starts. It is do or die in the Bayern Munich hot seat, for sure. But Kompany won't start to doubt himself for one second. Once a chief, always a chief, as you will learn from reading in these pages about his ancestor's history in the Democratic Republic of Congo.

Thank you and enjoy the book.

Frank Van de Winkel

This book was written as an independent project, however, it was always visible to Vincent, who was advised through Pierre, his father. Between them, they allowed me to work with complete freedom. *Kompany: The Making Of The Man* is, therefore, not a public relations story but a journalistically impartial portrait as I have nothing for, or against, Kompany and have only tried to understand him, gain insight into his life and clarify it for you, the reader.

Please feel free to share your thoughts after reading the book via *frank.vandewinkel@hotmail.com*

'Vincent Kompany, Van ket tot kapitein' first appeared in 2014 in Dutch, later in French as *'Vince Kompany, Prince des Belges'* and in 2024 has been translated, updated and edited by Edward Couzens-Lake and David Lane at Legends Publishing.

We have tried to keep the translation close to the original Dutch and French tone as so much of Vincent's early-years story was at the centre of that community and the use of language, and how the education system is described, is best explained as such. We thank all those individuals who have contributed to this book.

For details on other books by Frank Van de Winkel please visit his website at www.frankvandewinkel.be

CHAPTER ONE
DOZENS OF BOXES
OF BISCUITS

A handsome and stylishly dressed young man with a sparkle in his eyes proudly shows his pass as he strides onto the aircraft, ready to embark on one of the great adventures of his young life so far, a visit to the Congo.

Vincent Kompany, the son of a Congolese father and Belgian mother, is barely twenty years old and excited about what lies ahead.

He is many things on this day. Excited, yes. But also relaxed. Serious. Imperturbable even. And smart, his hair shaved close and short. He will soon be setting foot on ancestral soil for the first time. It is June 2006, and he is about to start a holiday that is, and will be, entirely different from the sort that so many of his peers are taking simultaneously.

How will he spend the time that this long flight will take? Will he sleep? Will he flip through his copy of the *Bradt* travel guide that is accompanying him? Or will he be reading a book about his father's homeland instead?

If he were to opt for the latter, then maybe his mood would darken, for it would tell him of a vicious cycle of war, corruption, lawlessness and bad governance – issues that have, over many decades now, left the Congo existing in poverty. Yet these are the very obstacles that have led Kompany to the excited state his mind is in, for he sees a challenge ahead, one he wants to face head-on, armed only with his unwavering sense for justice, one that is coupled with boundless ambition and a personal ethos that has always been based on deeds, not words.

Get up, stand up, stand up for your rights, remember?

In a video made for *Nike,* one of his sponsors, Kompany talks about what lies in wait for him.

'There are problems, and there will be solutions. You have to want to find them; that's my philosophy of things.'

He knows all too well that his native country is a potentially wealthy one because it is bursting, almost literally, to the seams, in valuable natural treasures. What other country can draw on resources such as cobalt, copper, zinc, tin, coltan, uranium, silver, iron ore, gold and diamonds?

Yet for all of this and the concept of a prosperous Congo, Kompany's eyes, now fix-ated on his guidebook, remain focussed on one particular sentence.

'The Democratic Republic of the Congo has written one of the saddest chapters in modern history: from the brutal political folly under King Leopold II of Belgium to the hideous corrupt kleptocracy of leader Mobutu Sese Seko and the blood-stained battlefields of Africa's First World War.'

Is *this* the country his father and family came from? And what feeling now prevails in the young man's mind at the role of his native Belgium in Congo's history? Injus-tice and anger? Outright contempt? Forgiveness? Or maybe even understanding? And yet another question arises, one that he has, no doubt, long pondered deep in his heart: is he a Congolese Belgian or a Belgian Congolese? And does he hope that this trip will provide the answer to that question?

There is so much to think about that the flight is over in an instant.

His heart may be pounding nineteen to the dozen; alternately, he may be as relaxed and calm as he has always been. We know that the plane has landed and the doors are opening, so, without any ceremony, he unclips his seat belt, reaches up for his carry-on luggage and steps down the aeroplane stairs and onto the tarmac.

Anyone who has ever been near the equator knows the clammy, sweltering heat that immediately hits you in the face upon arrival. Kompany feels it, smells it, he may even hear it, too. And he likes it.

'I like the atmosphere in Congo,' he will remark later on the *Congo WWS* channel. 'It's a loud country. Everyone sings, talks and is convinced they have something to say. And people carry on. That's what I do, too.'

Kompany has entered a new universe. Different laws apply here. The climate forces you to adopt a different life rhythm and worry less as a result. It is better to stay at home if you are afraid of a lizard, a colony of ants or a swarm of mosquitoes. And you're guaranteed to bang your head against a metaphorical wall if you have too little regard for African realities such as the different sense of time, the importance of family or reverence for palavers (patrons who offer you support) and elders.

And beware of the *féticheurs* (witch doctors) as they may be nothing more than con artists eager to exploit the young traveller. No, Vincent is determined, he will not make those mistakes.

Although he will still be regularly surprised, occasionally frightened even.

Besides, he isn't here as a tourist. He didn't board that plane to visit family, or arrive clad in a tropical suit to walk in the brousse (bush) or to look for the rare mountain gorillas in the Virunga National Park. He's here to undertake a study tour on be-half of *SOS Children's Villages*. First, in Bukavu, a border town near the hills near Rwanda, known for its overwhelming natural beauty. And then, in Kinshasa's raw, sweltering heat, he concludes the two 'duties' of his brief visit at the opposite end of the country. *SOS Children's Villages*, the organisation for which he has become an ambassador and has, for more than sixty years, been taking in orphans and other vulnerable people worldwide: all neglected, abused or abandoned children.

'My work for them is as important as football, and that became clear to me the first time I came here,' he later confessed to the Flemish television channel *VTM*.

'We took the first step in the co-operation with Vincent,' says Barbara François, chairwoman of *SOS Children's Villages Belgium* at that time.

'He was already busy doing something for the world, and we came at the right time in his life. During his first working visit to Congo, he was still very young, twenty, but already very mature. His ideas had already fully matured. For example, he wanted to establish sports grounds. He felt responsible and showed great interest in what we were already doing. Vincent was also open to ideas. And he thought he would achieve results quickly, although that doesn't come easily.'

That his ideas had already matured should hardly be surprising. In September 2003, when he was seventeen, Vincent was asked in the weekly *Humo* (a weekly Dutch TV and radio magazine) what an interview with him after his football career might be about.

'We will certainly talk about Congo, where I will have been many times by then and where I will have set up a number of development projects.'

Such self-assuredness at just seventeen years of age.

During his Congolese visit, Kompany used his name as an already well-known professional footballer to create goodwill in political and economic circles, including for the establishment of an *SOS Children's Village* in Kinshasa. In Bukavu, he gave the children and their caretakers a heart support machine, but he also wanted to experience what it is like in such a village. He will stay there for three days.

Barbara François: 'He did not behave like a star, even though he already was one. People knew him. At ministries, for example, we were let in immediately, almost at the moment itself, which is usually impossible. It takes you days to make appointments, and at the moment itself, you typically have to wait several hours. With Vincent there, we were seen in fifteen minutes. In those conversations, he impressed me with his pertinent questions. For example, Vincent talked on equal terms with the Minister of the Environment, not as a footballer who knows nothing about it. You saw that he was already mature, had something to say, and was being listened to. He also obviously possesses the gift of leadership.'

According to François, as prepared as he thought he was, Kompany had still received a culture shock in Congo.

'That's normal: he was born and raised in Belgium. And while Belgium remains among the wealthiest countries in the world, Congo remains one of the very poorest. When Vincent stayed there in 2006, Kinshasa was going through a difficult period. You saw soldiers everywhere: government buildings were extra secured ahead of the first democratic elections in over forty years. The administration barely functioned, if at all; the rubbish wasn't being picked up.

'Vincent responded by wanting to help everywhere, but that, of course, is not possible. For example, we visited an orphanage in Kinshasa that needed to be in better shape and had no long-term future. Our Children's Village project did convince Vincent for the longer term. We wanted to build fifteen simple houses where ten children live with a live-in maman. Maman means mother in French. There was also room for two schools and a medical centre. I did not see a single flaw in this young man during this trip. You can, for example, be disappointed by someone who suddenly blurts out something that does not go down well, but that was absolutely not the case'.

'He was perfect'.

Perfect. This is the Congo, remember. And Vincent Kompany is just out of his teens. It's not a weekend in Paris.

Vincent returned a year later, this time with carefully selected Belgian media in his wake, such as the newspaper *Het Laatste Nieuws* and the two largest Belgian commercial TV channels, *VTM* and *RTL-TVi*. *SOS Children's Villages* hoped that the resultant extra media attention would attract sponsors and donors for the yet-to-be-established capital Children's Village.

Why does Kompany want to put his weight behind this ahead of another organisation?

'Because SOS gives these children a chance to build a normal life in a simple but good way', he says. On the organisation's website, he explains that he hates injustice, perhaps above all else in the world.

'Millions of children in Congo are not given the chance to make something of their lives'.

Vincent considers that a downright crime. He started life at a disadvantage because '...even in Belgium, not everyone starts on an equal footing'. But he at least had escape options. He now wants to create the same opportunities for Congolese children so that they get a good education, learn values and norms, and are, in short, armed for life.

'I won't change the country with that, but they might do later on', he concludes. In Vincent's vision of society, everything stands and falls via a good education for all, especially for disadvantaged children.

The fact that Vincent's father taught for many years is no coincidence here.

What did Vincent himself expect from the trip back to the Congo twelve months from that first one? It would be simplistic to say that his main goals were to raise as much money and goodwill for the projects as possible. Yes, that was always an objective.

But not the exclusive one. Vincent also wanted to follow up on his previous trip to see how the projects he'd supported were progressing and, in doing so, raise their profiles and highlight the injustices that had previously been subjected to the children in Kinshasa.

But he remained open-minded. He knew that for every good experience or story he might hear about during this trip, he'd also be likely to be made aware of bad ones. His chances of seeing some of the more disturbing evidence of social injustice and deprivation were enhanced by the fact that he wasn't interested in the timetable for his trip being sanitised, with his 'presence' reserved for only the positively newsworthy locations.

He chose, for example, to visit the eastern Congo, where there was a lot of infighting and violence between opposing factions. If he was even the slightest bit fearful of going there, he didn't show it, by saying:

'I don't give a damn about risk and danger; I think those are unimportant details on a trip like this. Indeed, I would rather be in those places where no one dares to show up.'

This sounds more like the language of a soldier than a humanitarian. It sounds harsh and makes him come across in a similar manner. Tough, uncompromising, and even slightly irresponsible. After all, surely he should display some sense of duty as regards his safety as he was, at the time, a multi-million Euros asset of Hamburger SV, an employee of the football club who was only able to do what he was able to do because of the profile he had built for himself at the club and in the game in general? But no, he is not irresponsible, merely 'battle-hardened' in a different way, primarily from experiencing his parents' divorce when he was fourteen.

Indeed, as far as living through difficult times in the Congo, Vincent's father would have seen and felt a lot more than his son ever could have done from his time growing up in the country. Those experiences would have influenced Vincent, though, made him want to know and learn more rather than actively look to avoid them. So, he will invariably confront the consequences of what deprivation and conflict might inflict upon people. If anything, he chooses to seek them out.

In Belgium, for example, he decided to visit children who were seriously ill and close to death, not an easy experience for even those who spent their working lives with them. These were experiences that, he later said, touched him to the very core of his soul, adding, 'I can deal with that. I do not collapse; that doesn't make any sense.'

So yes, he is more sensitive than you might imagine. But he can absorb and experience the emotions they might provoke without them overpowering him.

Vincent's 2007 trip saw him initially fly out to Kigali, the capital and largest city in Rwanda, before heading westwards and onto Bukavu, situated on the south-western edge of Lake Kivu. His grandfather had worked as an electrician in Bukavu, where his father was born. Vincent was heading there as open-minded in attitude as he always is and prepared for anything – from great beauty to extreme misery. As things turned out, he experienced both, with the journey from Kigali to Bukavu immersing him into the 'real' Africa rather than the Africa as seen and felt by the tourist, an area where armed conflict is widespread.

Thus, as Vincent and his small accompanying party arrive at Rwanda's border with the Congo at around five past six in the evening, they find the border crossing has been closed for five minutes.

There is no 'official' way in which they can cross into Congo now, but that doesn't mean it cannot be done; it's just a question of knowing what to do in certain situations. So, aware of this, a member of Vincent's group discreetly approaches a Congolese border guard and gently speaks to him whilst, using remarkable sleight of hand skills, handing over some money to him.

The party now enters Congo via a bridge before, early in the following morning, returning to the border crossing where they can collect their passports. This sort of situation demands an open-minded approach to travelling which Vincent had adopted.

The Children's Village of Bukavu is ready for Vincent's visit. Many of the children there have lost both their parents due to the violent conflict that has characterised the area for so long. The village is now their whole life. They go to school there as well as eating and sleeping within its perimeter.

Vincent's visit has been long looked forward to, and he is greeted as he enters a kindergarten classroom with a song. He enters a first-grade, five-year-old's, classroom and is immediately aware of a child standing on a bench at the back of the room with his arm raised.

'How can I get to Belgium?' asks the child.

'It's much better that you take advantage of all your opportunities here,' Kompany replies.

'Try to get a good degree with which you can earn money later so that you can all quietly rebuild your country.'

A typical response: he advocates education as a lever for self-reliance and responsibility. When he joins them in their playground, it's time for a dance, with the teacher playing the drum to set the beat, Kompany standing amongst the children and clapping along.

It takes no effort for him to blend into the children's logic: he doesn't have to play a role. A little later, at the dinner table, he helps a little boy eat as if he had never done anything else: beans, rice and saka-saka (green cassava leaves).

All such interactions with the children come naturally to Vincent, even though he is not yet a father. Amongst them, of course, and to everyone's joy, there is also time to play football. There are no goalposts at the Children's Village yet, but the happiness of the young football players and their guests is no less for that. But he doesn't restrict himself to the football game alone, walking off to join some who are playing on a swing, joking with them as he gives the children a hearty push.

Vincent is clearly enjoying himself. Dressed smartly in a white T-shirt, beige three-quarter-length trousers and sneakers, he takes time out to fully appreciate his surroundings as the children run and dance around him. In the far distance, surrounded by green hills and mountains, lies the wondrous Lake Kivu and, on its emerald green water, he later recounts noticing thousands of sparkles from the reflections of the sun, observing that the beauty of nature is a pleasant change from the otherwise all-encompassing poverty.

There is a big difference between life in Bukavu and that in the Children's Village, he tells *Het Laatste Nieuws* (a Dutch language newspaper and the most popular in Belgium) a day later, after visiting a bidonville (shanty town), one of many experiences that he will never forget. In places like this, the children do not have the good fortune that those in the village share; they too will probably have lost their parents but exist, rather than live, in the poorest and most run-down and desolate of neighbourhoods. They are not only vulnerable to the dozens of illnesses that run rife in these areas but are also extremely likely to die, or disappear, without anyone noticing or even caring.

Vincent Kompany finds this visit has, as he'd hoped, been a great gift to him and a unique experience, one that is so much more fulfilling than any match victory. He will never hesitate to point out the bad things but always look for the positives in any situation. And, in Congo, he has had many life lessons. For example, he states that he has seen and learnt things he could not have known in Europe, adding, with meaning, that maybe that is a criticism of the sheltered Western European society of the time. He is also taken and will tell anyone who listens how surprised he was at the sheer physical beauty of Lake Kivu and the surrounding countryside.

This country and its people, he determines, deserve so much better.

Vincent knew that those very people needed to be the ones who were invested in the nation, local people with the knowledge and nous, an appreciation of the areas they live in who will be the best ones to 'recruit' to help rebuild the country. Much depended on what was decided in Kinshasa, a diplomatic reference to the obvious influence of the then President, Joseph Kabila. Kompany couldn't, after all, start making decisions or determining policy without the approval of Kabila. Yet, politically, he likened himself more to Patrice Lumumba, the fiercely inspired first Congolese Prime Minister who briefly held office in 1960.

Like Kompany, Lumumba had an aversion to injustice, a man whose outspoken charisma and political insights came from his family background in the Kasai region; he and Kompany shared the ambition to change things for the better.

There is one difference between the two men's characters, however. Kompany takes a much less impulsive approach than the former Prime Minister, choosing his moments to express his outrage and only dabbling, at best, in politics – and certainly never as a politician.

However, it is possible that one day, he and his father might be two of a kind, as Pierre was a member of the Brussels Capital Parliament and the Parliament of the French Community, becoming, in 2018, the first black Belgian mayor of the Brussels municipality of Ganshoren. Vincent's mother Joseline's political influence couldn't be discounted either.

Until her death in 2007, she was working at the Brussels Employment Service, a representative of the French-speaking socialist trade union FGTB. She was a woman with a very combative temperament. The Kompany's are not the sort of politicians who use their positions to mix with the rich and famous; however, status, perceived or otherwise, never appealed to them and neither did civic receptions with canapés and caviar.

Their motivations were to defend the interests of those at the bottom of society, using their intelligence to outwit and convince potential political adversaries or bureaucrats to swing over to their cause, polite when necessary, of course, but far more likely to be razor-sharp with their analysis and conclusions.

On the eve of his first Congo visit, Vincent was quoted in *Het Laatste Nieuws*, talking about his father's home country as follows;

'If I even hear the name Congo, I already feel regret. It hurts to realise that such a country has been unable to show its potential. Regarding resources, it is one of the wealthiest countries in the world, and we go there today to help children who are dying. How is it possible that Kinshasa is one of the world's dirtiest and worst-organised cities? Why are other countries shovelling billions of dollars from the Congo's subsoil while there is so much poverty? I don't understand the rampant corruption.'

'I have never been there, so it would be overly pretentious of me to lecture the Congolese from Belgium. I only know that the country is in a negative spiral that is difficult to reverse. We need people from all sectors hard at work. There is no other option. It would be my greatest disillusionment if Belgians give up hope of making something of their former colony, the country they got so much from.'

In this brief analysis, it is striking that Kompany simultaneously calls a spade a spade while also navigating a cautious approach to the problems he sees as tainting the Congo. He is clever enough not to mention the Congolese government or the head of state but subtly indicates that the Belgians not only have a historical responsibility but also a historical debt to repay in Congo, namely by stating '…the colony they got so much from'.

It may be a coincidence, but it is convenient that he refers to 'Belgians' and not 'Belgium', thus avoiding making fun of the Belgian head of state and government. Kompany formulates issues as positively as he can, ensuring that few, if any, people can read his words and feel he is being publicly critical about them or the position they hold. He could have used much sharper and cutting words but chose not to, deciding, again, that, in the long term, the circumspect approach was the best one.

Yet, as far as Belgium's former 'relationship' with the Congo was concerned, maybe he could have been harsher as Belgium didn't just 'get' what it wanted from the Congo; it stole what was needed and to hell with the consequences, short, medium and long term, some of which Kompany was now beginning to address.

But he won't point an accusatory finger at the Belgians for letting it happen, saying that '…it would be overly pretentious to lecture'. Playing any blame game won't benefit anyone now; Kompany just wants, and quite literally, to roll up his sleeves and get stuck in, although there are some who won't avoid the sharper end of his tongue.

'Unfortunately, it is not the Congolese who benefit from that wealth, but shady businessmen who smuggle valuable raw materials out of the country. Because now all profits are flowing out of Congo: the big companies there are in the hands of multinationals that don't pay a cent of tax. And then there is also no money to organise education or set up healthcare. I wish I could put an end to exploitation. I inherited that from my mother and father: an aversion to injustice. My mother was very socially committed. She always took sides with the weak'.

Kompany returns to the road and heads out to the bidonville of Ciriri, the team's white all-terrain vehicle bumping over the dusty brown and orange dirt roads. He sits in the vehicle's cargo bay, sun hat and sunglasses on, as relaxed as he can allow himself to be before, within seconds of arriving in Ciriri, being confronted by yet more bitter poverty and an anguishing statistic to accompany it: a quarter of the children in Ciriri reportedly never celebrate their fifth birthday. Malaria and AIDS are prevalent, and many children are dying of malnutrition. Dozens of youngsters and adults look up and approach as the billowing dust announces their visit. They crowd around the car. Visitors of any kind are rare here.

Vincent hangs out of the window, carefree and curious. He talks loudly and clearly, supported by hand gestures and facial expressions. He tells the growing group around the car that he has access to funds but cannot, at that precise moment, help absolutely everyone in need. A maman is, by now, standing closest to him; she must have been made aware of the visit in advance.

'You must respect that I am giving money to maman and am here to help at least some people this way anyway. If I hear that you challenge maman's decisions, that there will be arguments or if people threaten maman, then it's done immediately. Understood?'

Maman reaches out for several hundred Euros, a fortune by Congolese standards, and hides the bank notes in her colourful green paan before moving away and out of sight from Vincent's still-growing audience. It will never be enough. But at least it is something.

This direct approach is Kompany's way of reacting to a situation. He saw the poverty; he handed out money to the person who, for him, might best be able to put it to good use – in the case of Ciriri, this was the maman. Kompany always behaves like this, exuding a natural authority whilst being disarmingly honest.

The supervisors at *SOS Children's Villages* don't believe their eyes and chastise him for it; they had advised him against handing things out to anyone. Especially money, given the risk of infighting in the community over it and maybe even casualties as a result. It would be better, according to them, to identify everyone eligible and give each of them a voucher. With that, they can collect their gift without pushing and shoving.

Anyone who knows Congo even a little would not be able to comprehend why Kompany is taking so much risk by giving the money openly to someone. At the same time, so many other people are standing around who get nothing. Fortunately, the situation does not escalate, but elsewhere, it does when he arrives with dozens of boxes of biscuits in the back of the vehicle.

'Il y a beaucoup de biscuits', he says.

There are a *lot* of biscuits.

'Oui!!'

The happy response sounds expectantly from dozens of children's mouths.

'But....' Vincent cautions, '...there are not biscuits for everyone'.

Now, there is a murmur. After all, Vincent has not bought all the biscuits from Bukavu '...because I don't have enough money for that' . The hopeful murmur swells. 'Shhh,' demands Kompany, who emphasises the sound by bringing a finger to his mouth. He starts handing out the biscuits, sometimes a box for maman and then again a few biscuits per child. Initially, everything went as hoped. The children react excitedly, joyful and happy. Until suddenly, there is pushing.

Kompany responds angrily. 'Now I want you to be quiet!'

It doesn't help. A guy pops up from nowhere and snatches a packet of biscuits from the loading bay. The loading bay fence is now down, and eager people, young and old, almost storm the car. Thankfully, there are no injuries, but it is painful to see children and adults push each other out of the way, such is their desperation and hunger. One child, empty-handed and frightened, looks around desperately for something, anything – but to no avail. Kompany has, very unusually for him, been caught off guard. The contrast between the children of the Children's Village and those from the bidonville is stark: the former will always act obediently but those from the shanty town jump in, regardless of others, starving and desperate for any loot. Barbara François remembers it well.

'The biscuits incident? That's the spontaneous side of Vincent. He was struck by the misery and wanted to help. So, with his youthful drive, he loaded a van full of biscuits, intending to hand them out. He did this with the result that some adults pushed the children over and stormed the pick-up. In the scuffle, journalists and cameramen also lost some of their material, though you can hardly blame those poor people'.

'Unfortunately, Vincent had not announced his initiative to us and acted independently, so we didn't have time to react. It could have turned into a terrible drama. Vincent had not thought through the possible consequences. Imagine that children had died in the scuffle: that would have led to dramatic consequences. For him, too. That was wrong. We clarified to Vincent that you should never take this kind of initiative in poor neighbourhoods. *Faut pas le faire*, don't do it, not that way anyway. The idea of giving biscuits might be good in itself, but you have to think about how you give them. Vincent now knows it is best to consult with residents and his SOS supervisors'.

'Besides, when a Children's Villages ambassador goes somewhere, there are always crowds around them. So we need to do more than let them go where they want. Stars can usually do whatever they want, but this kind of trip is something else.'

The next day, everything seemed peaceful again. Kompany went to the Children's Village to say goodbye and brought football jerseys for them as a gift. There is no chaos here: the children all wait their turn. Meanwhile, as all of this is happening, something seems amiss in the car park. A soldier is beating a young man hard enough to draw lots of blood. No one intervenes until it becomes clear that the young man is suspected of having stolen a camera operator's mobile phone a day earlier. Kompany himself now steps in and pulls the two men apart.

'Bring him to the police', he asks the soldier. Vincent fears the soldier will kill the alleged thief and gives the soldier sixty Euros, so the message gets through. Sixty Euros is a fortune in Congo – and everything can be arranged with money.

Barbara François: 'Again, the same situation. Vincent notices that something is going wrong, wants to help, thinks, looks for a solution and says he can prevent bloodshed by donating some banknotes. Of course, that amount was disproportionate. But we have to look in hindsight. The military was hardly being paid at that time, and they went looking for money in every possible way.' Giving a few Euros, okay, but that much money?

Most Congolese don't earn that much in six months.

It always comes down to the same bottom line: when you are in a poor country, you want to help because the poverty pokes your eyes out, and you sometimes act impulsively to help make it disappear.

Especially if it makes you feel uncomfortable or even guilty about your own wealth. But it can be a more complex solution, as you need to temper your own feelings of largesse with an appreciation of your host country's culture. So, there is a learning process involved, even with regard to giving aid; it just isn't that straightforward, no matter how good your intentions might be. Vincent is learning fast and has already turned the page, taken it all on board and moved on. And he was respected for how he handled any criticism, admitting to being responsible and learning from his mistakes. But, as he might have said, "...those who do nothing never do anything wrong".

So, lesson learnt. But the brutal violence Vincent has witnessed does affect him. In Congo, the law of the jungle prevails, and it is an eye for an eye, tooth for tooth. Vincent isn't going to change that overnight. But how can you break this pattern? There is time enough to ponder that question when, after three days in Bukavu, the delegation boards the boat that crosses the beautiful Lake Kivu to the northern city of Goma. Vincent sits on the stern and enjoys the cool breeze and sweeping views. This time, he talks about his identity.

'I am Belgian in Belgium and Congolese in Congo,' he declares. 'At the same time, in Belgium, I am a Congolese and in Congo, a Belgian.'

In other words, to outsiders, he is always on the bridge between two cultures but is never quite a member of the 'club'.

From Goma, he drives west to Kisangani to catch a plane to Kinshasa. The capital is the final destination of the journey. As Kompany is about to take off with *Air Congo* in Kisangani, he sees children playing on the tarmac and a man working beside the runway in a vegetable garden.

In Congo, everything and everyone is multifunctional.

Two hours later, they are in Kinshasa, a fast-growing city with almost as many inhabitants as Belgium. There are no *SOS Children's Villages* here yet, but amongst the ten million inhabitants, there are hundreds of thousands of orphans and vulnerable children – and a great deal of them are homeless. Kompany visits two orphanages. But he does not want to judge the parents who abandon their newborn babies on the streets but, rather than that, he wants to focus on the children and show them his compassion.

Sadness drips from the walls of the second orphanage, especially when he enters the dormitory. It is small and crammed to capacity with twenty-four double bunk beds that sleep a total of ninety-six children every night – this means two are squeezed onto every mattress. Full to capacity. Vincent has seen more than enough and speaks to a journalist. He also gets a friend who is travelling with them, Rodyse Munienge, to pass on five hundred Euros to the orphanage. Munienge is well chosen for looking after the money; he is an extremely well-built guy with experience in the security sector and has also worked as a bodyguard. So he's a natural 'pick' when it comes to looking after financial matters.

The institution's director, meanwhile, needs to learn how to thank his benefactor when he is handed the donation.

As valuable as he is, visibility-wise, Vincent is very well aware that if he can persuade some more well-known faces to work alongside him, it could only ever benefit the Children's Villages and other projects he has in mind.

So he takes time out to meet with Werra Son, a founder member of the band Wenge Musica and one of the most well-known Congolese musical talents ever. Always one to press home the point, Vincent wears a white T-shirt for the meeting, one that promotes the SOS Villages but, at the same time, perhaps mindful he wants Werra Son to see he is here to talk about business rather than compete in the fashion stakes, he leaves his cap and expensive sunglasses behind. They meet and speak on a terrace, the whole thing witnessed by a cluster of cameras.

'We are going to set up a village for two hundred and fifty of the poorest children who no longer have parents,' says Vincent. He talks calmly, without faltering, in a clear voice. 'I've heard that you also do a lot for children?.'

'That's right,' confirms Werra Son, who makes a quiet but powerful impression. 'I have my own foundation.' He then confirms his support and even invites Vincent to a concert later that day. On that occasion, he walks onto the stage, shouting and asking for help for his foundation from his audience.

Papa Wemba, another Congolese musician who has been described as the 'King of Rumba Rock', also receives a visit from Vincent while he is rehearsing for a show. Vincent has to walk to the venue this time; there is no tarmac road here, but, instead of that, a flattened earth track. And it is teeming with people.

Women and men are selling fruit and vegetables as children play football around them, their voices buzzing and combining as if they were all living in some giant beehive. There is rubbish on the street, including a car wreck, which has seen its roof, bonnet and some of its entrails removed. On a nearby wall, there is graffiti in beautifully lined letters with the message, 'Beware of scammers, thank you'. All of life, as the saying goes, is here.

Papa Wemba warmly welcomes Kompany. The dashing man with outsized sunglasses is pretty much the champion of Congolese rumba music. Even when he is rehearsing in the open air, dancers infectiously sway along to the live music.

Unlike Werra Son, Papa Wemba is a talker. Kompany is not the quietest either and tries to make his point three or four times. Still, Papa Wemba talks constantly and quietly throughout the interruptions, seeing some irony in the situation they find themselves in.

'He is a child, and he could be my child,' he smiles, looking at Kompany. 'And he already takes care of children. I applaud him. I say thank you'.

Kompany's initiative has made Papa Wemba look into his own heart.

'Why don't we Congolese decide to do it ourselves? Apparently, a foreigner has to come here to set things right in our place.'

His Belgian interpreter listens intently as Papa Wemba continues, 'Nevertheless, we have the means, and we have the imagination. But it is not happening. What legacy are we leaving for our children? If we do not build this country, which is so beautiful...'

He breaks off his sentence.

In *RTL-TVi's* clip of the conversation, Kompany gets kudos.

'I say bravo and thank you'. Papa Wemba taps his heart for a while to witness the emotion provoked by Kompany's initiative. And then the cameras have captured enough. Papa Wemba takes the young footballer by the shoulder and beckons him away. You hear him tell Vincent twice more. 'It's your country'. Does Vincent not feel that? When Papa Wemba has waved him off, Kompany is bewildered.

A dozen youngsters shout that they want money '...because he is a star'. Kompany is at a loss but hands out some Congolese coins like a Father Christmas, after which one of the youths asks him who he actually is. This should come as no surprise at all. Kompany is not yet the world-famous football player he is destined to become, so he is certainly not known to the average man in the street yet. Few football players from Hamburger Sport-Verein are famous in Congo.

On Vincent's last day in Kinshasa, he travels out to the rural district of N'Sele, which is situated towards the east of the city and is very similar to its nearest neighbour, the community of Makala. A new Children's Village is planned here, but there is no sign of any construction or an area cleared and ready for building, just knee-high grass and the ever-ubiquitous cattle. It's not as if it's even the most basic of construction-ready sites that could easily be missed; the whole area that the new village will take up is set to cover five hectares. Kompany, dressed in a very sharp suit, is due to lay the foundation stone today, but that will take a while. So, this is a significant setback.

Clearly, patience is more of a virtue in Congo than in most other places. Despite his obvious disappointment, Kompany accepts the ownership document proffered to him and says, 'I have not been able to lay the first stone, but, hopefully, I will'.

His week in the Congo has, on the whole, gone well. It has opened Vincent's eyes to myriad problems, maybe more than he had ever anticipated, but he has not, for all of the sights witnessed, and frustrations felt, ever lost his composure, although, as with the visit to N'Sele, he has not been afraid to show his disappointment when things do not go to plan. He has been witness to poverty, hunger and disease; he has seen people who have been horribly mistreated as a result of the internal conflict that continues to ravage the country, especially young children.

This has all added up to him realising two things: firstly, how grinding poverty robs a person of their humanity, as they will do anything to survive, which is what he witnessed when he was giving out the biscuits, a small gesture of kindness that nearly led to a riot and, secondly, and in connection with this, how many of the country's political and cultural leaders do not care that this sort of thing is happening, that the poverty they let their people endure on a daily basis is in danger of leading to violence and even more unnecessary deaths. The 'suits' whom Vincent meets love a photo opportunity and the chance to be seen wanting to have something done, but, more probably than not, once he has left their company, they will slip back into their well-established ways.

Some may even suggest support but, in reality, see him as little more than an interfering Belgian 'busybody'. Fortunately, there are those, a growing number, who see there truly is more to Vincent Kompany than that and that his heart is genuinely in the right place; they've also noted that, unlike so many that may have come and gone before him, he never asks for money, only support.

Despite the apparent challenges, Vincent prepares to depart the Congo more determined than ever to help its people in any way he can, even if, as has now been well and truly shown to him, doing so effectively will require an extraordinary amount of patience, energy, creativity, powers of persuasion, vigilance and courage to get things moving – and to keep them moving. But, far from being deterred, he is evermore keen and determined, no matter what the obstacles are. He has attempted to follow the right path all his life and sees this as something of a moral crusade, something he *has* to do.

Vincent also realised that if he was to come anywhere close to succeeding, he had to stand out and not be seen or heard to complain or be negative about anything at all, saying, 'I was often tired, but I couldn't possibly complain about that because I saw people stumbling up a mountain every day with a fifty-kilo bag on their backs. Men and women working from morning to night for miserable wages.'

Whichever way you look at it, Vincent Kompany is a positive role model and representative for the Congo through his steadfast support for SOS Children's Villages; one of the reasons for this is that if he sees something that immediately needs to be done and that he has the wherewithal to make it happen, he will get his wallet out and pay for it himself, in cash, right there and then.

No messing about. Straight in. Like Vincent Kompany the footballer.

'I had five thousand Euros on me. I cannot help the whole country, but I had resolved to give money along the way to people who I felt could use it. Directors of orphanages, chiefs in poor villages, and small communities. Five hundred Euros is a lot of money for such an orphanage. A bag of rice costs thirty dollars – do the maths. I certainly didn't want to be seen as the Good Samaritan; it was simply that I had the opportunity to affect a situation positively, and I therefore did it. The gratitude I got back is worth much more than those five thousand Euros,' he concluded, speaking to *Het Laatste Nieuws*.

Vincent Kompany's life has never been the same since his encounters in Congo.

'I always think big. I recommend it to everyone: doing good for others makes you extremely happy. Sometimes I think it makes me happier than them.' But, for now, at least, he will stick to his commitment to *SOS Children's Villages* because there is also work to be done.

But he still thinks about other roles in Congo in any sector: political, social, cultural, sporting – but that's for later on. But 'thinking big' works. And, on this occasion, it can be seen to work in the Congo. On June 5th 2008, the foundation stone was finally laid at the SOS Children's Village in Kinshasa. A Congolese minister was given the honour and carried out the job, albeit with some pristine work gloves on. Vincent looked on smiling – his dream was quietly becoming a reality.

He is wearing an immaculate dark blue suit with white pinstripe and purple shirt, then puts on a white safety helmet before screwing an out-of-shape white brick onto another, with bare hands. It is a profoundly symbolic gesture that is a sign of progress, with the Congolese Government handing over the documents detailing the final building permit on the day of the ceremony.

'In Congo, you don't buy land...' Barbara François explains, '...you acquire a conces-sion. Before, there was a Presidential regime; now, we have a Parliamentary system. So, the President cannot donate land anymore; the Congolese Parliament has to decide on it. The land we had been 'given' by the government was also subject to a decree in which it was initially planned as a national park. But there was not even a tree on it, only a few bushes.'

In retrospect, therefore, it's easy to work out why, when Vincent originally arrived at Kinshasa to symbolically start the work on the village there, he could not do so. Consent for even the most worthy of projects in the Congo needs the signatures of both the Environment and Foreign Ministers, and, as seems to always be the case with bureaucrats, these things take time. Vincent's presence and growing status in football could, at least, be used as some diplomatic leverage to try to speed up the process and the need for the document as mentioned above, and he will, if it is es-sential, use his name to try and get things moving in the right direction.

Which he did here, albeit with caution. Yes, Vincent can afford to say certain things that you and I might not be able to get away with. But there are limits on what even he could say without causing offence and the immediate extra delays that this would create for everyone.

François adds, 'Vincent will want to continue to mean something socially after his football career: he certainly won't just become a businessman, that's clear. I do not see a politician in him, but social commitment is right up his street.'

What the Chairwoman of *SOS Children's Villages* also appreciates in Kompany is his forward-looking attitude and that he does not seek contradictions but transcends them. For example, he remarkably says little about Belgium's role during Congo's colonisation or the Belgian involvement in the assassination of the country's very first Prime Minister.

Barbara François realises he has opinions on these issues and events but says he deliberately wants to transcend the past to seek solutions for the Congolese living today.

François: 'I don't think he thinks negatively and one-sidedly about Belgium's role in Congo before and after independence. He recognises that Belgians and the Congolese in the past decades have made mistakes. Of course, there is corruption, as in all poor countries. But it is not easy to govern that immense country so full of land resources. Vincent recognises that building Congo is going to be a long-term job.

Moreover, there are signs of improvement. The Chinese are providing momentum, but not only them. For two or three years, many small businesses have sprouted up, so more people are getting back into jobs. For a few years now, there have also been new, younger ministers in power who have had an education, often abroad. They travel, realise how abroad looks at their motherland and are trying to turn the tide. For Vincent, that can only be an incentive.'

Carla Higgs, who will eventually become Vincent's wife, had previously visited Congo and the SOS Children's Villages, seeing them for herself just before the pair married. Vincent wanted to show her the country his father came from and to which he wanted to commit. When Vincent's father met his future wife, he'd asked precisely the same thing of her, and Joseline went to the Congo to get to know her husband's country.

Kinshasa's *SOS Children's Village* saw its first residents arrive in June 2011. A year later, it was officially inaugurated in the presence of Vincent Kompany.

CHAPTER TWO
PIERRE KOMPANY'S STORY

On their paternal side, the Kompany's 'belong' to the Baluba, or Luba people who were settled in Kasai, the major diamond mining region in Congo. The Baluba of Kasai have had an extremely eventful history, one that once saw them captured in huge numbers by the African-Arab slave traders from East Africa. That constant danger saw many of them flee from Katanga to Kasai, in the west of the country, where, ultimately, they rebelled against their Belgian rulers when they were forced into manual labour to extract rubber for the benefit of King Leopold II.

Many died from the hard labour that had been unremittingly forced upon them and from hunger and deprivation. Some, perhaps seen as potential 'trouble makers', were sent back to Katanga to work in the copper mines. It is a long history of persecution and of repeated fleeing but, for all that, continually demonstrating enormous resilience and determination has contributed to them gaining a great deal of respect within the country to this day.

The Baluba-Kasai are dynamic people who quickly adapt to new situations and respond to modernity. They'd initially realised that it would have been impossible to drive out their Belgian occupiers straight away, much as they would have wanted to, so decided they would use the presence of the Belgians to utilise the opportunities it might bring them. This meant sending their children to the best available schools, advancing, as best they could, to the highest possible positions allowed in a colonial society, climbing, as they did so, the social ladder. As a result, they achieved economic and social superiority over their peers in the rest of the country.

The Congolese historian Isidore Ndaywel è Nziem writes that the Belgian colonisers treated the Baluba-Kasai as 'superior' because of their dynamism and intellectual manpower. This had internal consequences as the Lulua, for example, looked on as the Baluba-Kasai became, in their eyes, 'the slaves of the whites', and even, because of this, as collaborators. When they (the Lulua) faced food shortages, they hoped the Baluba-Kasai would want to help. Still, very little happened, a sign of their growing arrogance within Congolese society, according to the Flemish historian of Congolese descent, Zana Eziza Etambala:

'Unfortunately, they turned their social condition, which gave them wealth and awe, to use it to scornfully look down on those who, for them, remained in their huts or lived hidden in the forests. This superiority complex towards the Lulua, their masters and protectors of yesteryear, is one of the elements that on the eve of independence gave rise to a race war without mercy.'

Yet the situation, which seemed irreversible, did change. This was because, in the run-up to Congolese independence, the Belgian rulers were concerned that, rather than having the peaceful changeover they wanted, the Baluba-Kasai would seize political and economic power by force – not a totally ungrounded fear as most of the Baluba-Kasai wanted independence quickly.

On the other hand, the Belgians did not want that to happen, so they put into place 'divide-and-conquer' tactics, which meant they were suddenly seen as supporting the Lulua. Etambala, a Professor at Katholieke Universiteit Leuven, commented before his retirement, 'As soon as the end of colonisation was in sight, the Lulua said, "You Baluba came with the whites (Belgians), and you are leaving with the whites. You have been given that leadership role by the whites, who never asked us."

The Baluba-Kasai had not thought the Lulua would chase them away and had underestimated the problems. They believed they had the knowledge and authority to take over governance at independence because they had studied and cooperated with the Belgians.

Did things ultimately calm down after Congo's independence, something everyone would surely have wanted? Sadly, this did not turn out to be the case. The regions of Katanga and South Kasai, with their rich underground resources such as the diamonds in the Kasai, tore themselves off from the Republic of Congo as early as 1960, the very year of independence. Belgian writer David Van Reybrouck, in his book *Congo*, considers as a reason for the liberation of South Kasai the fact that the Baluba-Kasai in Katanga were considered 'undesirable elements, invaders, outsiders, profiteers, strangers, people who did not belong.' Moreover, the Baluba-Kasai were simply not liked by the Baluba-Katanga. These ethnicities, too, despite commonalities, fought wars with each other just before and just after Congolese independence in 1960. War and flight. Rinse and repeat.

Belgium ultimately supported the two 'independent' states that came into existence due to Congolese independence, primarily because it felt that was how its own economic interests could best be served. But the Congolese Prime Minister Lumumba did not want this split in his country to become established, or, worse than that perhaps, accepted by the rest of Africa and the world, promptly deploying his Congolese forces to nullify the uprising in Katanga. However, this goal was not as easily attainable as he might have expected, and it was nearly three years later, in January 1963, that Katanga's bid for independence was undone. From his perspective, a similar operation in Kasai was more successful but at a terrible cost as, in the process, his loyal Congolese troops massacred the Baluba with the then United Nations president Dag Hammarskjöld speaking of genocide.

South Kasai's independence didn't last long either, being brought to an abrupt halt in September 1962. As this was happening, and in Katanga, thirty thousand Baluba fled in fear of reprisals from the new rulers in Katanga. An exodus ensued that, according to Van Reybrouck, created 'the first large-scale refugee camp in Congolese history'. Etambala added that 'the Belgians and missionaries deployed trucks to bring the Baluba to safety. Otherwise, so many of them would not have been able to flee.'

So the Baluba-Kasai do undoubtedly carry with them the suffering of persecution and migrations – although the cynic will note that '...this is true of more Congolese peoples and that the Baluba-Kasai have not always behaved nicely either'. That is an interesting point of view. What is more explicit, however, is that they did not make themselves popular by acting frankly and freely and declaring independence. On the contrary, while they felt that independence was the best way to protect themselves from further calamity, other tribes blamed them for selfishness, monetary gain and disregard for the rights of different populations.

On his paternal side, Vincent was part of the Baluba-Kasai, whilst his grandmother belongs to the Mushi, coming, as she did, from the eastern region of Kivu, near Rwanda and Burundi. That mixed ancestry is a great asset, as Vincent's father Pierre Kompany told me when I interviewed him for the newspaper *De Standaard*: 'I can embrace my country. Originally, my family comes from Kabeya-Kamwanga in eastern Kasai, specifically the town of Bena-Kazadi – which is also the clan's name since one ancestor was called Kazadi.'

Bena-Kazadi is located fifty-five kilometres south-east of Kananga. Pierre's ancestor Kabanza was chef de village there, the chief. Nothing unusual, family-wise, about that, though, as Kompany senior further advised, 'We've always been chiefs', further explaining that, one day, Vincent will inherit that title.

A village chief is the central authority's representative and acts as a judge, ruling in disputes between villagers. According to Pierre: 'Bearing responsibility brings with it a certain sensitivity; you have to be able to empathise with everyone. When I was a child, my grandmother told me I was too sensitive and should stop being so because I would become a chief. "If two villagers come to you with a dispute...," she said, "... you will vindicate the person who can best defend his case and talk the nicest. While the person who cannot explain it well will speak the truth."

Then again, Pierre's grandfather worked for the Miba, a mining company, collecting money in their shop network and being put in charge of accounting.

Pierre says that: 'Because there were no cars yet, he was sometimes carried around in a tipoi, a sedan chair normally reserved for whites.'

Etambala sees Pierre's story differently: 'I don't know how this ancestor of Vincent became a chief. Is it through blood relations? In Africa, including Congo, you have to be careful about that. It may be that the chief was a chef médaillé, a medalled chief appointed by the Belgians. Perhaps the man was the village chief of some forty to a hundred people and a dozen huts. In his village, a village chief was the boss, but outside it, he was nobody: compare it to mayors with no powers outside their municipality.'

Pierre Kompany says his family were chiefs from before the Belgians invaded there, so the Kompany's are not chefs médaillés.

Throughout history, the Kompany's have moved from East to West Kasai. The closest family on their father's side comes from the villages around Kananga, the capital of West Kasai, which before independence was called Luluabourg. Pierre's family had three brothers, but when their father remarried, he had another four sons and four daughters. Pierre's mother took charge of the household and childcare while finding time to cultivate a small field.

Pierre: 'She was a sensible woman who took life philosophically'.

François, Vincent's brother, was interviewed in the weekly *Sport-Voetbalmagazine* and was able to further elaborate on the Kompany family name and history.

'Our name comes from my great-grandfather. He was a kind of district chief in Congo, overseeing logistics on behalf of the big companies and so often came into contact with employees and residents. Over time, they got to know him well, and whenever they saw him, they would shout, "Look there, the company arrives!" And in time, he was thus Mr Kompany.'

In his definitive work on his country's history, Georges Nzongola-Ntalaja, a former professor at Howard University in Washington, does not have a good word to say for the Compagnie du Kasai, which had a trade monopoly that allowed citizens to sell their rubber only to that company which used some 285 auxiliaries who acted as collectors and buyers of the rubber.

They were armed.

Nzongola-Ntalaja: 'These African mercenaries were quick to use the gun to oppress villagers and to force them to produce more rubber.'

Did the Kompany's ancestor have anything to do with this?

'No,' says Pierre Kompany. 'He was a chief. Full stop.'

Incidentally, what historian Etambala writes about the Baluba in Kasai does line up with the duties that Pierre's grandfather performed, with Etambala claiming, 'The Baluba there had integrated themselves into the white dynamics, they had become a kind of collaborator to the state and commercial agents.'

Joseph, Pierre's grandfather (Vincent's great-grandfather), was undoubtedly able to climb the social ladder. In Tshikapa, the capital of the Kasai province, he worked as a clerk at the Forminière (a lumber and mining company), a respected position for anyone at the time, let alone a Congolese national, whilst Leon, Joseph's father, was a serving and active member of the Congolese-Belgian forces who served in Brussels during World War II as an electrical engineer, specialising in Morse code and radio transmissions. Whilst he was based in Khartoum, the capital of Sudan, he further served as a member of the Force Publique in fighting the Italians. So, clearly, and this barely touches upon the rich and very involved lives of Vincent's family members going back to the earliest decades of the twentieth century, this already suggests that the Kompany family were always going to be prominent in society and to have a natural instinct for leadership. Something that Pierre clearly demonstrated and which Vincent showed in his role as captain of Manchester City and in managing Burnley to promotion to the Premier League and beyond.

What does the long and occasionally distinguished, yet always visible, history of Kasai-Baluba and the Kompany family tell us about Vincent? One answer is that he is clearly, in the most positive sense, something of a throwback, a man who has, in abundance, so many of the qualities that were held (and revered) by his father, grandfather and great grandfather. Resilience. Pride. Ambition. And a natural inclination to lead. The Baluba-Kasai are, rightly or wrongly, known for those and other qualities, but, rather more negatively, are also perceived as being haughty, arrogant and dominant. Vincent Kompany is often told he has some of the attributes of both sides of the Kasai-Baluba.

Pierre Kompany is, like his son, a strong and frequently opinionated man. But he never raised his voice whenever I spoke to him. When, for example, I asked him about a critical moment in Congolese history, he referred to the fierce anti-colonial speech given by Prime Minister Patrice Lumumba on 30 June 1960, Independence Day. Shortly afterwards that day, Belgian King Baudouin called Leopold II, the King of Belgium from 1865 to 1909 and, during that time, quite literally the owner of the Congo, a 'genius'.

'Lumumba's speech had the advantage of clarity,' Pierre Kompany says resolutely: 'You shouldn't necessarily want to please everyone. Lumumba spoke from the heart and spoke the truth about what the Belgian coloniser had done. Had that speech made it impossible to live together peacefully? No. On the contrary, telling the truth and coming to terms with history and yourself just has a purifying effect. It was a great speech', concludes Pierre in *De Standaard Weekly*.

Pierre Kompany believes Congolese independence made sense. 'Surely it was absurd that we should have waited another twenty or thirty years. Independence could have no price either; there had to be no quid pro quo in return.' That after independence, the country struggled for a time, he said, was at least partly due to the Belgians who had inadequately prepared the Congolese. 'Belgium had yet to create high cadres. Very few Congolese with university degrees could run the country.'

Joseph Kompany speaks out in the same vein. He was grateful to be granted political asylum in 1975 in Belgium, but that does not take away from his stinging criticism of the former occupier of his country – while Pierre usually just shows great caution, Joseph testified in *De Standaard* that he felt 'we were not at home in our own country, it was like we were slaves.'

He had studied Agronomy (specifically the science of field crop production and soil management) and worked as a typist in an office full of Belgians.

'In the Belgian Congo, the division between the Belgians and Congolese was absolute. I did a lot more work but earned a lot less. The Flemish, in particular, made you feel you were 'only' a Congolese. Belgium did not encourage emancipation.'

Pierre's parents, meanwhile, stayed relatively safe in the Kivu region. Until 1967, his father and his electricity company prospered: he travelled to neighbouring countries such as Uganda and Tanzania to buy equipment. But in 1967, it was war again: mercenaries led by Jean Schramme and Bob Denard wanted to overthrow the regime of President Mobutu. They did not succeed and retreated to Bukavu in late 1967, where they fought violently with the Congolese army.

Much of the region's infrastructure subsequently broke down, and one man's death was regarded as another man's bread: harsh but straightforward. Grandfather Kompany was allowed to repair electrical appliances or supply new products, 'but a General demanded a bribe whenever he issued invoices.' Pierre recalls, 'My father, by nature a rebel, refused. He never got his money, and his business broke down because he had already paid all his suppliers. Eventually, he moved to relatives in Kinshasa.'

At school, Pierre emerged with the missionaries as an intelligent student and decent footballer. When he started his university studies in Kinshasa, he initially played 'only with the boys from the neighbourhood', with his dribbling skills standing out. By his own admission, he got more than one offer to join a club, although he had no real desire to take up football as his profession.

'I played football for fun and read a lot as I wanted to study.'

On one occasion, he buckled and accepted an offer, ending up being drafted into the attack of a team playing in the Congolese third division, where he not only won a championship but also ended up as their top scorer. When he later returned to his native region, he said, 'I was a fan of the Amicale Sportive Dragons club in Kinshasa, but my studies forced me to move to Lubumbashi.'

Always on the move, Pierre Kompany did so yet again. His team would miss his goals, but he had many more academic ones of his own to achieve.

But, once he had settled in Lubumbashi, he found his football boots again, playing as a centre forward with the University team, was spotted and opted to sign for FC Engelbert, later to be known as Tout Puissant Mazembe, a Congolese club par excellence who had won national titles in 1966, 1967 and 1969. Mazembe performed well in the in the African Cup of Nations Champions, the forerunner of the African Champions League. Pierre Kompany played into the early 1970s as a striker at this club. But however much he liked playing football, he ultimately opted for his studies because he feared that his football career would always be hanging by a thread because of his political commitment.

And, as many people claim, sport and politics do not mix – but his memories of his time excelling at the sport are mixed. He missed being selected for the Zaire squad that qualified for the 1974 World Cup in West Germany but not, by any stretch of the imagination, because it may have been felt that he wasn't playing at a high enough level as several players from the Mazembe team at that time, including goalkeeper Mwamba Kazadi, as well as defenders Mwanza Mukombo and Tshiman Bwanga (the African footballer of the year in 1973) made the Zaire squad.

Zaire's one and only, to date, World Cup ended in disappointment. Indeed, the team did not even score a goal in any of their three matches at the tournament, with the team conceding fourteen goals in total, including nine against Yugoslavia, performances which inflamed the ire of President Mobutu, the man responsible for changing the country's name from the Democratic Republic of Congo, to Zaire, in 1971.

By 1974, any hope of democracy in the country were long gone. Mobutu had seized a more than iron grip upon the land, establishing a one-party state seven years earlier. Then, in 1969, he sent the army into a University campus to quell students who'd been demanding both University reforms and more political freedom. Despite the military sealing all entries to the University campus, a number of the students broke through and started a peaceful march towards the city centre. One of the students taking part in the protest was Pierre Kompany. At the time, he was studying to be a civil engineer and was, in his own words, 'not violent... just a bit explosive.' However, their demonstration was in vain as the army began to fire live rounds on the protestors and, sadly, some were killed. Shortly afterwards, Mobutu decided the University must be closed.

Pierre Kompany: 'In 1967, I had started a preparatory year of civil engineering in Lovanium. I was active in the student movement and helped organise things. How does that happen? You are young and protest because the regime is heading for a dictatorship. We, too, were ignited by the global student revolt of May '68 that had started in Paris. In 1969, the army shot dead dozens of fellow students in the centre of Kinshasa. At the time, I was on the last bus coming from the University and heading for the city. But the military blocked a roundabout, and we could not drive through – that's how I escaped. I no longer felt free in the capital.'

Pierre headed south-east to Elisabethville. But events soon started taking a turn for the worse there as well.

'When students in Kinshasa wanted to commemorate their fallen comrades, Mobutu closed the University again. In solidarity, we refused to attend classes in Lubumbashi. The regime gave us a choice: either go to class or serve seven years in the army. Most chose to attend classes, but 206 students, including me, refused. We were punished by being sent to the Centre d'Entraînement de Kitona, a military camp. Officially to do army service, but (Pierre claims) it was a punishment camp.'

He went on to say they were mistreated there from arrival. For the next fourteen months, he was made to stay in Kitona, with Mobutu doing everything in his seemingly limitless power to grind the students down.

'It's an experience that marks you forever.' The only 'advantage' this internment might have given Mobutu is that the students were not allowed to handle weapons, as he feared they would be used against him. Only after sustained protests were the students allowed to continue their studies again.'

By the the end of July 1972, Zaire was going into an ever-deepening decline. Companies owned by foreigners were expropriated and given to the Mobutu faithful. Often, these people needed help understanding business management, and the consequences were disastrous. Especially when Mobutu decided, two years later, that the companies must be transferred into state hands. The economy collapsed partially due to the global oil crisis and the fall in copper prices. Many people lost their jobs, and purchasing power deteriorated sharply. Corruption was growing. Young Pierre Kompany no longer wanted to live in a dictatorship without much prospect of improvement or a decent job. The choice was quickly made. Pierre wanted to build a future elsewhere and thought it could succeed. Fear also played a part. He feared he 'could still be called before a military court, summoned as a former Kitona student.'

His plan was anything but obvious. As a tourist, anyone could briefly enter another country, but to settle there as a resident, with the rights of all the other citizens, is rarely easy. Pierre knew how to get a certificate in Kinshasa stating that he was suffering from an illness. For that, he would need care in Belgium. A professor from the Université Catholique de Louvain-la-Neuve in Belgium helped him. Pierre had, by then, forgotten the name of the 'illness'. But his subterfuge got him out of the country.

'That's how I came to Belgium in 1975.'

CHAPTER THREE
A NEW LIFE
IN BRUSSELS

Pierre Kompany was not the first family member from Congo to move to Belgium – other family members preceded him in the 1960s. He initially applied for the status of political refugee, but, in his eyes, it would take forever to be recognised. All he could do was grit his teeth and be patient. After a while, he was given a temporary residence permit, which saved him from pending deportation. But, for the first few years he spent in Belgium, the thought of being sent back to Congo (Zaire) was never far from his thoughts. For thirteen months, he lived in Brussels as an illegal immigrant, a sans-papier, recalling, 'officially I couldn't do anything… because I needed documents for everything.'

Pierre survived by working shifts in a factory, doing odd jobs, and even tutoring. Anything and everything he could find, or was offered, just to keep his head above water. But eventually, on one unforgettable day, he was ordered to leave the country after the authorities discovered that he had not been genuinely ill when he'd crossed from Africa.

'One evening, I came home, and a man at the door said I had no rights and had to leave the country. He even handcuffed me,' he told *De Standaard*. Meanwhile, Mobutu's youth organisation, JMPR, approached him about returning to the country. 'It would not have made me poorer. But I didn't want to; that was against my principles.'

He had considered 'cashing in' on his footballing talents in Belgium. He had all the qualities needed by any first-class team but he felt he could not take the risk: there was a real chance he would, given he'd then have something of a public profile, be caught and given a single ticket back to Kinshasa.

Pierre was content, instead, to train with the reserves of the second-tier side Racing Mechelen before, later on, dropping down into the provincial divisions in Flemish Brabant. Finally, in 1982, after seven years of residence in Belgium, he obtained the status of political refugee.

'I understand very well what refugees go through,' he says. Pierre wanted to return to his studies and obtain a degree in industrial engineering.

Just before he'd received notification of his updated status, Pierre met Joseline Fraselle, a woman from the wooded village of Champlon-en-Ardennes, a borough of Tenneville in the region of Marche-en-Famenne. During her studies, Joseline travelled to Brussels to visit Pierre and ended up staying, with the two marrying in 1982.

34

Pierre and Joseline shared the same left-of-centre political ideals. Vincent has since said that his mother, just as his father had always done, could spend hours debating politics and world affairs, observing, 'In a discussion, she will never let her guard down. And my dad is like that, too. I don't undercut either,' he told the newspaper *Het Nieuwsblad*.

When Vincent started to earn good money at Anderlecht, his mother made him 'clearly understand that he should pay his taxes,' according to his father. 'She convinced him to give things back to society.'

Discrimination was something she hated. When the Kompany's youngest son, François, told her that a teacher had made a racist remark, his parents sent a letter to the school management and to the neighbourhood police, with Pierre recollecting in Raf Willems' book *Sympathy for the Devils* that; 'We gave Vincent and the other children a sense of pride. They were not allowed to act on unfair treatment and were not allowed to remain silent.'

Regarding them being considered left-leaning, the political 'label' that would most accurately describe Vincent's parents is perhaps Socialists. However, as a Catholic, Pierre undeniably embodies some Christian Democratic values as well. During our interview for *De Standaard Weekly*, Pierre was more emphatic about his political positioning.

'I am, and remain, a man on the left. My examples are Nelson Mandela, Mahatma Gandhi and Martin Luther King. And I support Professor Albert Jacquard, a left-wing thinker-writer and specialist in ethnographic genetics.'

He rejects any theory about the superiority of races and peoples, adding, 'my values? There are three: solidarity, solidarity and solidarity.'

Joseline was working in the heart of Brussels at ONEM, the National Employment Service. It was the government service in Brussels for residents looking for work. She was a delegate for the largest French-speaking trade union in Belgium – the highly militant Fédération Générale du Travail de Belgique (FGTB) – in which the department of public services, the Centrale Générale des Services Publics (CGSP), played an important role.

Pierre Kompany and Joseline Fraselle settle in the north quarter, in a flat almost on the border with Schaarbeek, between the North Station and the Brussels-Charleroi canal. The neighbourhood still bears scars from the house clearance work that took place there in the 1960s, the time when politicians thought the future of cities consisted of a combination of skyscrapers and highways, nothing else. Brussels, it had been decreed, must look like New York.

A desolate wasteland and dilapidation was the result. Yet, over time, more and more of the neighbourhood was being returned to its residents, recovering slowly from the errors of the past with the city government and some associations making significant efforts to introduce lots of social housing. In addition, public spaces were improved and made tidier, greener and, significantly, much safer. Vincent told *Het Laatste Nieuws* that the neighbourhood looked 'much better' and it eventually became one of the nicer neighbourhoods in the area.

'It is proof that if work is done on the appearance of a neighbourhood, the mentality of the residents changes.'

When Vincent and Joseline had initially moved into their flat, the district looked more like something from the old Wild West. The owner of the flat they occupied was a social housing company, the Lakense Haard. They erected six residential towers from 1974 to 1978, all of which are still standing. The total of 601 housing units consist of studios or flats containing one to four rooms, with the Kompany family renting flat P on the sixth floor at number 35 Helihaven Avenue. When I visited them in the tower on a Monday afternoon, I didn't expect any trouble, which might have been the case when they first moved in. But this is no longer a well-worn social housing cliché where you find yourself stumbling over the myriad piles of dog shit, litter and used heroin syringes – neither are you accosted by whores or worrying whether or not your car will be broken into – that's if you weren't the victim of a car-jacking before you'd even parked up!

The neighbourhood might look different at 11 o'clock at night, but it is still and quiet. One of the first things you might notice is that Helihaven Avenue is still a traditional-looking street with cobblestones. The second thing that might strike you is that the six residential towers are nicely painted in soft grey paint, unlike other apartment buildings further along where the paint is peeling off. The third thing you might notice is how clean the blocks and the surrounding areas are. A street sweeper would have little work there.

If you enter the hall of number 35, you will see that it also looks neat, there's even a recycling bin for the waste paper next to the letterbox for the advertising junk mail. Alphabetically, all tenants are listed with their surnames on an outside wall and in the hall. Of the 103 flats, all with balconies and spread over fourteen floors, most are occupied by people with a North African name, with those that originate from the Congo also very well represented. Yes, there is still some work to be done. There is, for example, an area set aside that contains play equipment for children, plus a communal lawn and vegetable garden, but it all looks a little run down when I visit. However, the colourful community centre in the middle of the site does stand out, complete with its sole graffiti slogan, *Nique la police* 'Fuck the police', a strong and very clear message.

At the community centre, you can drink, talk, take away brochures on burglary protection of your home or take a hundred-and-one different courses in French and Dutch. A social assistant is always on hand if you need help or advice on anything, whilst fathers are urged in posters to take paternity leave. The community centre looks cosy and warm, and toys for most small children are always ready to be played with and enjoyed whilst, for the adults, the library is open. Next to the residential towers are some well-maintained relaxation areas that might be envied by those living in a more salubrious area. So it is a district of contrasts – tired and worn out in one respect, bright and inviting in another. I step down a wooden bridge and see, among other things, two basketball courts with a big fence around them so the ball doesn't get lost and a mini football pitch on synthetic grass that is playable all year round, which includes iron goals with nets, something I had never seen before, which all look top quality.

There is also a table football and table tennis table; a children's sandpit with play-things neatly bordered by a large fence; a large rope climbing frame and a car tyre swing. Few children in Belgium have such a playground in their municipality. In a so-called deprived neighbourhood, you find it all together and in excellent condition. A child cannot be bored here and certainly not a Kompany.

As I walk back towards the town of Schaarbeek, I notice a child-composed wall fres-co, a glowing message of hope, on which they have painted the story of the neigh-bourhood, in French, and promote precepts of life. 'La terre mérite notre respect, le quartier aussi', which translates as 'The planet Earth deserves our respect, and so does the neighbourhood.' Another one proudly states, 'Notre quartier n'est pas une poubelle!'... 'Our neighbourhood is not a dustbin!'

Local residents are taking control. There are also many new buildings, including some low-energy 'green' housing. Thus, for several years, the neighbourhood has been metamorphosing, reportedly due partly to Vincent Kompany's financial contri-butions. Yet, back in the 1980s and even early 1990s, a pleasant living environment like this was hard to imagine as waves of vandalism took place in the residential blocks of the Lakense Haard.

In 1989, the housing companies and government agreed to free up eight hundred square metres of play and leisure space next to the residential towers that would grow into the play paradise I've just seen for myself, something that ultimately turned out to be very much used and admired by the extremely active three-year-old Vincent and his equally agile five-year-old sister Christel.

An organisation that counsels children and young people follow on, and the plans are to house it in a residential tower next to the Kompany's. It'll be known as *La Maison des Jeunes L' Avenir*, the Youth Centre for the Future. The non-profit or-ganisation offers entertainment and homework help, a great mix of work and play. Quite how much of either is needed, *L' Avenir* makes clear on its website.

'The North Quarter has many migrants. Most households are single-parent families or families with more than five people. Our young people are vulnerable socially, eco-nomically and culturally. This makes them easy prey: they are absent from school, sometimes even dropping out altogether. Families and young people live by them-selves, folded back on each other, in their community, cut off from the outside world. That ghetto favours the creation of organised gangs for whom violence is the only means of expression. Young people are also caught in the seesaw between two cul-tures and usually lose their identity. They do not feel completely comfortable with their parents' mentality but don't quite feel accepted by the native Belgians either.'

Initially, it is difficult for the still-young Pierre and Joseline to survive in such circumstances. Especially when they had little money, which was undoubtedly the case when Pierre returned to his studies.

'I then set myself a time limit: try for one year, and if I passed most of the subjects, I was allowed to continue.'

Pierre's strict target for himself worked out. He is allowed to skip the first year; the other years, he spreads over two more – except for the final year. He studied for five years at the *Institut Supérieur d'Ingénieurs industriels de Bruxelles*, obtaining a degree in Industrial Engineering Aerodynamics. During those years, he took classes during the day and worked as a taxi driver on weekdays from around six in the evening until just about midnight. 'It was hard. When you are young, you never keep that sort of commitment up. You can maintain that discipline only when you are older and have a wife and children.'

On 15 March 1984, Christel was born, the first child in the family. Vincent arrived two years later, on 10 April 1986, at the Edith Cavell Hospital in Uccle, near Brussels. Pierre will have to work even harder now and do whatever it takes to help support his growing family.

Historian Zana Etambala reflects on Pierre's story: 'There are few Congolese men who would work below their degree level. The outlook of the Congolese is usually: "I am a civil engineer, I am a doctor... so I only want to work at my level." Not Pierre; he became a taxi driver to earn a living. There are contrasting stories about fathers of top Congolese-Belgian footballers, but Pierre kept his cool and remained grounded.'

Two children became three on 28 September 1989 when François was born and, whilst many young parents called upon the 'Bank of Mum and Dad' to lend a hand, it was obviously more difficult for Vincent's parents to do that. Pierre's family were mainly in the Congo – although he had relatives elsewhere in Belgium – and Joseline's parents lived more than a hundred and twenty kilometres away in the province of Luxembourg.

The children sometimes went to stay with Joseline's parents and were always happy to do so. Their maternal Grandfather, Jean Fraselle, was a gendarme and, in the Sixties, an amateur footballer. He was a man who could look back on a memorable achievement: he played with his club Royale Étoile Sportive Champlonaise from 26 September 1965 to 5 November 1967, fifty-six matches in a row without losing whilst, in 1966, he was a member of the team that won promotion to the second (provincial) division.

Whilst studying, Pierre Kompany picked up the thread of a possible invention that he had been thinking about for some time. His idea involved a wind turbine that turns even when the wind blows in the opposite direction, as well as functioning in water. The windmill worked with four horizontal, curved blades with concave and convex sides. The concave side caught the wind and set the mill in motion. Thus, a rotational movement was created because the convex side of the blades offers less resistance to the wind.

This was already well known, explained the newspaper *De Morgen*. But Kompany mounted the blades so that wind blowing against one blade was diverted through that blade as if they were inside a hollow tube. There, the air meets the next blade perpendicular to the previous one. That wind gives it an extra push, increasing its efficiency significantly.

The mill was environmentally friendly, silent and non-polluting. Moreover, it cost far less than traditional mills, and both wind and water can drive it. Pierre hoped that developing countries would also take advantage of it, for example, to pump water or to supply electricity. His self-confidence got extra publicity during his internship at Sorelec in Orléans, France, a company specialising in environmentally and energy-friendly technology. Pierre worked there on a heating system with water that was based on solar panel technology. His ideas were well received, and his final paper was the best of his year. But turning it into a commercial success was difficult. 'No, that doesn't frustrate me,' Pierre told me, 'if you are not a philosopher in life, you are an idiot. The invention has not destroyed my life and has taught me a lot. Nor did I ever want to beg on my knees to only get little pennies for it.'

Eventually, he decided to teach mechanics, technology and technical drawing.

In 1988, when he was forty and Vincent just two, Pierre graduated and worked as a general mechanics teacher in the secondary *Ecole des Arts et Métiers* of Erquelinnes, in the province of Hainaut, on the border with France. He, his pupils, and fellow teachers built his first water windmill there. But the distance from Brussels made his journey to work tiring, and he spent around two and a half hours commuting every day.

A year later, Pierre got a new job in Diegem, just outside Brussels, leaving teaching for the US courier multinational, DHL. As well as the considerable savings on his travel time, he was now in a job that paid him more money than the previous one. At first, he was a stock manager. Then, three years later, he moved up to the quality manager role in the aircraft spare parts department, where he managed a team of ten people. He also spent a lot of time travelling: he might be in Stockholm one day, London the next and, a week later, somewhere in the United States. But, for all that, he was at the beck and call of the company 24/7 and was sometimes called at midnight to go and carry out a specific task. He was beginning to feel that his work came at the expense of his family, there was a problem. Especially as he wanted to fully fulfil his responsibilities as a parent. Combining her job with caring for the children was also challenging for his wife, especially when Pierre had to go on business trips. Eventually, the issue came to a head, although not through Pierre's making, as, in 1996, when Vincent was ten, DHL fired Pierre Kompany. He received a 'hefty' severance but regretted his dismissal, although he claimed that his world did not 'collapse' because of it. Perhaps, he goes on to say, he was not accommodating enough for them. Pierre remained unemployed for the next four years.

He did, however, fall back on his invention and did everything he could to find a company that would put his mill on the market. But that cost money. He spent €7,500 on a prototype that he presented at the Geneva Invention Fair and diligently continued working on an improved version. Gold medals were won at invention fairs in Brussels (1997) and Geneva (1998) which reinforced his conviction that his project could succeed, but, frustratingly, a large-scale commercial application still failed to materialise. However, he founded the company Eco-Turbines and continued to promote his concept. But it was not all bad news as Rochefort invested €500,000 into the project and later installed two turbines.

Financially, things picked up when Pierre started teaching again at the *Ecole des Arts et Métiers*. Not in Erquelinnes, but this time in Brussels, a few minutes by tram from their home on Helihaven Avenue. It was a surprising choice because engineers as skilled as Pierre had other options. But not only that, *Arts et Métiers* was not immediately known as the most accessible school for teachers. Teaching and dealing with young people was what Pierre loved to do, although unlike previously, he wasted less time on commuting. Saving time was vital for a parent with three children, especially during the three-and-a-half months of holidays each year.

The children in the Kompany-Fraselle family are very active after school hours. They play outside, meet many other children as they do so and get involved with and play many different sports. There is no question of them just staying inside their flat or just 'hanging out' in and around their block. Vincent explained that all of them were very sporty because of their parents, who had encouraged them to do as much as possible.

Christel was requisitioned to be the goalkeeper whenever the brothers played one-on-one matches. In the beginning, this was done with a plastic or foam rubber ball, which they could also play with inside their flat because it did not make any noise or do much damage. So it was in this active, sociable, environment that Vincent's parents looked to guide their children's choices regarding their free time and bring them into as much contact as possible with their peers in other neighbourhoods and communities. They often chose to travel over to the north-western municipalities, where there was more greenery and more Dutch spoken, an easy enough thing to do as, by public transport, the children could be there and involved in a game of something within fifteen minutes.

They soon became members of the Dutch-speaking Scout group in the village of Ganshoren. Vincent was a Scout between the ages of seven and twelve, enjoying not only what Scouts were expected to do, but also what they were expected not to do. For the young Vincent Kompany, this involved climbing up onto the roofs of various buildings, with Vincent recalling, 'We did everything that was dangerous and were not allowed to do.' Pierre approved of their joining the Scouts as he thought it was important for children to be members of a youth movement because it taught them the social skills that would be so important to them later on in life. Of the three Kompany children, Christel turned out to be the most sociable, admitting as much to the newspaper *Le Soir,* saying, 'I am slightly more impulsive than Vincent, less closed too. He is more cautious in his dealings.'

That scout group, known as Knights of St Martin, called their premises 'the little farm' after the origins of the building. There was a vast wasteland beside it whilst, immediately behind the building, there were plenty more green fields and room to play in. In that quiet area of Leopold Demesmaekerstraat, you could easily imagine you were deep in the countryside.

Sander 'Bison' Raemdonck, who remained a Scout group leader until his early twenties recalls; 'When I joined, at around the age of eight, Vincent was already a member. All the scout groups were mixed, but Vincent was not a guy who had much contact with the girls; he was less concerned with that then. We met every Sunday from two until five, then once a month from ten to five. In our group, there were twelve to fourteen of us. Every year we went on a camp, and he was there a number of times, Vincent happily wearing the uniform, a beige shirt and tie.'

'Vincent was the odd man out, especially in the beginning. He was one of the first black children to go there, and you could also hear that he was of French-speaking origin. Of our little group, most of the boys went to the same school. That couldn't have been easy for Vincent because he went to a different school. But he was certainly included. He wasn't a cocky kid, more of a loner. Was he pleased to come? I have contrasting feelings about that. In the beginning, it was at his parent's request, although he was certainly not reluctant, but whether he really looked forward to it, I'm not so sure.'

'We played many ball games, which Vincent enjoyed, as well as tug-of-war and pot-stomp. He was more out of his comfort zone if it were other games. The same applied to games that involved language. Vincent would get worked up if there was cheating or if he was falsely accused of something. He also quickly felt he was being mistreated. He could not handle that very well and sometimes behaved so angrily that he was scolded by the leaders.'

'I remember an incident at camp in the Ardennes. We went into the woods with the group, and Vincent arrived a bit later. When we returned, all our air mattresses were flat... apart from his. So we suspected he had done it, but he denied it, and we never knew who caused it.'

'I recall that his sister Christel was a very busy petite mademoiselle. If she saw a tiny spider, she started screaming. And François, who probably joined at the same time as his brother, could go down very theatrically during a football match like professional footballers do when they want a penalty kick. We made it clear to him that things were not that serious, but the Kompany's didn't understand that we took football less seriously.'

The Kompany children often went to the Laarbeek forest on holiday – to the village of Jette, which was teeming with play facilities. In the summer holidays, and for seven or eight years, they also drove to La Ciotat, a French seaside resort near Marseille. The family did not have much money, says Vincent in *Het Laatste Nieuws*, but they lived like a 'normal family'. He saw these trips as a highlight of the year, especially as spending time with his father meant lots of exercise, especially swimming, whilst, with his mother, he went to museums and did some general sightseeing. At that time, he had little interest in cultural tourism, but recalls; 'I know the Pont du Gard, the Roman churches and the lavender fields of the Provence.'

Vincent was also charmed by archive TV footage of Olympique Marseille, who in his childhood were one of Europe's top sides, winning the very first rebranded Champions League under the leadership of the Forest-born (Forest is a municipality of Brussels) coach Raymond Goethals in 1993. At the club, the legendary Marcel Desailly was an outstanding central defender and equally adept as a defensive midfielder. The family Kompany made plenty of trips to the stadium to watch matches and, whenever they could, training sessions with Vincent getting photographs of himself with Robert Pirès and Ibrahim Bakayoko.

Vincent also particularly enjoyed watching westerns on TV, with macho cowboys overcoming assorted villains very much to his liking, but especially, the horses. He was not the only Kompany child who loved horses, so it was a pity for him and his siblings that horse riding was so expensive. He is also a lover of *The Godfather* film series, the Mafia epics that he watched at the Kinepolis cinema paradise in Brussels. Then, later on, and as an older high school student, he became hooked on the North American Basketball League, so much so that he scheduled his studies through the night to allow him to watch the NBA games at around three AM.

It was not out of a love for the area that Pierre and Joseline rented a flat near Brussels' North Station – it was basically what they could afford. However, the rent was capped, which allowed the family to make ends meet and put things into perspective. Clearly, their problems were not as bad as others were experiencing, so they were grateful for what they had.

But no matter how much humility you display, it still wasn't an ideal neighbourhood to have three children growing up in. But at least Vincent's parents found something positive in that; their children were living with and growing up alongside people from very diverse backgrounds, and confronting the poverty that came with this was something his parents found very important. Vincent's mother emphasised the importance of becoming familiar with and learning new languages. She had seen, day after day, how difficult it was for monolingual unemployed people to find work. Therefore, from early on in their lives, the Kompany children were encouraged to be bilingual, with Pierre also taking Dutch evening classes.

In an interview with *Humo* magazine, Vincent recalled, 'I was lucky to grow up in different cultures. That's how you get an open mind. The more cultural baggage you have, the more tolerant you become. If you confine yourself to your room, you assume your rightness. The most important thing in their upbringing is that children develop a personality and develop their talents as much as possible. Parents should insist on politeness, on respect, but not submission to authority figures, on citizenship, on being sporty and making an exemplary effort at school.' Assertiveness is often a characteristic of the verbally articulate and the sharp-tongued Kompany was no exception: talking, discussing and forming an opinion were instilled into him and his siblings.

Vincent: 'If there is something I disagree with, I say it. I won't be silent to anyone.'

Is what he thinks typical of the Kompany's is my subsequent question to Pierre.

'We don't have any complexes. Each individual is at our level. The children are also taught self-confidence, belief in their abilities, and pride in who they are and their origins. I told them family stories every night at Christel's bedside and Vincent and François's bunk bed. They needed to know what happened.'

'Like the story of my father, who refused to pay bribes. He never got the money he was entitled to, and his business broke down. He eventually moved to Léopoldville, now Kinshasa, and died there.'

On their bedroom wall, the brothers François and Vincent put up football posters of AC Milan, Marseille and Barcelona. They made it a game of supporting each other's club's biggest enemy: if one was for Barcelona, then the other was for Real Madrid. Or if one was for Inter, then the other followed AC Milan.

In an interview for the weekly magazine *Story*, François confirmed the passion of the Kompany's: 'We inherited that from home: our parents wanted us to learn to stand our ground. We are also stubborn. We got that from our mother, who comes from the Ardennes, and they have that trait there. We want to make it in life.'

Vincent agrees wholeheartedly in the weekly magazine *Knack*: 'According to the people from the region, I have some typical traits: I am a 'biter', a hard worker. Actually, the stereotypical image of the Ardennes coincides with that of the Flemish people, the Dutch-speaking. Only we are also stubborn.'

Pierre recognises that injustice shocks Vincent, although his son still attributes that trait mainly to his mother. 'Like my brother…,' Vincent believes, '…but one trait I definitely have from him is that I can't stand injustice. That makes me furious. I often got in trouble at school for standing up for someone.'

He certainly did. Sometimes, Vincent would even fight about it. But usually, he is very calm, remarkably calm even, claiming; 'I am someone who rarely fusses about things.' Those who don't know better would mistake it for languidness or lameness.

'I am cool, relaxed and never radiate an overdose of energy. That's something my mother can get annoyed by,' he tells *Het Laatste Nieuws*. He then adds that everything had to be done quickly for her, while '…I always want to show that the situation is under control. Even when it is not at all. My composure is undoubtedly hereditary: my father and uncles are like me. The women, in turn, are the opposite.'

Vincent may (or may not) be a 'biter'. But he is also a thinker, as he explains when talking to *Humo*. 'I am constantly weighing up all the pros and cons. I have great pride and a big ego. Sometimes that is a negative trait, but it also helps you. I am cautious, and therefore, I reduce the chances of someone taking advantage of me.'

Kompany is fairly macho but, simultaneously, a sensitive boy who dreams of an ideal world... but he soon discovers that the reality is very different.

'Ideally, I would love to be a flower power boy, but I had to find out quite young that the world is full of hypocrisy.'

Mother Joseline did not gloss over Vincent's sensitivities and weaknesses. When asked why he was often late for appointments, she replied in the weekly *Sport-Voetbalmagazine* that, in her view, it was out of absent-mindedness.'

'Getting up was always a big deal for him.'

She admits that Vincent '...has always been lazy, sloppy even. But, in his defence, it should be said that the Kompany's are not exactly people who crawl into bed at nine in the evening.' But absent-minded he most certainly is, she stresses, calling him a 'dreamer'.

'It often happened that he would run into a pole in the street because he was once again lost in thought.'

Nor, as it turns out, did a week go by without Vincent forgetting to take his football boots to training or leaving his kit in the dressing room.

It is absent-mindedness, she stresses again, not a lack of commitment, as Vincent never perceived punctuality as necessary in his upbringing. Also it has nothing to do with nonchalance.

'I look nonchalant, but that is not who I am. I am a quiet boy, but that is something else. It doesn't mean I am constantly dreaming uninterestedly or being a slob. My room, for instance, always looks pretty neat.'

Pierre and Joseline raised their children quite strictly, with clear rules about what could and could not be done, but at the same time, Christel, Vincent and François were given a lot of freedom of opinion and respect for their parents' personalities.

Pierre: 'We let them do what they felt like. That was also his mother's wish.'

And of his children, Pierre adds; 'They are here because we wanted them, so we must guide them well. We also followed our children closely because you never know what happens in such a big city.'

Vincent also recalls: 'They were worried about us, but because I grew up in a multicultural neighbourhood, I have much less prejudice,' he claimed, speaking to the daily *De Tijd*.

During holidays, the children often attended sports camps, with Vincent becoming an interschool champion volleyball player. But he also roller skated, rode horses and tried kayaking whilst, at school – predictably he enjoyed participating in all sorts of competitions. Although when he joined Anderlecht, they preferred to see him train with his mind entirely focused on football rather than compete in other sports with his school teams. However, Vincent did not let that get to him; he knew he was already indispensable to Anderlecht and had no fear of reprisals. He was also pleased to carry on going out with his school friends.

François and Christel were also sporty: they competed in athletic events, although François, who also played football, soon gave that up. Vincent had already joined a football club by the time he was six, but until then, according to Pierre, he was more into cycling and skateboarding.

The children's many extracurricular activities demanded a driver, especially to pick them up in the evenings, as taking the Metro or a tram back then was considered too risky. So, after work, Pierre spent a lot of time in his car on certain days of the week; this included taking François to KV Mechelen, Vincent to Anderlecht and Christel to the athletics club in Brussels.

Vincent, like François, also played football around the flats where they lived. When he was six and seven, he regularly played there alone. At that age, he was usually one of the youngest children there, and sometimes, he looked somewhat lost. Later, he played for a local team on Sunday mornings, a club consisting solely of Congolese players. He was already taking a very professional approach to his regular games, being the only one in the team with studded boots.

His enrolment in that football club ended up providing an excellent solution to how best to bridge the age difference with the neighbourhood boys and his shyness: he was now learning the basics of football in the process and, by the age of six, Pierre had already got him a membership card for the Royal Sporting Club Anderlecht.

Vincent then combined football and athletics, with Anderlecht referring him to the Excelsior Brussels club a few kilometres from his home, at the Victor Boin stadium in Laken, where he competed during football's close season three times per week: on Wednesdays, Fridays and Saturdays. His athletics trainer, the amiable Francis De Buyst, recalls Vincent signing up with his mother and father.

'His father was ambitious, but both parents were simple people with a heart for children. They were very strict and demanded discipline and politeness. Il faut dire merci, the children were told... You have to say thank you. Vincent made an undeniable impression. 'I remember him as a polite and respectful lad who did not apply himself to just one event but sampled all athletics disciplines, which was best for his overall development.'

Vincent not only competed in the traditional running events, but also participated in the long jump and javelin. He became one of the best athletes at the club due to his sheer willpower to do well. He succeeded at everything he did and achieved good results in all the competitions.

Vincent also quickly picked up his trainer's tips, then applied them swiftly to whichever discipline they related to.

His sister Christel was perhaps even more talented in athletics than Vincent, or so Francis De Buyst believes.

'She quickly made her way to the top of the Belgian youth group, but had to drop out with knee problems. She had the talent to become an elite athlete. We had a lot of fun with her: she liked to tease. My mother tongue is French, and I speak Brussels-Dutch. She often laughed at my language antics and corrected me. She also wanted to win but showed a little less doggedness than Vincent.'

However, at around 12, Vincent quit athletics as he found it impossible to combine the training with football, but he is pleased that athletics made him more robust physically.

Back in the North Quarter, the neighbourhood is changing, it no longer resembles the Bronx from the 1970's, but neither has it become an idyllic paradise. Kompany admits that he did not see people from his neighbourhood who were successful at anything. He found that hopelessness was very depressing.

Perhaps it explains why Vincent had to find his ideal role models elsewhere, thousands of kilometres away, in the form of Muhammad Ali and Pelé, two men who reached the top despite enduring, like Vincent, modest living conditions in their youth.

'When I see the road they travelled, I knew I could emulate that.'

What also helped Vincent on the road to success was, as he described himself in *Humo* magazine; '...an almost arrogant dose of self-confidence. I am who I am and have never imposed limits on myself.'

'You don't get it handed to you on a platter – success depends on yourself and whether you develop your talents. Everyone has the opportunity to work their way up, only here it is not easy.'

So, he is not engaging in fatalism. Taking destiny into your own hands and seizing opportunities is what it comes down to. However, he glosses over some of his more painful experiences in the neighbourhood.

'I have experienced things, but I don't see the point in discussing it. Because I don't want to be a victim.'

He goes on to say how his physique has helped him.

'If anyone insulted my friends or commented about my brother or sister, they had to stay away from me. Congolese, Moroccans, Turks, we all lived in harmony. You observed daily that the differences between people have nothing to do with up-bringing. It was a matter of being given opportunities.'

Vincent's best friend, Rodyse Munienge, was nine when they met, one year after he and his single mother with five children had come to Belgium from Kinshasa. He lived at number 33 on the 11th floor, Vincent at number 35 on the sixth. Even then, according to him, Vincent had a habit of walking around in his '...famous Anderlecht tracksuit', he told *Sport-Voetbalmagazine*. Everyone called Vincent 'Anderlecht', by the way.

Munienge thinks Vincent had one big flaw:

'He always wants to be correct. People sometimes got annoyed when he stubbornly wished to have the last word. I often stopped talking during a conversation because I knew it was a wasted effort. When the big boys of the neighbourhood came to our little square and told us to give them our ball, he went up against them.'

Vincent looks back at happier times in *Humo*.

'Compared to most comrades in my neighbourhood, I had a super childhood. My parents did everything they could to keep us, the three kids, off the street. In fact, we were almost only at home to sleep. We went to good schools, to sports clubs, to the scouts.'

At almost three years of age, Vincent took his first lessons at school in Miss Inge's reception class at Het Klavertje 4. At that tender age he dreamt of becoming a fireman, then a little later, he changed his mind by writing 'engineer or the army' in an excercise book – things were ultimately to end up very differently for Vincent however.

CHAPTER FOUR
THE SMART AND PLAYFUL STAR AT SCHOOL

Vincent did not have to walk far on his very first day of school, it was just across the street from his parents' flat.

'Vincent knew what he wanted: if he had a goal in mind, he went for it. He was also a little rascal,' says Inge Devos, his teacher in the reception class. 'He sometimes pulled a bad boy prank, but he was never really naughty.'

He stayed for the entirety of that first school year then started the first kindergarten class with new teacher Miss Ingrid, before moving to another school the following year.

Pierre Kompany remembers: 'Pre-school care and Kindergarten was offered by Het Klavertje 4, but primary education wasn't available. We waited until a place became available at the Dutch-language-speaking school Maria-Boodschap, which Christel already attended. It's not that my wife and I preferred a Catholic education.'

There were also Flemish children as well as French-speakers in his class.

Teacher Inge: 'Vincent was active and sociable. His mother tongue was French, like many of the children in the class, but learning Dutch went reasonably smoothly for him. When I compare his face now with that of then, it strikes me that it hasn't changed much. As a matter of fact, he was also always elegant and smartly dressed.'

The new school wasn't as close to the Kompany home which, at around two kilometres away, was too far to go on foot for the young children, meaning their mother took them there by public transport. This journey involved crossing the busy Place Sainctelette, which was near the former Citroën garage and the Brussels-Charleroi canal on the border of the village of Sint-Jans-Molenbeek. The school is in the lively Dansaert neighbourhood, replete with its many fashion shops, wedged between two houses and secured with large double gates during the day.

Vincent's Kindergarten teachers constantly praised the atmosphere in what was nicknamed 'mini-Mabo', which had relatively small classes of no more than twenty children, all of whom got to know each other well, with many also playing at each other's homes. This meant, in turn, that the parents all got to know one another too, with many firm and long-lasting friendships forming as a result. One of the teachers, Jeanine Borremans, now retired, watched 'Vincent-ke' or little Vincent, a name she pronounces in French, for about ten years, from first Kindergarten through to sixth grade.

'Vincent was no small fry, he was quite big for his age,' she recalls. 'He was no longer a toddler but a pre-schooler who could already do everything except sit still for a long time. He did listen well and always did what I asked... never less than that. In fact, you had the feeling that he only did it to please you. When he was done, he soon became restless. "Go and play with the ball outside," I sometimes told him, even during class. "Play with the ball; swing your legs and arms in the air!" And when it was time to return inside, I would tap my right hand with my wedding ring on the window... He was a special one.'

'Vincent liked to compete with the girls...,' she says, '...and they didn't let him do it. The actor was in him, even then, with all his charms. He could get angry all of a sudden, though. And he was careless sometimes. Then I'd say: 'Vincent-ke, don't throw your bag down there like that!" He was the étoile (a French word which means the star) because of his size and energy; he could also be so sweet. In gym class, everyone was already looking at him because he was a special one, you know.'

At the time, the Brussels school did not have many children with a background like Vincent's, but Miss Borremans doesn't think Vincent was ever teased. This was a great strength of Brussels and something that lay at the very heart of the city, one that is proud to have a long-established multicultural society.

Miss Jeanine kept a close eye on Vincent's progress, which was easy enough as the second-year Kindergarten class was right next to her class.

'I would see him standing outside the classroom door, and I would say, "Well, Vincent-ke, have you said something you maybe shouldn't have again?"

'"Yes!" he'd admit. Although he wouldn't have done that with me because he knew how far he could go.'

Jeanine Borremans also observed; 'We organised socio-cultural activities and, at first, he was always there. We went to the theatre or museum, dressed up, modelled, played football... later, between one and half past one, he left with his mother, often with a long face because, at six years old, Vincent joined Anderlecht football club to train.'

'When he played football in the playground, he couldn't stand losing, and sometimes he would walk away angrily and go and sulk on a bench. François was much calmer; he didn't show the same abandon, although he was also a sweet and good boy. Christel also stood out less than Vincent; she was more of a leader-type figure who'd happily organise and encourage the other children to play rather than, as Vincent would, wanting to be at the centre of action all of the time. '

Jeanine Borremans also saw Vincent outside of school on several occasions. For example, Vincent's father once gave three teachers grandstand tickets for an Anderlecht match, and she was there, as was Master Johan of the first grade who Vincent sometimes ate his sandwiches with at lunch time. She also attended training and practice matches, where Vincent would often come over and give her a hug. She also wouldn't miss watching a Belgian national team match on television for all the money in the world whenever Vincent played.

Jeanine contacted Vincent once to ask how his own daughter was getting on, but she was unsure whether she would receive a reply. But she needn't have worried. Vincent, clearly surprised to hear from her, asked if she was following him on social media? Then she wanted to see him again, so, in 2013, she did just that at a Red Devils' fan day.

Vincent recognised her immediately, instructing the security people to '...let the lady through', before giving her a big hug as she made her way through the gate that kept the fans apart from the players. Jeanine recalls, 'I told him I was very proud of what he does for the youth of Brussels, like with the BX Brussels football club, which he founded, where children, regardless of their origin and level, are allowed to play football together.'

Vincent spent the year of his second Kindergarten class with a teacher who asked for her name to be withheld. However, she did say that he was not particularly quiet in class but stood up and asserted himself. A leader type. He took the initiative in most situations, for example, leading the games they played with a ball. But, whilst Vincent was upfront and central when playing sports, he could have perhaps been more visible when it came to other tasks, such as cleaning up the classroom.

For Vincent Kompany, even at this tender age, sport meant everything to him.

The teacher added that she has never encountered a young child with the sporting attributes that Vincent clearly possessed in all of the thirty-seven years she was in teaching. Like Jeanine, her fellow teacher, she had to try and control his inevitable restlessness, so if, for example, he was playing up a little, she'd say to him, 'walk around a bit outside so you calm down.'

This teacher also taught gymnastics to his class, and she noticed how exceptional he was, saying, 'he had strength and was very agile and fast. He could have become a runner or a triathlete.'

Whilst he was in class, Vincent often seemed restless, but it was evident to everyone who taught him that he was eager to learn. Vincent participated in everything, including the perceived less valued subjects like drawing and handicrafts, even though he wasn't particularly keen on either. Language-wise, Vincent steadily improved his mastery of Dutch, which gave him an advantage over many other children in Brussels and it became his second language. There were of course many Flemish children who attended his schools, so it was easier for him to make friends and be able to mix socially.

According to another of Vincent's teachers, '…the teachers spoke exclusively Dutch, and I never translated (for the children). But if the children knew that the teacher spoke French, there was a chance they would make little or no effort to speak Dutch.'

Joske Gezels, who was Vincent's teacher in the third Kindergarten class, recalls a performance that was put on in a local sports hall by the school as part of their yearly festival, which featured the song 'Swimming In The Pool' by Belgian pop group *The Radios*. Part of that show saw young Vincent appear in his swimming costume, giving him, according to Ms Gezels, the opportunity to be part of something that, '…suited him as it allowed him to release his energy.'

In that first grade at Maria-Boodschap, Vincent was one of over a hundred and fifty children drawn from more than twenty different nationalities. The school is at the same address as the Kindergarten, so his physical transition to 'little Mabo' went smoothly. It's a place that is respected for being one of the Flemish anchor points in the city centre, one that makes it's Dutch-speaking identity a trademark.

Because of this, its intake includes many children whose parents might be considered part of the Dutch-speaking 'elite'. For example, highly-placed civil servants, businessmen and women and staff members from Brussels' social and cultural sector, such as film director, actor and screenwriter Dominique Deruddere, composer and musician Walter Hus and fashion designer, Marina Yee, sent their children there.

The head of the school was Paul De Prins, who had, during his time as headmaster, chosen to maintain the school's Dutch-only speaking policy, asking the parents of French-speaking or immigrant children that this requirement had to be strictly adhered to at all times. Thus, if a parent committed to at least one of them learning Dutch (along with their child), they would have a chance of enrolling that child at the school, with De Prins commenting, '…as a school, you can do two things if you have a relatively significant school intake who are less familiar with the language. Either you adapt to those children and lower the quality standards and thus the level of education so that those children can cope with the level. Or you maintain the language standards and encourage the children with a different mother tongue to bring their Dutch to the same level as the Dutch speakers.'

De Prins chose the second option. This also meant that the school gave the children, providing they were prepared to commit to the language, extra support so non-native speakers were not left to their own devices.

An advantage of the presence of French-speaking children in 'little Mabo', in turn, was that it obliged the school to make French lessons more challenging for them. As a result, the level of French lessons was pushed up considerably, and the Dutch-speaking children, in turn, were obliged to go the extra mile in their French classes.

It seems very strict, even unreasonable. But it was also, linguistically speaking, a win-win situation where the children are concerned. Vincent's parents endorsed this philosophy, with De Prins saying, '…strictly Dutch-speaking was not an issue for them; from the first day they were behind our project. Mother Kompany spoke decent Dutch, and Vincent's father always showed himself constructive, respectful and wholeheartedly supported our approach.'

De Prins went on to say that all of the Kompany children '...swam through primary school like happy little fish', with Vincent being the most extrovert of the three, a genuine go-getter who was always positive in his approach.

'Yes, Vincent was behind the occasional mischievous prank – but he was never a naughty boy. If we had to inform his father at the school gate of an incident, as we sometimes had to, he could react so strongly against his son that we sometimes considered it might be better not telling Pierre what had happened.'

'Vincent was told off by me if his actions merited it. He always had respect for his teachers and for me, but he was not a follower; he didn't hide from anything and was very articulate. So yes, he possessed a strong character but still needed guidance. Sometimes, you could not talk to him in the heat of an argument with his fellow pupils – you had to leave it and bring it up again at a quieter time. But he would always listen.'

If there was a conflict with Vincent when the headmaster intervened, it was often related to a feeling of resentment or injustice. 'A situation that seemed unfair to him. More often than not, it was a disagreement during a football match where Vincent got himself very worked up.'

Master Joost taught Vincent at the end of his elementary school days. He had to sometimes separate fighting parties and, when doing so, allowed Vincent to calm down rather than administer instant punishment. He preferred to discuss the issue with the protagonists in a different setting. For Vincent, it was imperative that disagreements were talked out so that they always understood each other, even if, perhaps, they didn't always appreciate the other person's point of view. But at least they understood each other. Master Joost felt it vital to always offer Vincent a clear and honest explanation about decisions that involved him, feeling that if, as inevitably it was, the issue was soon forgotten and Vincent would be back on track.

Vincent began his first year at school in the class of a male teacher, Johan Vanhooren, who got to know Vincent very well right up until he was in the sixth grade. Master Johan also looked after the children on Wednesday afternoons, where Vincent was a regular attendee.

'I think I could be very strict,' he recalls. 'With Vincent, that was sometimes necessary. But then alternating with a more pleasant role, I also gave the children freedom when the circumstances were right. But, occasionally, you'd have to say enough is enough'.

'Vincent needed that more pleasant approach, by the way. I sometimes allowed the children to push the boundaries a little more, albeit within limits. But when the limit is reached, we were extremely consistent in our response'.

As Master Johan had realised, this more relaxed approach worked well for Vincent because he would respond in kind as a genuinely pleasant and playful child. He, like Vincent, loved football, and that brought them even closer together. For many years, they'd play against each other in the playground at break times, with Vincent dashing down the stairs to get outside to play as quickly as possible. For him, every minute he wasn't playing football was a lost minute. He'd made the most of those break periods, playing until the last possible second, even when the other children were already neatly lined up to return inside after the bell had rung. Vincent often had to be dragged back inside, almost literally. Everything revolved around football and competition.

Until he was eighteen, Johan Vanhooren had played as a goalkeeper for the amateur club SK Halle. So he knew a little bit about the game and could already see something special in his pupil.

'Vincent could do things I had never seen in his peers.'

Vincent loved nothing more than kicking penalties. Scoring a goal against the master, who was a 'real' goalkeeper! Even though the ball was plastic, Vincent could hit it very hard and according to Vanhooren: 'He would often play a trick with the ball, so, sometimes, it would be spinning as it came towards you. It was difficult to prevent him from scoring!'

'At the end of his primary school years, Vincent already had enormous power in his legs. Even in the third and fourth years of school, he already had such a kicking technique that, as a goalkeeper, you could make a fool of yourself, so to speak.'

'For a kid of his age, it was tough to kick the ball between the posts. As an adult, you do take up some space in goal. Plus I already had experience as a goalie, but Vincent was particularly talented. He could juggle the ball, keep it high, and I'd end up being amazed at what he could do'.

'And no...', scoffs Vanhooren, 'I never 'gave' Vincent a goal'.

'I'm not like that. Vincent wouldn't have appreciated it either.'

Vincent put his heart and soul into all the matches he played. For him, it was never 'just' about winning. 'No', says Master Johan, 'He was looking for a challenge, which forced him to get the best out of himself in order to improve. He wanted opposition worthy of the name because, otherwise, he would get bored. He also always wanted to join the weakest team. He would pick sides saying, "That one and that one plays with me – all the rest go on the other side!"'

If the difference in scores between the two sides playing became too wide, Vincent would usually suggest a reshuffle of the teams to make it more exciting and, if necessary, deciding that a good player who was a teammate should switch teams and play for the beleaguered opposition. This often occurred, and people became used to Vincent choosing and constantly rearranging the two sides. He'd always stand out as an individual and used to enjoy going on long dribbles with the ball, but he may have found it a little too easy as only some of the other children were even close to being as good as him. So, given the choice, Vincent would play alongside Murtaza, a classmate of his, in a two versus two game against Masters Johan and Joost, games that were a lot more challenging, which Vincent enjoyed so much.

More than twenty years later, Johan Vanhooren still remembers Vincent using the walls around the football pitch to kick against so he could control the rebound when the ball came back at him. He'd even use that tactic against opposing players, using them as something to play the ball off in much the same way as if he was using the wall. But it didn't end there. If a penalty was awarded against Vincent's team, he would swap places with his own goalkeeper and face the penalty himself. Master Johan recalled how, during every academic year, the third Kindergarten class would take part in a match against the first Kindergarten class, something that was an extremely big deal to Vincent. Again, Vincent would suggest that he played for whichever team was seen as the weaker in those games.

Johan Vanhooren has nothing but praise for Vincent and his peers.

'They were a dream of a class. Vincent had no competition regarding results among the other boys, but the girls performed exceptionally well against him. That couldn't have been easy for someone who always wanted to be out in front. In terms of his level, Vincent was just below the very best. At no point did he struggle with anything, although he did have some limitations. For instance, he was certainly not among the fastest readers, but he did like to read.'

Vanhooren recalls how ' I taught Vincent Kompany to write his name!' He also remembers once having to tear up a written practice sheet of Vincent's but does admit that, in any written failings, Vincent's handwriting was always 'neat and tidy.'

Ultimately, mathematics appealed more to Vincent than the written word and he went on to show an excellent flair for the subject, as well as being fascinated by various world religions. As for subjects such as arts and crafts, these were, as we have already seen, not Vincent's speciality, at one point dismissing them as being more suitable for girls than boys! But, at that time, as with most boys of his age, he preferred the company of his male friends as they had more shared interests.

If he had to team up with another child for any sort of school activity, he'd invariably choose one of his close male friends, possibly because he knew there'd then be an element of competition involved. But, much more than that, he enjoyed being part of an active group, described by Vanhooren as a 'group animal' who always wanted to initiate things and looked set to be a natural leader even at that early age. Vanhooren remembers one particular example of this.

'If we were putting together a performance, say on Wednesday afternoons, he wanted to be featured in all the songs. If, for instance, an interview took place in such a show, he wanted to lead it and resolutely took the microphone in his hands. Likewise, in plays. He never hid. Of all the boys in the class, he was always the one who took the initiative. He also wanted to claim the lead role, although it always had to be something tough.'

Vincent also wanted to respond quickly, claims his teacher: he liked to see immediate results. If there was competition involved, he revelled in it.

'In one particular language game, the children had to read the letters as fast as possible and, if they knew the answer, put a card in the air, which really suited him. I also like to bring variety, which for children of six, is very necessary. For example, I would teach for half an hour, then I would get out my guitar, and we would sing songs. Vincent usually went into overdrive in the process, even though he didn't like to sing. But the sillier he could be, the better. That was usually the problem for him: he possessed a lot of energy, which he had to release. After all that singing he'd done just that. He then fell silent again.'

Even in the first year of school, he was eager to prove himself right. Vincent was already very articulate and comfortably fell into conversation, even with adults. This meant he could always explain himself and, when needed, find a way of talking himself out of a potentially tricky situation. Master Johan gives some kudos to Vincent's parents for his conversational skills, as they had clearly encouraged him to talk to people from a very early age.

'Vincent always said goodbye to me before he left. His father and mother insisted on that, even if I was at the other end of the playground. I always appreciated that.'

In that first year, Master Johan used different colours for the marks in school reports. Red was nine out of ten, yellow was eight and blue meant seven out of ten.

'Vincent was usually a 'yellow-blue' child: seven to eight out of ten and, as a result, typically one of those children about whom you didn't have to say much about during parents' evenings. On one end-of-term report card, for example, Vincent's total marks reached just under 90%'.

So, every Wednesday afternoon for six years, Master Johan and Vincent saw each other in a group of about fifteen to twenty children. They often all played a game of football together, and on more than one occasion, Vincent would also talk to his teacher about the game. Vincent was, by then, a fanatical supporter of Anderlecht, whilst Master Johan supported Standard de Liège, and he'd often tease Vincent if his team was doing better than Anderlecht.

But Vincent was more than able to take the criticism thrown his way about his favourite team and, ultimately, had the last laugh every time Anderlecht became champions of the Belgian First Division (which they did in 1991, 1993, 1994 and 1995), usually leaving Standard de Liège in their wake and with high calibre players such as Marc Degryse (who later played for Sheffield Wednesday) and Luc Nilis.

But there would be times when, as much as he wanted to play football, there might, for one reason or another, be no training at Anderlecht for him on that day.

Master Johan: 'If Vincent had the rare misfortune that there was no training at Anderlecht, the children in school had to go inside the gymnasium with the toddlers. Then, I took out four or five board games to play with. He then became as motivated to win those games as he was in any football match. But, content as he was, he'd be a lot happier once his parents had picked him up, as that meant he could finally go outside even if it was raining. Rain was, for Vincent, a disaster as it would mean having to stay indoors when all he wanted to do was go outside and play. His teachers soon became familiar with his pleas on any rainy day...

'Come on, Master, it's not raining much. Can I go outside and play?'

The following year, Vincent was again directly supervised by a male teacher, Master (Joost) Meskens. This was a significant time for Vincent as he was baptised during the academic year and also took his first Holy Communion. Then, in his third year, Vincent was taught by Marleen De Wilde in what turned out to be a relatively small class, where he constantly produced work of an extremely high standard.

He was, by then, even more eager to learn and would complete his work quickly without ever letting those standards slip. He also got used to, and excelled at, more in-depth pieces of work in both Mathematics and Languages, becoming, in the process, a very bright and always active eight-year-old who wanted to play a prominent role in whatever might be going on in the school at the time.

At this time, there was another Vincent in the class with him; his name was *Petit Vincent*. The two Vincents soon teamed up and ended up doing everything together, especially playing football at break times. As always, these games were always very competitive and, such was Vincent's urge to win, he'd sometimes end up verbally clashing with Petit during a game if it wasn't going his way – his complete and utter absorption into their game meaning that he would still be distracted once he was back in the classroom as his and Petit's conversations about their game would continue long after they were sat back at their desks.

This didn't come as a complete surprise to Marleen De Wilde, who was very well aware of his need to win and discuss things afterwards... even if he felt compelled to do so in the middle of a lesson.

'I couldn't shout "Vincent" because the duo would think it was about the other Vincent. One time, I introduced the names Jansen and Janssen (referred to as Thomson and Thomson in the English translation), the detectives with the bowler hats and walking sticks from the *Tintin* stories. That is what I called them from then on; when I wanted to bring them back to the point, I'd call out 'Jansen and Janssen.'

In third grade, the children learnt addition by practice, plus long division, multiplication and subtraction. Vincent had no trouble with any of those disciplines. He had insight and could assess problems logically, which meant that, in this class, he was among the higher achievers. De Wilde recalls that, in particular, Vincent always wanted to do better than the girls.

'If he didn't have a ten out of ten, but felt that he deserved that grade, he negotiated half a point back that I had deducted because of sloppy writing, which they are no longer allowed to do in the third grade. Then I said, "Vincent, even you can see it is not correct", but even then, he'd keep arguing.'

In addition to football, Vincent loved the classes that taught local history, as De Wilde fondly remembers. 'We studied the history of Brussels and often took a look around locally. It was about the origins of Brussels, the Black Tower, the Fish Market or Grand Place. Vincent always listened with keen ears.'

'He was equally delighted when geography was taught. There was a globe in the classroom, which he was very fond of. He enjoyed finding countries.'

As his knowledge grew, Vincent's character traits were also becoming sharper.

You could see he was a leader. In the playground, he'd say, ' that's what we will do'. He divided the children into groups, which was agreed immediately. Sometimes he did get opposition from the girls, who thought he shouldn't always be in charge.'

Jealousy was no stranger to Vincent either.

'The children made little pieces of artwork... But if someone didn't like his work, he'd take revenge by not liking that child's work in return. But his painting or drawing (not his favourite subjects) was still good, as long as he could be busy.'

Teacher Marleen remembers Vincent Kompany, despite his competitiveness, as always being very polite and someone who liked to help.

'For example, if someone was needed to move tables, he'd volunteer immediately. It was only on rare occasions that he'd keep quiet at such times, but that would be when he was tired, and she then knew he'd have to be left alone for a little while. If he had been in the wrong over something, he'd soon admit to it and was swift to say that he shouldn't have said or done something in particular. He had his moments, but he was never a naughty boy, never a rascal. He preferred to take the initiative in things rather than to rebel. This sometimes involved bringing in a book from the library that was maybe not meant for someone in his age range, but, for whatever reasons, something about it genuinely fascinated him, he wasn't trying to show off.'

The children felt at ease in her class and always did their best. Marleen De Wilde was steeped in the oft-lauded Mabo philosophy. 'There was a family atmosphere. Things had to happen naturally, so the children did not have the impression that they were learning. They also had to be quick to ask for something: I felt I had to be available so that they would see the school as an extension of their home.'

Sometimes Vincent was taken to school by car, but mostly he walked in. He would sit in the study until five, when Anderlecht would pick him up in a van for football training. But, by the fourth and fifth years, he had started using public transport to travel alone to these sessions.

Marleen De Wilde had already had Vincent's sister Christel in her class and later taught François. Christel was, she says, a 'softer' version of Vincent. 'Always very sensible and easygoing, proud, tall and pretty, she stood above the other children. And always beautifully dressed. Mother Kompany was not only very kind but also very caring and had great taste.'

Vincent finished in that third grade with a final mark of around ninety per cent, whilst the class average was about eighty per cent. He was, again, amongst the best students in the class.

Vincent's fourth-grade teacher (1995-1996) was Jaklien Deliens. She, too, found Vincent very driven and ambitious. She swiftly distinguished between what was important in Vincent's eyes and what was incidental. If the latter was the case, he could be nonchalant, getting off-topic easily and quickly devoting his attention to other things. For example, he remained uninterested in handicrafts, a discipline which tested his patience. He much preferred learning quickly and factually.

According to Deliens, Vincent was something of a precocious student who would sometimes be silent, even if the energy that radiated off him suggested that he was right... and even if it had been told that he wasn't. Other children couldn't control themselves as well as he could in similar situations and might have been be outspoken. But not Vincent. He didn't argue so much with his classmates then (unless it was about football) and preferred to avoid conflict, choosing to be more of a conciliator. So, whilst some children could be very hard on each other, he never showed this. This inner calm may be because Vincent already knew about the world. He was often charming, as Deliens remembers...

'In the class photos, I see his disarming smile, and that smile alone could melt you away. He thought, too, that it would get you on his side. That smile was part of his persuasiveness. But you had to have valid arguments to convince him. That proved he was a sensible guy. He could also laugh internally if you joked, like he was laughing secretly rather than exuberantly. You could call that reserved.'

'Vincent had a natural charm and seductiveness. He also had a strong sense of justice, plus he was ambitious and driven. Why? Because he wanted to be somebody.'

Only one incident with Vincent caused a stir. It happened during a gymnastics class, something that he enjoyed. In the gym were some safety cabinets with a fire alarm, which activated if you smashed the glass. During a gymnastics lesson, the alarm had gone off. The Headmaster pointed to Vincent as being responsible and was upset about it and with him. But Vincent felt unfairly accused. He was punished, but insisted he had not done it on purpose, which the gym teacher agreed about. Whilst jumping over the trestle, he had accidentally hit that box.

'He could be very indignant about such things,' teacher Jaklien admitted. 'But he didn't resist the punishment. I wasn't there, so I have to be careful what I say. And yet Vincent must surely have felt that I was on his side, but as a teacher, you didn't go against the Headmaster's decision.'

'Vincent is not a pupil I have particulary special memories of', says teacher Danielle, from the fifth grade, who has asked me to stick to her first name.

'I was at school when father Kompany came to enrol his children. That was before Vincent was in my class. As a Dutch-speaking school, we were instructed to speak only Dutch. Mr Kompany addressed me in French, and I replied that we only spoke Dutch at school. To which he suggested we switch to English (laughs).

'But Vincent was a pleasant child', she says, looking at a class photo.

'He looks very nice, smiling. A white and red striped jersey, blue jeans, trainers, very short curls: a handsome little guy. He was not a chief, but he didn't let himself be fooled. He had something to say. I thought he was precocious: he always showed a sense of responsibility and duty.'

By then, Vincent was wholly immersed in his football, and his school results were beginning to suffer as a result. He was aware of his undoubted football skills and was convinced, even then, that he would make it as a professional footballer.

Although he never came home with bad reports, he now only thought studying was necessary on rare occasions. Consequently, his grades slipped and no longer matched his abilities. It is normal for a child in the increasingly rigid fifth grade to drop a few per cent in terms of marks, but he yielded far more. Nevertheless, his parents wanted Vincent to perform at school.

Vincent's reduced work ethic manifested itself mainly at home, in his homework, and when he studied after school. Sometimes, he would come home tired and lost the desire to study in the evenings. However, in class, he remained engaged, interested and active, still a reasonably easy-going student who was interested in many things. However, he was still quick to react if something happened that he believed was unjust.

'For example, during football matches in the playground he'd appeal decisions... "Teacher, that was hand ball!" he'd shout out. He was always honest. He wouldn't appeal if he wasn't convinced. Even so, the Headmaster did not always take to that side of Vincent' teacher Daniëlle confirms.

'The Head did not take it well whenever children were too confident and somewhat arrogant in his eyes. Vincent always argued when he thought he was right and putting the brakes on him was difficult, especially if he felt he had been treated unfairly. Some adults don't put up with that behaviour.'

Argument in the playground seemingly became more important to Vincent than learning. But Danielle had a solution if this manifested in the classroom, saying, 'if things did get out of hand with that football talk, I stopped the lesson and discussed the incident with him.'

All three Kompany children had big egos as far as Danielle was concerned.

'Ego should be seen as self-awareness, mixed with a dose of pride and the demand for respect. Vincent knew he had something special and was proud of his achievements.'

But was he vain with it?

'Yes! Vincent told us, for example, that his grandfather was the village chief in Congo. His father had that self-confidence too, but without giving an impression he was better than anyone else. But when the Kompany's enter, you know when they've arrived.'

Vincent's parents were not prepared to sit back and watch their 'little man' ground down by others with more money, higher status, a different skin colour, more power or a perceived superior network. It made them and their children especially sensitive to the issue. This explains Vincent's stubborn resistance at school to everything that was, in his eyes, unjust. When he expressed his opinion against another child about their actions, the teacher, or Headmaster, became unimportant in his eyes.

As Vincent reached his eleventh birthday, his 'big ego', as the teachers began to refer to it, became even more apparent.

The more Vincent developed as a footballer, the bigger the place it took in his life. And the more his performance was compromised at school. But was the school versus football clash the only reason for some poorer school performances? Possibly. But not definitely. Another possible explanation is that Vincent was already at the early stages of puberty with new hormones to contend with too. Yet the clues were there.

Sixth-grade tutor, Joost Meskens, remembers many of Vincent's football skills and numerous antics.

'When the children played football, Master Johan was sometimes referee. If he whistled for a foul that Vincent thought wasn't one, Vincent could react vehemently: become angry, turn red, even cry. He was sometimes a choleric and explosive little fellow, dripping with sweat. And he felt he was always right. He knew more about football than Johan because, after all, he played football for a club. I agree that many children react that way, but Vincent could go too far sometimes.'

'On one occasion, he had lost a game. He was sweating as usual and was very angry with his fellow players. He felt that the girls were to blame and that it was always the same: his team would have won without the girls. In those moments, he did not realise that there was anything else in life besides football. In the sixth grade, he already knew what he wanted. He had his goal in mind and would achieve it at any cost: become a top footballer, he would make it. Other children looked up to him. In the gymnastics class, it was the same thing: he was the fastest. Vincent wanted to be the best at everything. He didn't succeed in his studies, but in sports, he did.'

Master Joost adds: 'Vincent surpassed my own footballing abilities in no time. But I also did weightlifting, and he knew that. Vincent respected my strength and called me "the strongest master". When he was about fourteen, he came to school with friends again and pointed me out, which I thanked him for'.

Bernadette De Luyck, Meskens' wife, also became acquainted with Vincent when she joined her husband on a two-night school trip to stay on their farm in the countryside.

'I remember being told that Vincent played for Anderlecht and hailed as a footballer who would go far. When his class stayed here, the other children came to say "hello" to me, but not Vincent. He was playing football on the lawn, which was all that interested him. Even during the barbecue that was the conclusion to the farm visit.'

At the end of their short break at the farm, Pierre Kompany picked up his son and a few more children in a black BMW. According to Meskens, Kompany senior was 'a super-polite man. Attached to the farm at that time was a shoe factory. Pierre shook hands with all the workers there.'

Most of the time, however, it was Joseline, Vincent's mother, who the teachers got to see.

'She was stricter than the father. She'd sometimes make it known at parents' evenings that she felt, at times, Vincent's attitude towards certain things in life wasn't always acceptable. His parents were very committed to their children and expected a lot of them: they had to dress stylishly, their hair had to be nicely combed, and their bag of books and school things always had to be in tip-top condition.'

Vincent might, you suspect, have been increasingly distracted as he got older, especially as he was a popular young man who looked after himself very well.

Master Joost recalls that '...in class, Vincent always wanted to sit next to a boy, even in the sixth grade. His interest in girls was low because girls were less interested in sports. At that age, this is understandable. Nowadays, some sixth-formers have a girlfriend. But Vincent was not interested in that sort of thing. It was just football, plain and simple. François was completely different: he was already interested in girls. But not Vincent, not at this stage.'

'To Vincent, a girl had a different value to a boy. No matter who they were. One consequence was that the female teachers had more trouble keeping Vincent in line as he preferred the masculine approach. So yes, he accepted female authority less. Then again, the women of his family were sacred, especially his mother. If he was called "a son of a bitch" by a fellow pupil, he'd fly at them. I sometimes had to separate the fighters, and at the age of twelve upwards, that's not always so easy.'

Vincent was always interested in hearing stories about people's lives, especially those of people like himself, including the lives of the people in the Congo, where, at the time, his interest was growing and affected by the civil war.

Vincent felt that it was unjust that King Leopold II had made Congo a Belgian colony and, as a result of that, had stripped the Congo of its natural resources, ivory, rubber and diamonds, amongst many other commodities – a policy that benefitted Belgium as it helped to finance luxury projects like the expansion of Ostend. When the Belgian Congo had gained independence in 1960, Vincent said this was a good and just thing as the Congolese could, '...take matters into their own hands and fend for themselves.'

Meskens told the children in Vincent's class many harsh, real-world stories, such as about his father's farming job and the help he'd had. Tales about frozen hands during the leek harvest upon which the workers urinated in order to warm them and about working day and night because, at night, the vegetables had to be taken to Brussels for sale. He spoke of the sometimes cruel handling of animals, so much so that animals would often die and the unhygienic conditions in which cows had to calve. He told them about the power of nature against which nothing or no one can take a stand. He'd also recall anecdotes about the world wars during which Vincent hung on his every word, especially one about a German soldier who'd been beaten to death close to the school during World War II.

Vincent loved stories like those, about things that had happened or events that he could learn something from – no matter how tragic they might be.

Outings greatly appealed to Vincent, especially those which allowed him to use up some physical energy, such as those that took place in a nearby forest. These trips were an opportunity to also have some fun with his friends and do the sort of things expected of young boys at the time, including climbing trees. Which wasn't an activity on the school's agenda.

'Vincent!', Master Joost would shout, '... don't climb the trees!'

Master Joost recalls his words were often in vain.

'If you gave him free rein, he would disappear into the forest, build a camp, and you would see him come back only when you gave the whistle that it was time to go back.'

Vincent might have lived in the city, but he was a nature lover, and even bad weather didn't bother him. 'He was rock hard: rain, cold, or snow, nothing stopped him.'

The football-school combination was, almost inevitably, becoming a tough assignment for both Vincent and his teachers. Master Joost suspects that, in those days, Vincent was training three times a week at Anderlecht and, on top of that, he also played a match at the weekend, a commitment that severely curtailed his free time.

'He no longer had time to read. Every month, the children had to read a book. Well, with him, it was never finished. He was candid. "Master, I don't have time for that." I always turned a blind eye because I suspected he would succeed in life in some other way.'

Vincent, according to Master Joost, was now only an average student. In second grade, he'd estimated that Vincent had marks of around 84-85 per cent, near enough to the class average. When he graduated from primary school, he had 77 or 78 per cent, while the class average was 78 to 81 per cent.

However, no one else in his year had a 'leisure activity' that required his attendance four times a week for two to three hours each time. It was as if Vincent had a part-time job during term time, which he had to fit around his studies. What made this commitment even more demanding was that this particular activity was both physically strenuous and exhausting for him despite his tender years.

Vincent was clearly having to manage his time, and sometimes, unsurprisingly, he simply ran out of it. Something had to give, with the unread books at school being a prime example.

And let's not understimate how high a bar the school was setting.

Vincent shouldn't, therefore, just be seen as someone whose grades dropped as he moved through the school years. Throughout his time at the school, he remained one of its brightest and most promising students, certainly regarding all-round ability and most definitely amongst the boys. Without his football distractions, could he have pushed on and become, for example, a Doctor, Lawyer or Civil Engineer? When I put this question to Master Joost, his answer was emphatic.

'Vincent was an intelligent boy with a lot of ability. He would certainly have made it in another sector if he had focused on something other than football. Vincent's parents had above-average intelligence'.

'The tree doesn't grow too far from the apple.'

'In retrospect, that sixth year of learning must have been among the best years for Vincent in his youth. He could play football as much as he wanted at school and his club without much stress. He could combine football with his school results... plus his parents were still living together. And with teachers like me, he had a master who could be strict but, at the same time, understood his football passion and personality, those outspoken boyish mannerisms included.'

CHAPTER FIVE
'HE WAS SO GOOD, WE HID HIM'

In early 1992, Pierre Kompany looked for a football club for the then almost six-year-old Vincent to join in the neighbourhood of his employer, DHL, in Diegem. Joseline, his wife, would take Vincent to training, then Pierre would pick him up again after work. Pierre duly made inquiries at Strombeek, Vilvoorde and Mechelen, but things didn't work out at any of those clubs for one reason or another.

Anderlecht were different with their response, offering Vincent a three-week trial. He duly impressed as he joined in with training along with the club's other young players at their youth complex situated in the Neerpede district. Vincent enjoyed himself and made rapid progress, but it wasn't until two years after he'd started training with the club that he first really acknowledged that the Vanden Stock stadium (now known as Lotto Park) was the home of the club *he* was playing for.

Vincent had always thought he was training with FC Neerpede, the football club who were based in the neighbourhood that shared its name. Things have changed since then and the Anderlecht Youth Centre is now officially called the RSCA Belfius Academy, but it's still referred to as simply 'Neerpede', by many, hence Vincent's misunderstanding of his playing affiliation at the time.

Neerpede is the last remaining rural green area in the city of Brussels. If you happen to visit, you will find it contains many farms, especially those which are dedicated to growing fruit, as well as the famous Luizenmolen windmill in Anderlecht's Butterfly Street. There are many winding footpaths and fields, all full of partridges and trees, mainly willows, in a landscape that has remained largely the same as the one that sixteenth-century artist Pieter Bruegel so vividly brought to life.

It is, amidst a bustling city, an oasis of peace and quiet, an unexpected rural idyll appreciated and enjoyed by many.

From Anderlecht's home stadium, you can head for Neerpede via a narrow road before moving on and eventually leaving the park by following the tracks of tram number 56. You will, at first, end up in Vijverpark, another charming area that is a wide strip of land replete with several ponds that are surrounded by natural vegetation and frequented by many types of waterfowl and adjacent to Pedepark where, for a while, there stood a floating windmill which Pierre Kompany made. Next door to Vijverpark is a sports area that includes tennis courts, a riding school, hockey and rugby pitches as well as an artificial ski slope. It is an exceedingly pleasant area of Anderlecht, far removed from the urban sprawl that is Brussels, so it is perhaps no surprise that Vincent couldn't easily connect Neerpede with Anderlecht, the great city club with an illustrious history.

The RSCA Belfius Academy looks very different to how it did during Vincent's childhood, in fact it has been transformed beyond all recognition. When Vincent was training and playing there, from 1992 to 2003, the dressing rooms were, to say the least, 'atmospheric', breathing a charming air of past glory at best and in dire need of replacement. This sense of neglect was symbolic of the few chances that youth players were given to progress to Anderlecht's normally star-studded first team at the time.

Change was desperately needed and, finally, in the autumn of 2011, the current three-storey facility opened its doors. It included a 500-square-metre weights room; a rehabilitation area with a swimming pool; sauna; Turkish bath and jacuzzi as well as a rest and relaxation area, and a restaurant, all for use of the Under-15 team upwards, with the first-team players also regularly training there on its well-maintained, heated pitches.

However, when Vincent first trained at Neerpede with the national A-team, who practised there regularly, his working environment was somewhat different to those his counterparts enjoy today. Neerpede offered little more than primitive army barracks standards, with one written account describing them as 'old fashioned with absolutely no luxuries', something which, apparently, made them 'cosy', with concrete-lined showers that were roomy enough for forty players, their loud voices bouncing off the stark walls as they rushed through their ablutions.

During training in those early years at Anderlecht, the priority for young players was always focused on individual development and performance over results. The better a player is, the more likely they are to play their matches in a higher age category. So, for example, an exceptional sixteen-year-old may find themselves playing in under-18 or even under-21 age group matches. It was an approach that suited both Vincent and his parents. It rewarded progress, but there was a greater emphasis on mutual respect for both teammates and opponents – one that took their fledgling careers seriously. It required every player to be fully committed to the club and its ethos, including possessing enormous amounts of personal self-discipline, as well as being polite and courteous at all times.

Anderlecht traditionally did very well in games against the equivalent age groups of other Belgian teams. The range and quality of their opposition was somewhat limited however, as most competitions at that level were played on a regional basis, meaning Anderlecht's schoolboy and youth teams were primarily playing against teams from the surrounding towns and villages. And, because Anderlecht had invariably already signed up all the promising players from in and around the province, these early games in Vincent's time at the club were mostly little more than opportunities to practice what they had been learning in training. Anderlecht tended, even at their most junior levels, to play a very attacking-minded, offensive style in all of their matches, encouraging a consistent match philosophy even during the young players' earliest years at the club. This might, in retrospect, now be seen as something of a disadvantage in their development as such persistent dominance against weaker opposition meant that their players were rarely put into a position where they had to learn to cope or how to play and react when competing against opposition who were far more competitive than they might have been used to.

At Neerpede, the young players were initially tutored into playing in a 3-4-3 formation, with three defenders, four midfielders and three strikers. This formation is one of the most difficult to learn, tactically, and is only suitable for technically adept players whose natural game is to be offensive and dominant in possession. It's a line-up that can be vulnerable to counter-attacking football from an otherwise beleaguered opposition.

At the top level of Dutch football, it is a formation that had been adopted by coaches like Rinus Michels with the Netherlands national team, Johan Cruijff during his time as coach with Barcelona and Louis van Gaal with Ajax. The common denominator there, of course, is that those are all examples of highly adept and very technically proficient teams who would be easily able to adapt to a tactical approach that gave their coaches the flexibility to change things during a match, whilst less gifted sides might prefer a more simplistic 4-4-2 line-up, where each player's role is fixed, and they retain it for the entire match with little to no flexibility.

Anderlecht therefore picked a 3-4-3 formation in all competitions for their U-11 to U-14 teams before switching to the more familiar 4-3-3 line-up from their U-15 teams upwards. Both formations allowed for intelligent, attacking, technically refined and, overall, easy-on-the-eye displays, the type of 'champagne football' that Anderlecht prided itself upon. Both systems have ingredients to allow a game that is played at a high tempo, with players switching positions throughout a match and collectively pressing the opponent from the top of the pitch, thus starving them, as much as possible, of possession in potentially dangerous areas. Again, it is not a style that any team can adopt, and any player who can do so will have an excellent chance of playing at the highest possible level of the game.

Vincent was fortunate that his time in the game began just as the Belgian Football Association was encouraging the same style of play amongst all age groups and levels. Albert Martens, a family friend who coached Vincent from the age of nine to twelve, recalls that 'In around 1999, they started playing national elite football for players as young as seven or eight. They used to play Anderlecht against local teams, and we would win 10-0 or even 20-0. Our three or four best players made the difference, and better ones did not need to replace our mediocre players because we were winning anyway.'

Such was Anderlecht's dominance at the time.

But also, it was important that the style of play and training regime allowed the best players to stand out whilst the not-so-good ones could still grow. It was an approach that benefitted Anderlecht's young players and spread throughout the game in the nation as a whole, with Belgian football ultimately taking great strides forward as a result. The evidence of this remains clear, with the national teams' improved show-ings at European Championships (quarter-finalists in 2016 and 2020) and World Cups (quarter-finalists in 2014 and third place in 2018) in recent years. Martens claims this is all down to that consistency of tactical approach, with all players now being given the same instructions from the age of nine or ten upwards.

'In the French top tournaments, we *(Anderlecht)* competed well for years but never lasted until the end of them. That has changed. I remember a tournament where we won against Ajax, and afterwards, they asked if they could touch the ball. Back then, Anderlecht had a lot more talent running around than Ajax. But in the Netherlands, their clubs competed on a regional level, as we do in Belgium now, until the players were fifteen or sixteen. Belgian football wasn't progressing because we also needed the structure in our club game to do that'.

There was one significant difference between the attitudes of those two nations when it came to their younger players at that time. In the Netherlands, a promis-ing youth player got an opportunity at first-team level at least three times whilst, in contrast, Martens believes that, in Belgium, the same player may not even have had one opportunity, with clubs, like Anderlecht, preferring to source their play-ers as the finished product from elsewhere. That is until those same Belgian clubs suddenly started to feel a financial pinch in around 2010 and had to start giving op-portunities to the players who had come through their schoolboy and youth ranks.

This shows just how much of a talent the young Vincent Kompany unquestionably was as he was given his first team debut with Anderlecht in 2003, when he was just seventeen, with his international debut for Belgium coming shortly after his eigh-teenth birthday. Clearly, he was an absolutely exceptional player, identified as such, from a very early age.

Vincent's earliest years in the game often saw him playing as a defensive midfielder, but in his final years in youth training, he played more and more often as a central defender. In that critical position in the team, he was seen as the 'bolt on the door', the last player between his teammates and his goalkeeper. So he had the responsi-bility to cover for any mistakes made by his fellow defenders and, overall, to protect his 'keeper as much as possible. It's therefore a role that demands excellent game insight; exceptional pace over short distances; anticipation and the character to re-main calm and in control at all times – essential qualities for any central defender to possess, but very rare for anyone to possess all of them.

Marcel Desailly, Paolo Maldini, Rio Ferdinand.

Vincent could already boast these essential attributes. At Anderlecht, he wore the number three shirt (nominally a left-back number but, in a three-man defence, that of the left-sided centre half) plus the number four shirt, which is more traditionally that of a defensive midfielder. Yet, like all of his teammates, his positioning on the pitch was interchangeable. Thus, if he was playing in defence, he had the freedom to push forward and support his midfield and, alternately, if he was playing in midfield, he'd be expected, when necessary, to fall back and help out his defenders. His skill-set allowed responsibilities for a wide-ranging role in the team and the ability to play a cross-field pass to the feet of a teammate; enough confidence on the ball to include playing it out of defence with his feet and making runs into opposing teams' territory. He was also able to control and play the ball equally well with both his right and left foot.

So just how good was Vincent as a young footballer? I asked that very question to several coaches who'd worked with him at that time.

'We urged Vincent to choose his moments very well when he wanted to go into the attack from position four,' said Werner Deraeve, a former Anderlecht player (1969 to 1974) and his youth team manager when Kompany was at Neerpede.

'Sometimes Vincent would run forward, and a gap would open as a result, allowing the opponent to easily advance. It was better for Vincent to play in the three as a defender. He couldn't run as a four *(midfielder)* needs to because he didn't always have the stamina to get back into position'.

'If you are wearing number four, you have to play in midfield – but you are also helping the defence. But he wasn't a marathon man! Playing him at three meant he could be a pure defender, someone who was not constantly on the ball, a player who has to run fewer kilometres in a match than a midfielder and someone who can keep an eye on the game because it usually takes place in front of him.'

Martens still acknowledged that Vincent would have been more than adequate as a defensive midfielder but was convinced, even at that early stage of his career, that he was more suited to playing as a centre-half in a defensive line of three. But he wanted to push Vincent, which meant not always playing him where he might have felt most comfortable.

'With me, he never played at the back because he was far too good for that already. Improvements in training are often achieved by not letting a player play in his best position, but rather where he learns the most.'

'We wanted to make it difficult for him.'

As a defensive midfielder, Kompany saw a great deal more of the ball than he would have done playing as a centre-back and, purely through playing in matches in that position, he got more and more used to the myriad in-game possibilities that might affect a midfielder, learning, in the process, how to deal with them.

'This wasn't a position he was most comfortable in. He needed to be challenged more. He had stature and duel strength; he used his body well, anticipated excellently and learnt, as a midfielder, to always think ahead. He was not a pure defender who tends to run backwards all the time, but wants to build up play as quickly as possible. He was also fast, agile and flexible.'

Vincent started his football education playing as a forward and regularly scored thirty to fifty goals per season. But even when he was primarily a striker (between the ages of six and eight), he still never spent an entire season just running around in attack and scoring goals. Pierre Kompany remembers Vincent's first game at that age, playing against Dilbeek. The 'devils' of Anderlecht that season had won almost everything and were playing a tournament elsewhere. Boys who had yet to be allowed to play in those games, including Vincent, got a chance in this extra game, and they won 4-0, with Vincent, the stand-out player.

By now, Vincent's personality was already beginning to emerge. When he was still only nine, he was interviewed by *Canal +*, the French TV channel on the day of a match between Anderlecht and Standard de Liège. Standard are one of Anderlecht's biggest rivals but Vincent chose to say that he didn't like how Anderlecht focussed on bringing in players from all over Europe rather than relying on developing and playing those that had come through their schoolboy and youth ranks. His thoughts on the matter didn't surprise Martens, who responded by saying that, for Vincent, it was never about himself but how the team itself might benefit.

Vincent's confidence showed that same season after a team containing Anderlecht's second-year schoolboy intake played a match against RWD Molenbeek and lost 3-0. The first year intake, which included Vincent, was due to play them shortly after this game.

Martens remembers Vincent saying, 'Coach, we'll beat them'.

'He wanted to show that the first years were doing better than the group immediately ahead of them. He was right. They won 2-0; he scored the goals and, as a stopper for the defence, ran the game.'

Vincent's friend Faris Haroun, then at RWD Molenbeek, talks about another duel between the two clubs.

'Early in the match, I benefitted from a refereeing decision that affected Vincent so badly that his reaction saw him get a yellow card – and yellow in youth game means you are straight off the pitch. We'd been playing for barely ten minutes.'

Other legendary tales of his unbridled zeal tell how Vincent once dared to say to a coach at half-time that his tactics were wrong. Another time, he asked, completely deadpan, to be replaced because he felt his performance was not good enough. He didn't just show his emotions in matches either; if, even as part of a training routine, he was on the losing side in a game, he would sometimes burst into tears, cursing the whole world, something Albert Martens soon became very familiar with.

Anderlecht's head of youth training, Werner Deraeve, had started watching Vincent's matches more regularly from the time he was nine. He observed, 'The technical ingenuity of some very young Anderlecht players is initially relatively limited, possibly because they are naturally clumsy – which can be a particular characteristic of tall boys. It eventually works out well for them, although they sometimes need more time than boys of average height. Vincent, however, as tall as he was, already had good technical ability and an excellent overview of the game.'

'He did not like to head the ball though.'

Albert Martens explains further.

'By playing 'Anderlecht football', with the ball played along the ground, the young players didn't have to head the ball so much. Before the age of thirteen, they were supposed only to head it infrequently anyway. In the beginning, Vincent tended to pull his head away. We worked on this, but I never expected him to become as good as he became in the air. His ability to hang up there for a second longer than his opponent evolved tremendously.'

According to Deraeve, Vincent preferred controlling a game situation with the ball at his feet rather than taking the easy option and just heading the ball away. He liked to challenge his opponents by playing football; this meant he took risks, and sometimes, he might have taken too many. But his overall ball control was 'good'. He had a 'tight pass', always wanting to do things correctly. Vincent was predominantly right-footed but could easily play as a left-sided defender as well. Martens believes that, at the time, and despite being marked out as a central defender, one of Vincent's most significant assets was his ability to pass the ball well.

'He could make a stretched pass over twenty metres on the lace of his left foot,' he recalls, adding that 'Vincent used his body very well. If you wanted to go past him, it was equally challenging to do so on either side. He had extra-long legs.'

If Vincent did not like the position he was playing in the team, he would soon speak up and say so. This meant he'd frequently get into arguments with his coach. Some of his coaches would accept this spark from a young player whilst others couldn't deal with it very well at all. But Vincent wasn't being argumentative for the sake of it. If he questioned the role he was expected to play, he wanted his coach to explain why he was in that position, often firing off one tactical question after another in support of his cause – and they were usually the right questions. He loved to discuss these points, and, much more often than not, his observations would prove to be the correct ones.

However, Vincent soon began to question his coaches' decisions to such an extent that Deraeve felt obliged to intervene as he couldn't always accept these 'rebellious' statements or, more usually, some other aspect of his behaviour. Vincent could, for example, have punctuality issues. So he made a point of reminding Vincent that in training, the coach is the boss and, during a game, the referee, not Vincent Kompany.

Despite his competitive spirit (in even the most light-hearted games), Vincent remained very sporting towards opposing players. If he accidentally hurt or injured an opponent during a game, he was the first to ask them if they were alright, to apologise (even if he was not in the wrong) or to help his opponents back to their feet. This was an approach he quickly took up with referees as well, making sure he was always polite to them in the heat of a game – even if some of these 'polite' enquiries as to why a match official might have made the decision that he did might have ended up with him getting a yellow card for his actions. Vincent may well have been courteous with referees, but even arguing with them politely often earnt a sanction against him. That need for lucidity from officials has stayed with Vincent to this day as, with officials, the one thing he has always expected, as both a player and a manager, is clarity.

If he has that, then he is happy, even if, on occasions, he might still disagree. If, on the other hand, he feels an injustice has been done, or that someone on the field is stirring things up a little, either with his teammates or match officials, he will react. It is part of his on-pitch persona that has stayed with him from his schoolboy days to his time as a senior professional with Manchester City and Belgium and as a coach with Burnley in the Premier League. One such example came after Burnley's 1-1 draw with Nottingham Forest in September 2023 when, after the match, he commented on a goal for Burnley that had been disallowed by VAR, feeling that sufficient explanation for the decision had not been given.

'I have to get used to it. In the Championship if it's in, it's in. I have a decent business and coaching brain, but when it comes to law and legality, I switch off. Handball this way or that, they come and explain it to us, but I have made a decision to trust what they are doing... it is not something I want to discuss too much, I cannot change it now.'

Ambition has always fuelled the fire that burns within Vincent Kompany, and he is as ambitious today as he was thirty years ago. He is always seeking a new challenge (one can easily suppose that is why he agreed to become the coach at the then recently relegated Burnley in 2022, a career decision that certainly surprised a few people in the game) as, when things get a little too easy, he soon becomes bored. Even in his earliest years in the game, he had to have a sense of responsibility and targets to meet. And woe betide anyone who tried to hold him back.

His coaches at Anderlecht soon realised this and realised that there might be a few difficulties working with someone with such an ambitious and assertive attitude to life and football as a whole. They had, in order to establish some sort of harmonious working relationship with Vincent, to find a mutually agreeable way of doing so, and quickly, for, as Martens says, 'With Vincent, you have to be standing alongside him as well as ahead of him at the same time.'

Vincent was always the first player in a team to want to learn something new. Coaches who realised this and worked with him, such as Martens, would soon benefit from the end results. If Vincent found training boring and believed he wasn't learning anything from a session, he'd quickly lose interest. And it wouldn't be subtle; he would do so quickly and very visibly. He liked to push himself to the absolute limits at all times and demanded that from his teammates throughout his playing career – so if they didn't share that commitment, his interest in them and the session would swiftly evaporate. This is something that the players he coaches today will almost certainly be familiar with.

Upon reading this, you may think that Vincent Kompany was never the easiest person to work with, even as a young boy training at Neerpede. If, for example, he didn't believe that a coaching session, or a match tactic would benefit him or his team, he'd dismiss it out of hand and refuse to be convinced otherwise.

He wanted to lead rather than be led, a part of his character that was already very clear when he was only six years old. His personality, then and now, seems a rich mix of the most vital characteristics of his parents: the renowned stubbornness so readily associated with the people of the Ardennes that comes from his mother, combined with the easy nonchalance and adaptability of his father.

Vincent displays the best of both worlds but does not offer these strengths for free and will always demand something back from the coaches he is working with.

Vincent kept his parents fully appraised about his experiences in Neerpede. More often than not Joseline, his mother, agreed with his thoughts and actions, even if, on occasion, they might have gone against the sporting grain of Anderlecht. She was, as a trade union militant, someone who was not easily impressed by the 'cult' of football and the obsession with celebrity it has at the highest level. She saw many of Vincent's peers as pampered individuals who, for her, behaved as if they were the eighth wonder of the world, demanding (and expecting) adulation but, more often than not, offering little to no social commitment in return for their life of privilege.

Joseline Fraselle also questioned football's privileged position in society, the endless intertwining of politics and sport, and subsidies for clubs which benefit from tax-payers' money, whilst they continue to pay their players exorbitant wages. But she also found Anderlecht's demands on her son excessive, especially when she noticed how his school was adapting to the demands of the football club rather than, as she quite reasonably expected, Anderlecht to adapt to the needs of the school.

But, despite what this might have made people think, Joseline Kompany was not anti-football; she was, for those reasons and more, anti-elite football. And it occasionally showed. At Anderlecht for example, people found her occasionally lacking in subtlety, however, to her credit, she was always happy to talk things through, with husband Pierre glad to smooth out the edges when needed.

'I have always been opposed to what I call the dictatorship of clubs,' Joseline told *Sport-Voetbalmagazine*.

'Neerpede is the prime example of that. The youth coaches told us every year that school was the most important thing. That was a bit hypocritical: in reality, education always came second, after the football.'

She sometimes got a rebuttal, although, at Anderlecht, they realised they had to be careful when dealing with the parents of such nuggets of gold as other clubs would have been only too willing to take Vincent on if Anderlecht ever decided they could not cope with their demands any more. This was the primary reason why Vincent's frequent lateness for training and other appointments was only sometimes treated seriously by most club personnel – except for coach Eddy Van Daele, who was a little more unforgiving of his charges, including the multi-gifted ones.

'I trained Vincent for four months at the beginning of the 1996-97 season,' recalls another coach, Luc Spaepen.

'He was playing at the provincial youth level then. Vincent was ten and trained three times a week. They did not play in the national league then, but did play against the better teams in what was then the province of Brabant. And you could immediately see that he was intelligent by how he reacted and handled things in the game. You could also count on him. He was among the best footballers and had everything within his game to succeed. Yes, even amongst ten-year-olds, you could see his footballing intelligence stand out, especially with his positional play. Many players at that age are drawn to the pack, where the action is. He didn't. He tried to look where he could best position himself tactically.'

Vincent was also exceptionally fit and strong, even at that young age. His jump was higher than his peers; he could also hold onto the ball and was not dispossessed easily. What also stood out with Luc Spaepen is that Vincent did not take advantage of the fact that he played better football than the others. He didn't act as if he was a better player than anyone else and focused on improving his game.

Outbursts were, as a consequence, almost completely absent.

This was the first year that saw youth players play eleven-against-eleven games on a standard sized pitch, albeit for two halves of twenty-five, rather than forty-five minutes. This was quite an adjustment for most young players to adapt to, but Vincent met the new requirements of him effortlessly. On a big pitch, organisation, intelligence and initiative are suddenly more critical as there is more space for players to find or run into. Equally they can see that same space and 'hide' from the game as well. Vincent made the very most of all the space that he had and never hid; he was mostly playing either as a central defender or in midfield, although, as we have already seen, he was primarily deployed in the back four as this gave him a great view of everything that was going on in the game. He would occasionally make his way further up the pitch.

'We never stopped him from making his way forward... and he scored goals,' says Spaepen.

'You could also place him in attack. If you did, he scored regularly and effortlessly. Vincent had the advantage of knowing when he could and should slot in, position-wise, during a game, no matter what role he started in. But, and primarily playing at the back, it became important for him to learn when and where to push himself up into the midfield rather than just doing so on a whim and we paid a lot of attention in training with him to learning that.'

Another coach who worked with Vincent at this time was Michel Punga.

'In 1994, I started training with Vincent at Anderlecht. I gave individual technique training to the top talent and coached Vincent once a week for three years. It happened more than once that he was fed up with his coach and would walk over and came to train with me on another pitch. That, or one of the other coaches were fed up with what they saw as his bad behaviour and sent him over to me. Whenever this happened, I always told it to them straight, "You don't know how to handle stars."'

73

Vincent was clearly still prone to criticising certain aspects of the sessions he attended, saying, on one occasion, he didn't 'see the point' of a particular exercise they were doing. Michel Punga didn't accept this.

'You can't say that, Vincent.'

'I told him not react that way but to always behave decently. Vincent learned with me by training hard until the tears were in his eyes. And I didn't teach him to take the ball, stop and see what he would do with it, but to execute everything in one flowing movement... taking the ball on and sending it immediately and directly to where he wanted it to be, accelerating the game instead of slowing it down. We practiced endlessly, over and over again, on ball technique alone.'

'It felt almost like child labour at times.'

Punga is convinced that some coaches do not know how to deal with the elite players, those who, he claims, wouldn't stand out if they weren't eccentric, stubborn or otherwise contrary to what is usually expected in terms of onfield behaviour.

'In Belgium, many coaches still cannot deal with the stars, and Vincent was 'unlucky' enough to be one from the age of twelve. Fortunately, Vincent was mature, perhaps ten times more intelligent than the other players. With me, he was always allowed to be himself.'

For Punga, one thing was preventing Vincent Kompany, an outstanding central defender, from becoming an exceptional defensive midfielder.

'Vincent's problem in becoming a real top midfield player was his slight lack of agility and mobility; he was a bit stiff because of his long legs, turning and turning, stopping and sprinting is a little harder for him than for those who are not as tall. Turning ten times in one minute is not his thing. He is more dangerous when he can leave with the ball at his feet. That is why he is better as a central defender.'

Even as a young teenager, Vincent was already beginning to stand out at Anderlecht.

Deraeve: 'He was the leader, the boss in the dressing room.'

His tall stature certainly favoured him amongst his peers. It was also that presence that saw him, from the age of thirteen, compete in the higher-age series competitions for Anderlecht. According to Van Daele, he joined the U-16 group and was soon the best player, even amongst them. Vincent had benefitted after a huge growth spurt at the age of fourteen that saw him grow a further thirteen centimetres. He was still playing as a central defender at the time, and this was a massive plus for him. But it didn't come without issues. Vincent's growth spurt caused him many problems, especially with his back and leg muscles, as Deraeve explains:

'The muscles did not follow the growth of his bones; they pulled and dragged everywhere.'

74

Vincent was susceptible to injury, and that particular issue remained one that troubled him. So he worked hard at strengthening his musculature, albeit very cautiously so as not to cause any more problems in the process. And, ultimately, he succeeded with this part of his development, with Deraeve now confident he would reach the top of the game.

'If Vincent had failed then, it would have been a huge disappointment for the youth coaches: if it didn't work out with him, then it would never have worked out with anyone!'

Vincent's ultimate breakthrough was crucial for another reason, according to Deraeve:

'We at the youth academy were frustrated because, after Walter Baseggio in 1996, no one from the youth side had grown into the in the A-team's starting line-up. Vincent was our calling card to show the others that it could be done.'

The youth players themselves had previously been highly frustrated at their lack of opportunity to progress into the first team, with Kompany telling the weekly publication *Knack*: 'We may have been playing with Anderlecht's youth side, but we could not, at one time, ever imagine advancing to the first team squad. It was always the same story: transfers took priority over our own youth. I had a tough time with that.'

'At one point, I even stopped playing football for a fortnight.'

He also struggled with something else. 'Boys of North African origin, as well as from Turkey and Italy, always get the same treatment when we play outside Brussels. Sometimes I can't believe my ears. The opposing boys' parents often have a go at us from the sidelines; some of us get called the most appalling names. Why do they do it? Perhaps, as Anderlecht have all the best players, they feel inferior, it made them agitated, so they reacted. They also seem to think I am older than the age given, so we are cheating! And, somehow, all of this continues to go on, and the referees never seems to notice it! That sort of thing in football, abuse and racism, revolts me, and I will always oppose it, whether I am seventeen or seventy-seven.'

Deraeve believes Vincent was very well advanced for one of (still) such tender years.

'You didn't always know everything about him and often had to push him for even the most basic information. He kept his private life hidden. That's one of his qualities. On the one hand, he is an open book; on the other, he will never fully reveal himself. He does things that even those around him don't know about.'

The fact that he has achieved so much is, according to Deraeve, precisely because of this side of his character, although Vincent is, first and foremost, someone with good intentions.

'Football is a team sport, and you learn best by being out on the pitch with your teammates. You can't affect that. He had to learn that not only on the pitch… but also outside of football.'

Kompany also knows where he is coming from; he has forced himself to keep that in the back of his mind. He sells himself very well, which gets him more attention. He always makes sure he is in control of whatever it is he is doing, even if he sometimes pretends otherwise. Eddy Van Daele praised his growing worldly intelligence as much as he does his game.

'Vincent was too wise for his age. I remember when he was eleven. We drove by bus to Paris for the Danone Cup, and he sat in the front. "There's the Louvre…" he pointed out, "…there you have this, and there you have that."'

'Like he was our guide.'

'How did you know all that?' I asked him.

'I was here with my parents a month ago.'

Vincent analysed that tournament for *Canal Plus*. He not only did so competently, he was also very impressive; it was almost as if he had been doing that sort of work for most of his life.'

Life was good for Vincent. But then the ground was knocked out from under his feet, and all the certainties he had woken up with every morning, not least the one that said he'd be with Anderlecht for the foreseeable future, was gone.

His parents were going to divorce.

It meant Vincent was suddenly, visibly unsettled at school, and at the club, Van Daele then had to put a lot of time and effort in keeping him on track. Albert Martens knows that the divorce weighed enormously on the Kompany children, especially as, at first, they had no contact with their mother for months, with Pierre suffering as well because he was suddenly alone.

Despite the sudden lack of income that came with the divorce, the Kompanys were still hesitant in accepting any attractive offer for Vincent from a foreign club. His welfare, as with all of their children, came first. So Anderlecht were able to keep Vincent 'on board', albeit with a renewed and substantial effort expected to continue to commit to his career and personal development, which was the best solution for everyone in what was a torrid time for the family. Vincent admitted to *Het Laatste Nieuws*, 'I have had to grow up and mature quickly. Five people lived on one income alone.'

'The atmosphere at home was very bad. If I had not succeeded in football, we would not have made it.'

'Of course, he suffered from the divorce,' Deraeve says. 'He was less focused, he was mentally absent, he never arrived for training on time.'

The lack of punctuality worsened, at both the football club and at school. For some, it became almost incomprehensible that the problem was allowed to drag on for so long. Vincent knew he was irritating others and that his tardiness was leading to other problems as everyone else now had to wait around for him. This was giving them, not surprisingly, the impression that Vincent Kompany considered himself more important than anyone else. But it was an issue that had origins that were far more straightforward than anyone might have expected because, for all of his life, punctuality had never been an important requirement of his otherwise fairly strict upbringing.

Van Daele admitted, during our conversations, that he was now 'ashamed' of demanding so much of a twelve-year-old when it came to timekeeping and felt as if he wanted to apologise to Vincent for making what he now considers to be unreasonable demands.

'I was too strict. I was always very punctual, and that was Vincent's problem. He wasn't. Demanding that he came in on time didn't make sense. It was not always his fault anyway, for example, public transport was sometimes delayed. But in spite of that, and with the entire group in mind, I still could not be seen to tolerate lateness. But Vincent still did everything at his leisure and was always very cool about it.'

'But he knew why we were strict with him: we knew he had the talent for the starting line-up, and with the better ones, you always have to be stricter than with average players.'

'He thought I was targeting him, but the opposite was true.'

Martens adds: 'I trained him the years before all this started to happen, but Eddy had him in his adolescence... and that is when youngsters start to rebel. I also trained the fourteen to sixteen year olds, who are completely different from the younger ones, they still look up to you and with me, Vincent never rebelled.'

Van Daele: 'Looking back, I was too strict, but on the other hand, I have no real regrets when you see where he is at with his career now. I never had to send Vincent home because he didn't feel like training on any given day. The hardest part was getting him on the pitch, making sure he had his training clothes and boots on, that his laces were tied...'

Martens: 'He challenged Eddy, he tried to go as far as possible. He wanted to play coach himself.'

Van Daele: 'Yes. He always pushed as far as he could go. Maybe a little further sometimes. But he always listened when we said that limit had been reached.'

Martens: 'I sometimes spoke to him about it; I also had many discussions with his father and mother. His mother didn't like Eddy – she felt he was over-strict with Vincent and claimed he didn't like her son.'

Van Daele: 'I drew lessons from that. After Vincent, I always told parents of really promising players that I was very strict simply because their son was an outstanding player. I should have said the same to Vincent's mother at the time. But I didn't because I thought she might tell him and he wouldn't take it seriously. That was a mistake.'

Martens: 'The Kompany's visited my home regularly. My son stayed with them on sleep-overs, and François sometimes stayed with us. They were friends, so I had a different relationship with them. But I often had to explain to his mother why we were strict with Vincent.'

'Pierre was football mad, but his mother did not always allow Vincent to play football. And you had to give time to the family: they demanded attention. His mother was correct, strict, and informed. Eddy is right, though, but mothers are mothers. Pierre wasn't always easy either: you had to explain everything to him, and he also liked to be in the spotlight; he liked you to acknowledge him. He could go on for hours about something that seemed very trivial. But he was always correct. And he did a lot for other children. If he had a sandwich, he would have given half of it away.'

'They were proud, but were also very good people.'

Martens: 'Vincent liked Eddy anyway; he thought he was one of his better coaches. But his relationship with him was sometimes not good; he said I had a better feel for him. Yes, I could restrain him... sometimes. I was more of a father figure. Eddy was the better on the pitch whilst I was more of a mental coach for him.'

Van Daele: 'Was he arrogant? No, never. He was, and is, the way he is. He won't do things he doesn't agree with just to create a good impression. Pointing out to him that he was late and nonchalant, I felt it was my duty, regardless of how he reacted. Also, I thought he would have similar problems later on if he did not learn it then.'

'Which turned out to be the case. He overslept in his first match with his later coach, Frankie Vercauteren.'

Martens: 'I did things differently to Eddy, far more diplomatically. I tried to gain insight and understand my players' life circumstances. With Eddy, everyone was equal, but I followed my own rules, and those guys never forgot that.'

Deraeve: 'Vincent worried about his parents' separation and what had happened; he had to let football go a bit at that time.'

'We realised we had to give him time. But he let himself go a bit, so then it was time to intervene. Vincent needed to be put on edge from time to time by giving him a kick up the backside. That would make him feel he had to show everyone what he could do on the pitch, he'd react in the right way. At one point, we also had to seriously talk to him to keep him here and avoid him doing athletics instead.'

'His mother preferred athletics. At a young age, athletics did not require as much training as football did, so combining it with school was much easier. Perhaps his parents tried to encourage him to take up athletics and leave his football behind?'

Deraeve's suggestion here isn't far off the mark.

Much later in his life, Vincent admitted as much to *Het Nieuwsblad*.

'When I was thirteen, I quit football for a few weeks because there was too much hypocrisy in the game for me. Athletics seemed like a new challenge, but I was fed up with it after just a few weeks. I found it too hard to just run with no ball and no goal in front of me. That's when I realised football was my thing. Looking back in hindsight, I'll admit that I acted awkwardly in those years.'

'That had everything to do with the fact that I find it hard to take criticism.'

Vincent had decided that being a professional footballer was genuinely what he wanted to do. But this internal realisation didn't come with a change of approach or attitude. As far as that was concerned, nothing changed. He still tended to complain to Werner Deraeve when he disagreed with another coach and could, on occasion, be furious in the dressing room with someone. But the next day, he would have forgotten about it.

In other words, he could be bad tempered or irritable, an aspect of his personality that would later soften into a much calmer approach to things, but even so, long-lasting rancour to anyone remained alien to him back then. And although his perception of football could not be more exemplary, he still realised, deep down, that it was 'only a game'.

Albert Martens seems a kind-hearted man, but, as a coach, was a demanding one who may not have considered football to be merely 'only a game' himself.

'I could be furious when things were bad. People often say, "Nice try," but trying is not enough. Children, too, need to know what they are doing. For example, we won a game against Club Brugge 7-1-and I tackled them hard afterwards because they had only sometimes done what I asked. And during training, we fought out some world-class duels. Always four against four, in different groups. Heroic matches they were, with a knife in their teeth, tackles included. And they'd weep! Vincent couldn't stand losing and got angry, but I had to teach him how to deal with losing.'

Vincent has spoken in interviews how that occupational therapy helped his character grow.

'When I was young, I sometimes didn't understand why they were so down on me,' Kompany told *Het Nieuwsblad*. 'Afterwards, they explained that it was because they believed in me. Now, I can only be happy about it, but when you're young, you don't always understand. I thought they treated us like adults very quickly and demanded a lot. That was difficult.'

'I was Vincent Kompany's coach at the U-14 and U-15 teams; he was part of a fantastic line-up,' says Peter Mommaert.

'Vincent was discouraged when he came to the U-14's because he didn't get along with his previous coach. However, he was a real football animal. I tackled him according to the situation: sometimes gently, sometimes a little more harshly, and in doing so, I drew on my experience and feeling as a physical education teacher with the peers of the players I coached.'

'This approach clicked with Vincent and his father.'

As we've discovered, Vincent arrived late for training many times, but that was quickly dealt with. Mommaert would tell him to train alone as well as making him carry the training equipment to and from the pitches. Or he'd send him straight back inside. Vincent soon got the message.

'Even as a thirteen and fourteen year old, Vincent was outspoken. Yes, he could be stubborn and contrary. I liked that he came out with his own opinions, this showed his strong personality and leadership qualities. As long as he expressed his opinion respectfully, I had no problem with that. If he expressed his opinion, it was never because he questioned your authority as a coach, because he respected that.'

'He said what he thought out of a genuine desire to do better.'

'Vincent was a central defender and was allowed to advance to midfield when the situation favoured it. He did that happily and always very capably. Vincent preferred to play as a defensive midfielder and made that clear to me. He had to drive forward – he was a born winner and wanted to put the pressure on in every match.'

But it was take it or leave it, Mommaert adds.

'At a top club like Anderlecht, players have to listen to the coach and don't have too many choices. He needed space; he could claim the ball and exuded calmness at the back. He was the lock on the door with his speed and good positional play. He also had a presence. In midfield, positional play is completely different, and in his drive, he would have run everywhere and soon found himself out of position. In midfield, even more collective responsibility is needed – he was better playing at the back as, when he came up from the defence with the ball at his feet, he was far more danger-ous than he might have been doing so as a midfielder'.

'Vincent was an all-rounder who had everything: technique, speed, insight, person-ality, mentality.'

And he was still, maybe even more of a leader.

'In the dressing room, he was attentive and focused. At half-time, he commented and motivated his teammates. Sometimes, even to the extent that Mommaert might interrupt him – "Hey Vincent, that's my job!" Vincent also applied that attitude on the pitch: he coached and encouraged his teammates throughout the game.'

Mommaert concludes, 'He could already read the game much better than his teammates and could think three steps ahead of them – although he still had a lot to learn. I experienced his appreciation of the work I'd done with him later on when I left Anderlecht. Vincent and his father had organised a farewell party. Pierre said Vincent had blossomed again as a person and footballer with me and had regained his good humour with it – also, that forward momentum in the game had recovered. That public appreciation gave me tremendous pleasure.'

When he was fourteen, Vincent made his debut for the Belgian U-15 national team under the watchful eye of coach Patrick Klinkenberg who combined the role with a job as a physical education teacher.

He regularly went along to Neerpede to look for up and coming talent and, on one such trip, he witnessed Kompany at work for the first time. It only took him a further ten minutes to know what a good player Vincent already was, admitting, almost to himself, that Vincent's technical ability and overall potential meant he'd probably shine playing for Anderlecht even if he was playing at a level of just 60% of what he was capable of, with Vincent only having to raise his own game to 100% in matches against the likes of Club Brugge, Standard de Liège and Genk.

Klinkenberg had now, he surmised, two potentially world-class players in his young squad: Eden Hazard and Vincent Kompany.

'When I saw Vincent playing at Anderlecht, he'd sometimes be playing as a defensive midfielder. And yet, I preferred him as one of three central defenders. That didn't convince him at all, but, eventually, Anderlecht realised that playing in a back three was the best thing for him. They could, of course, say what they wanted, he was their player, not mine, but, for all that, it was with me that he really started to focus on playing as part of the defensive three – although yes, I agree, he was more than capable of also playing as a defensive midfielder, the number four.'

Klinkenberg was already convinced that Vincent had the potential to one day become better than Marcel Desailly, another player who excelled as either, and primarily, a central defender or defensive midfielder and who, with France, ultimately became a world champion. However, according to Klinkenberg, Kompany saw himself as more of a player who got on the ball and distributed it within the game, much like a quarterback does in US football. He may, muses Klinkenberg, have been able to build a career as a midfielder in Belgium with Anderlecht or an equally dominant club, but it might have been a little bit more challenging for him to do so if he went on to play elsewhere in Europe and for an elite team, let alone, as Desailly had done, on the world stage.

Klinkenberg: 'He wouldn't be an ideal fit in a 4-3-3 playing system, because in that, the midfielders have to go to extremes for ninety per cent of the time because there are only three of them instead of four. They have to do an enormous amount of running; you need incredible levels of stamina for it. I explained this to him, and he gave the impression of accepting that explanation.'

It is striking how the tactical preferences of Deraeve, Martens and Klinkenberg are all similar – they all saw Vincent growing into the professional game as a central defender, with Klinkenberg emphasising, again, how he felt Vincent's game was not, certainly as a midfielder, suited to playing in the 4-3-3 formation that so many of the leading teams in Europe were adopting.

'I think of his dribbling, his dominance in the air, his shots from distance. He scores easily and is quick over the first few metres. He can infiltrate opposition defences, is good at the short game, but he needed to be able to watch a game unfold in front of him. He has a good kick and is very good on long balls. In a 4-4-2 perhaps, he could have functioned as a midfielder, but in a 4-3-3, it would have been difficult for him because of his running capacity – you have to be able to play for ninety minutes at a constant speed of twelve to fourteen kilometres per hour.'

'Vincent was not the man to have on the ball throughout the entire match.'

According to Klinkenberg, the first time Vincent came to the national team, he acted as if he had always been there. He had charisma and quickly felt at ease in what might have been a pressurised environment. But Vincent had good reason to feel relaxed and self-assured. At fifteen, he already looked like an adult and was bursting with talent.

'As a fifteen and sixteen-year-old, he played with the national team for about fifteen to twenty matches. Matches against club teams included. In the beginning, he did play as part of a midfield three, but mentally, he couldn't quite do that yet. So, I asked for a different attitude and more commitment. I left him at home for a while to make him realise what was expected of him. At that age, you must be very clear and make your demands. Players do have obligations to fulfil.'

'We select footballers because of their talent and capabilities, but talent alone is not enough. Whoever wants to make it also has to be good in terms of physical qualities such as stamina and speed, mentality and insight into the game – and they must work hard every day.'

For the final match of a European Championship qualifying group, played in Belgium, Klinkenberg opted to leave Vincent at home as he felt he needed to fulfil his role as a number three better. Staying at home, rather than playing, would give him time to think about his place in the side, but also reminded him that, as good as he was, he wasn't indispensable.

'He needed to perform in his role at number three in a much more responsible way. I wanted more discipline in his game, and he needed to defend more decisively. At that age, he had still not fully mastered the details of defending in a zone with four, rather than three, defenders.'

Vincent had been playing at Anderlecht in a 3-4-3 playing system, whilst all national youth teams followed the 4-3-3 model. According to Klinkenberg, Vincent needed to pay more attention to the tactical guidelines and paid the price by missing out.

'I didn't complain about his commitment, and I'm not going to say he didn't listen either, but you couldn't always convince him.'

The conflict between player and coach escalated.

'Indeed…,' says Klinkenberg, '…at one point, I told Vincent that he was no longer allowed to play for the national team. Because of disciplinary and tactical reasons – as far as the disciplinary reasons are concerned, I am not going to go into detail as what happens in the dressing room stays in the dressing room. But look, I am a very demanding coach, especially in terms of tactics. At that time, in Belgium, tactically, there was still a lot of work to do. Vincent had a lot of tactical freedom at Anderlecht, and I don't blame the club for that: it will always do what it thinks is best for the club rather than the national team, including at youth level.'

'But as coach of the national team, I had to serve the interests of the entire national team, not Anderlecht. Vincent was best as number three, and that role required tactical rigour from the player. And he was not used to this. He had to comply with individual and collective goals and did so insufficiently.'

'I had warned him several times.'

Klinkenberg now profoundly regrets that he did not know that Vincent's parents were no longer together and admits his approach would have been different if he had been aware of this.

'I would have been equally demanding, but in a different way.'

Marc Van Geersom, a former youth coordinator with the national teams, acknowledges that 'struggles' existed between Kompany and Klinkenberg.

'But I never intervened,' he says, 'Patrick and Vincent were mature enough to discuss their problems.'

Van Geersom wanted to uphold the national coach's position and autonomy – the players had to adapt to the coach, not vice versa. Van Geersom remembers Vincent '...as a great personality with innate leadership qualities. He was head and shoulders above the rest. He was precocious and had a mind of his own. His problems at home made him more independent than others, so you had to deal with him like an adult, albeit with some caution.'

'But sometimes you have to set an example to make someone come to an understanding.'

On the Royal Belgian Football Association website, Vincent's record as a youth international shows three appearances for both the U-16 and U-17 national teams, all six of these appearances coming in 2002, including playing in a 3-0 win over Poland U-16's that March and another 3-0 victory, this time over Slovakia in the Sirenka Cup competition six months later as part of the U-17's team. He was on the bench for the 0-0 draw with Cyprus that followed that match but, after that game, was never selected for the national team at youth level again.

Klinkenberg: 'He had not done so well during the first match of the Sirenka Cup (a 1-2 defeat to the Romania U-17's). Yes, he was on the bench in the last match, but you shouldn't look for anything behind that. The philosophy of the Belgian FA is that all players in the squad should be given a chance. Also, don't forget that we played three games in three days; that takes a lot out of the players.'

Interestingly, in their next seven matches, all of which were played without Vincent Kompany in the team, the Belgian U-17s didn't win a single one of them.

At the time, Eddy Van Daele was scouting a player in Eastern Europe along with Werner Deraeve when they heard that Vincent had played as a forward during the Sirenka Cup in Poland.

Van Daele: 'We nearly couldn't believe it!'

Nearly?

'At Anderlecht, the fact is that Vincent had played as a number ten, so we didn't think it was that much of a tactical masterstroke,' says Werner Deraeve.

Maybe not. But it still seemed indicative of the fragile relationship between Vincent and Klinkenberg, that he'd been played in a position that didn't best suit him or his game. Vincent had previously displayed his capabilities as a player who could get forward with Pierre recalling a game when, despite playing as a central defender, Vincent strode forward during the first half of a match, played a quick one-two with a teammate before hitting a shot that came off the crossbar. This meant, of course, he was now defensively exposed as the opposition regained possession. Despite this, you might think that Vincent would have got some praise for his attacking instinct and for so nearly scoring a goal – but no, at half time, he was scolded by his coach for abandoning his defensive duties.

Vincent had another potential setback to his career at fifteen when he suffered a severe knee injury, one that kept him from playing and training for several months. Klinkenberg did his best to reassure Vincent, advising him to take care at Anderlecht and to let his recovery take as long as was needed.

'We had nothing against a players' recovery taking time, it meant he did not come into the picture of foreign scouts. He could also recuperate from his busy life. Remember: he trained four times a week with the team then three times individually, and also went to school. Playing for the national team on top of that made it an even more hellish life for him, but anyway, it is what it is.'

But Vincent had already decided around this time that he no longer wanted to work with Klinkenberg. His feeling was that he wasn't learning anything new with the respective Belgian schoolboy and youth team setups, adding that he felt there was little to no communication between Klinkenberg and Anderlecht and that, as a consequence, he felt as if his best interests were not being served.

Deraeve: "Of course, at Anderlecht, we had nothing against Vincent pulling out of the national youth team. It meant that we could spend more time with him ourselves. I then received a phone call from Marc Van Geersom who asked me if I could persuade Vincent to return to the national youth team, specifically the U-18's, who he was then coaching. But, ultimately, that was up to Vincent to decide. It wasn't my job to intervene in that or decide for him. I told Van Geersom that Vincent did not easily backtrack on a decision. Anderlecht will, of course, always release a player if he is selected for the national youth team and I told him that. And of course, it's an honour for the player and recognition for our work and the player's market value can rise if he is an international.'

'But we would rather have had him in Neerpede at that time.'

Patrick Klinkenberg fears that some of these facts may have been misinterpreted.

'Did I have Vincent play as a number ten in Poland? Yes. Were we intending to launch him in that position? No, of course we weren't!'

'He was going to have a great career as a central defender; I always said so. But in that one game, I wanted to test Kompany at number ten, playing him just behind the strikers. It also had to do with balance in the team, injuries, and circumstances that every coach who has to put a team together before the final match of a tournament recognises. I can understand that Anderlecht were surprised at his playing there. It was an exception, a stopgap. In a youth-friendly tournament.'

'The story is untrue that I scolded Vincent for being out of position after his shot hit the crossbar. That would have been all too ridiculous!'

Klinkenberg is clear about that time in Vincent's career and decision. Which does not rest well with Eddy Van Daele.

'Sorry, but that explanation about Vincent up front is not quite correct,' says Van Daele. 'Marc Van Geersom told Werner Deraeve and I at the time that they wanted to make a striker out of Vincent. According to them, he could become a new type of Jan Koller.'

Koller was a tall and physically imposing Czechoslovakian who played as a striker for Anderlecht from 1999 to 2001.

Deraeve: 'I had heard from people in football that Klinkenberg wanted to put Vincent in the striker position; I am happy with that.'

Marc Van Geersom, meanwhile, categorically denied that he said this or that it was an option to retrain Vincent as a striker or number ten.

'I don't know what the people at the Belgian FA thought about it, but neither Patrick Klinkenberg nor myself ever had that idea.'

His comment drew that particular conversation to an abrupt close.

But one question remains: what was the young Vincent Kompany's recollection of all this? Is it possible that he misunderstood things and those misunderstandings have grown since then?

Did Vincent's preference for the number ten position play a role in the story?

Two weeks later, Anderlecht took part in an international tournament in Lille, France, which they had won a year before.

Vincent played as a central defender, his usual position.

Van Daele: 'He starts dribbling, loses the ball and the opponent scores. A bit later, he makes an unnecessary mistake; it's a penalty, and we are 0-2 down. At half-time, I ask what's wrong. His reply? "Well, sir, it's not my favourite position in the team." He still wanted to play as a striker.'

'There's your position, I replied, pointing at his fellow defenders. I let him cool down for five minutes and said: "Vincent. Listen. If we think that you're able to make a big career, it's there. And it's not the striker position!" He was angry at hearing me say that. He threw his shoes on the ground and yelled out his frustration. In the second half, he single-handedly made the difference. He provided the equaliser. He also never asked to play up front again. They had turned his head at the national team, making him a little crazy.'

Martens: 'With Patrick Klinkenberg, Vincent once said after a match with the national team that he hadn't learnt anything.'

'In turn, Kompany said he didn't even want to play for the national youth team anymore,' laughs Werner Deraeve. 'That supposedly suited his career development better. Yes, that boy knew very well what he wanted. But not long afterwards, in February 2004, he played his first match in the full national team, against France.'

In subsequent interviews, however, Vincent gave a new or additional reason why he no longer wanted to play in the youth national teams.

'School is important. I gave up the national team for a year and a half to concentrate on school,' he claimed in *Het Laatste Nieuws*.

'I had to repeat a year because I was always away.'

And that was something he didn't want to go through again.

'My father played in the first division in Congo but gave his studies priority. That's the way it should be.'

'I also had to be sidelined for four months with a knee injury. I was so disappointed that I often just stayed absent when I was supposed to be at the club to work on my rehabilitation. In the national team, I had been sidelined from the squad. At that age, I was also impressionable, often hanging around on the streets. I was really at a crossroads,' he told *Sport-Voetbalmagazine*. 'While my peers were away with the national team, I was able to catch up at school. I also trained three times as usual during that period.'

A challenging time for the still-maturing Vincent Kompany. But more was to come, only this time it would centre around his personal rather than professional life.

Vincent's side of his broken family was facing big financial difficulties around the time of his fifteenth birthday – Pierre who now lived alone with the three children, was unemployed and on state benefits. The situation came up a few times and, as much as they could, Anderlecht helped them out at the end of what would have been another difficult month on more than one occasion. According to Deraeve, Pierre greatly appreciating that help, giving his word he would now not look to transfer Vincent to another club. For every year that his son remained at Anderlecht, his transfer value went up, and the club stood, eventually, to earn more and more money from his inevitable departure to bigger and better things.

By the time he was sixteen, Vincent had signed a full-time contract with Anderlecht although, even before then, he was already receiving a substantial amount of money from them – this was despite Belgian clubs not being allowed to pay a player any kind of salary before he was sixteen. What was now making things potentially difficult for Anderlecht was that clubs in the rest of Europe could now sign on their young players as professionals before they were sixteen, something they were increasingly becoming very worried about as it potentially meant they could lose Vincent before really seeing the very best of him in their first team.

By then, Vincent was very clear about the route he wanted his career to take. At just sixteen, he told Van Daele, who ended up spending nearly three decades coaching at Anderlecht, that he wanted to be considered part of the first-team squad as, within a year, Vincent expected to be one of the players regarded as a member of the first team's strongest starting XI.

These were not unreasonable expectations on his part. Things were moving quickly, and with it came the visible recognition of Vincent's value to the club. Upon signing his first contract with Anderlecht, Pierre Kompany had been given a car, courtesy of the club. It was only a second-hand Mitsubishi, but it was a sign of what was to come. A short time afterwards, Pierre was able to trade in the Mitsubishi for an all-terrain vehicle whilst, a little while after that, he was driving a Mercedes, not the most common of sights in the city's North Quarter. After all, despite his car and newly enhanced status, Pierre still lived in social housing. As for Vincent, it was all that Anderlecht could do to curb his enthusiasm, talent, and voracious ambition, with Van Daele admitting, 'We were constantly working with Vincent on just keeping him focused.'

Little wonder. There'd always been distractions for both the player and Anderlecht. Vincent had long been the target of other clubs, many of whom had first shown an interest in signing him when he was only twelve. Ajax and PSV Eindhoven, two Dutch football giants, were amongst Vincent's earliest admirers, as were Lille and Le Havre in France, two clubs renowned throughout European for the reputation and success of their youth training centres. Paris Saint-Germain, not then the behemoths of the game they are today, added themselves to the queue of Vincent's admirers, as did Marseille, the club that Vincent had long since announced was his favourite. Then there was Juventus in Italy and, you can guarantee, interest from clubs in England, Germany and Spain, not to mention Anderlecht's major domestic rivals in Belgium such as Standard de Liège and Club Brugge.

Remarking on the growing interest in his son, Pierre Kompany, in a feature with *Het Laatste Nieuws*, said, 'We are not making a carnival of it. His mum and I never coached our sons as top footballers but as children.'

Vincent's luck may have been that his parents did not chase immediate wealth. The 'reward' for their altruistic approach had now arrived.

By the time he was fifteen, interest in Vincent from Bundesliga giants Bayern Munich became a tempting reality, with the Kompany's invited to spend time with them by the Bundesliga giants. Deraeve countered their interest by making it clear to Bayern's representatives that Vincent was definitely staying put as far as he was concerned.

'We pointed out that he had every intention of staying with Anderlecht, in growing with us. He also had excellent facilities here, not only where he could finish his schooling but also combine that with his football.'

'It came down to making Vincent feel good, by putting things into place that suited him best at the time.'

Anderlecht knew they had an asset on their hands and were going to do their utmost to protect it for as long as possible.

Deraeve: 'We had to work non-stop in order to keep him at Anderlecht. We increased his salary every three months once he'd started playing for the first team at seventeen. But we played it very open and honest with him whenever interest from other clubs came in and always left it for him and his father to decide what to do next.'

With the salaries, signing-on fees and perks that were openly being offered by other top clubs, Anderlecht's hierarchy soon realised that they were not going to be able to compete for Vincent's services for very much longer. Cannily, Vincent used the offers that had been made as a negotiating tactic whenever he and Anderlecht sat down to discuss his next contract, even though he was not primarily motivated by the money on offer, with Deraeve admitting, 'He was not too demanding. We always did everything we could. There was mutual respect, and I wasn't too strict either. Vincent has a lot of respect for people who, in his eyes, deserve just that. He will never mistreat you if you have looked out for him.'

'In Neerpede, I sometimes talked to Pierre and Vincent, about their family issues,' says then general manager Michel Verschueren. 'Pierre was always very amiable. In their difficult period, the club helped the family.'

Verschueren acknowledges that there were problems with the youth flow into the first team, but believed that the youth players should look at themselves in the mirror first.

'Often talented players left us too early. And they sometimes returned after a few years, full of disappointment. Why the flow of youth players from Neerpede to the first team was so difficult for many years, I really don't know.'

'You must have discipline, know what you want, and make sacrifices. In that respect, the Kompany family is an example: they had the patience. Others didn't.'

Pierre Kompany had, by then, started working as a teacher in Brussels. In addition to that, the club was working with him so that he could install his water windmill in Pedepark on behalf of the city council. Once again, the family were keeping their heads above water. Vincent, now free from some of the pressures he had been feeling, continued to improve as a footballer, not least because his school facilities were so ideal for his needs that, at specific times, he could concentrate almost exclusively on football.

Anderlecht then switched gears to an even higher level, with Vincent becoming one of the first youngsters at the club to receive individual training. This covered four disciplines: football, technical, physical and psychological coaching. The club invested in making that individual coaching as high quality as possible according to the scientific data available at the time and was collaborating with professor Kenny De Meirleir, an exercise physiologist at the Vrije Universiteit of Brussels.

Martens: 'Vincent became a star in the meantime. You have to be able to deal with that; don't underestimate it. If you go from nothing to the top quickly, who deals with that really well? If you suddenly earn ten, fifty or two hundred times what you previously earned? You win the lottery, but you have to keep getting up every day. I have always told them they are no better than anyone else when this happens, that they should always keep their feet on the ground and never forget where they came from.'

'You can, after all, only ever eat one steak at a time, and you certainly can't drive two cars at once. Anyone looking for pure happiness that way will soon find it unfulfilling. Vincent is one of the exceptions to whom that message has reached. The amounts earnt are also no longer proportional to performance: young players can earn €600,000 or €700,000 gross per year, which is not normal. And that also does not determine a person's value in society. But top players like Vincent are not so concerned with money; they only think about the game.'

Vincent trained four times a week with the player group, and on top of that, there were two to three additional individual training sessions.

Deraeve: 'That is a lot, even more than the professional players. But if you want to reach the top, it is necessary.'

Van Daele: 'At half past three, he trained with the first team and came to me at five. He was not obliged to return to me because he had already trained. Yet he always came, which characterised him: he wanted to be a better player. This was proof that he wanted to get to the top. His existing qualities were improved whilst his less good sides were also worked on, like practicing crosses with his left and right foot. He worked hard on his heading, too.'

Vincent admits that he needed that drive himself, adding, 'In my youth, I was always the one who represented the group off the pitch. That was also one of my great qualities.'

But as a coach, Van Daele points out that you had to make the training interesting and not just put on sessions for the sake of it. 'With Vincent, you had to make him do something for points or whatever, anything at all, something extra that always made it a bit more interesting because otherwise he trained nonchalantly. Vincent needed constant challenges. And he kept on arguing. Occasionally, I said: "Vincent, that's enough, stop!"'

Kompany agreed with Van Daele: "He is one hundred per cent right. I needed difficult situations to become stronger. In my youth, I could sometimes not step up in training. Some people said, "Oh well, as long as he is there during the big matches." But I realise now that you must play every match with the same attitude. If only out of respect for the opponent.'

He also started taking a step back verbally.

'When I now read all the things I used to say, I sometimes think: the young Vincent Kompany, he just said anything he liked!'

Kompany was coping with the individual training sessions and could handle the heavier training rhythm. However, at school, he sometimes fell asleep in class due to the physical workload.

Deraeve: 'He became so good we hid him from foreign talent scouts. That's why he was not allowed to play with the U-19's. It was almost a stroke of luck if he got injured. "Please, don't put him in the picture," I told the coaches. I was criticised for holding back his development.'

Eventually, Kompany was playing so well that it soon became irresponsible to hold him back and not to let him move on.

He was clearly more than ready for the big time.

Assistant head coach Frankie Vercauteren (a left winger who made over 350 first-team appearances for Anderlecht, as well as playing 63 times for the Belgian team) had long had an eye on him and, in consultation with head coach Hugo Broos, suggested moving him first to the B-team and then up to the first team. Thus, and still only sixteen, Vincent left the youth centre at a time when, as we have already seen, as good as he was, that club issue about their best young players not being able to break into the first team was still very evident.

Would Vincent rise above that particular glass ceiling?

Deraeve: 'Vincent entered the first-team dressing room with all his natural flair. Although a number of the older players thought he should listen carefully first before expressing his thoughts. But Vincent pushed himself; he is a natural leader. He had the innate class as a footballer, technically and physically: he was a magnificent athlete, always a little bigger than others his age.'

Michel Verschueren looks at the transition more broadly, including from the Kompany family's point of view.

'The combination of football and studies (for Vincent) had been tough and demanding, especially for a family that did not have it easy financially – with the story of his father, a political refugee who needed seven years to get the necessary papers and ended up living as a wanted man, working as a taxi driver for years to pay for his engineering studies. Plus looking after his three children. He has done it all. Well done! This is a family that fought not to get from nothing to something, but to reach the top.'

'No matter what difficulties they faced, in each and every case, they achieved success.'

CHAPTER SIX
'VINCENT WAS AN ACTOR, HE COULD PLAY ON THE STAGE'

The challenges Vincent faced combining his education with football, his wanting to excel at both, and the difficulties this caused him, have already been outlined.

So, how did Vincent manage at school as his football career went from strength to strength?

He was twelve years old when he exited the doors of his primary school on the Vlaamsesteenweg in Brussels for the last time. A few months later, in September 1998, his new daily journey involved a walk down a few streets from his home to a building on Mout Avenue, close to the Stock Exchange.

He was about to take his first steps at the Maria-Boodschaplyceum Senior school.

The school describes itself as a Dutch language hub where ideas and discussions are prompted through lectures; a cross-disciplinary school and an 'active' one which gives its students room to live and learn, a place where they prepare themselves for whatever they want to do with their lives.

Vincent already knew what he is going to do with his life.

Christel, his sister, was a 'veteran' of two years at the school who could, if and when necessary, show him the ropes. He was confident and soon felt settled, and, at first, all seemed well. He was smart, both school-smart and street-smart. He was taught in the same school group for all his classes, and even if he was already finding the combination of wanting to do well at school with progressing in his football career a challenge, it was an environment where he could only prosper as long as he got his head down and worked hard.

But, after only three weeks, and after a school sports weekend he spent in Tongerlo, his resolution wavered; he has become the leader of a group of boys whose modus operandi was to play practical jokes on each other as well as other members of the school. If, previously, he had erred, it had been at his smaller, more informal primary school, where his parents might have been able to keep a tighter hold over him. They offered him guidance on an almost daily basis, knowing that the school would, if necessary, ensure he was swiftly dealt with if his standards of behaviour dropped at any time.

This was not the case at his new school, where students were not so likely to be chastised for their errors, and it has to be said, to the disdain of many of the teachers who felt that this policy of laissez-faire was not going to be one that kept Vincent on track.

'With us, the distance between teacher and pupil did not exist,' says his former teacher, Simonne Pollet.

'The pupils respected the teachers, and we did not feel worth more than them. The mentality was open; children were allowed to speak their minds.'

Pupils were, therefore, rarely punished, and this was made clear to their parents upon enrolment. Headmaster De Gols' approach was talking to wayward pupils so they realised they were doing something wrong and modified their behaviour voluntarily rather than have the school take punitive action against them. Some teachers felt that they could resolve any issues they were having with Vincent by sending him to the headmaster, a course of action that, at many schools, usually resulted in a feeling of trepidation, even terror, on behalf of the wrongdoer. But not in this case. If Vincent was sent to see Mr De Gols, he knew he wouldn't be punished for whatever he'd said or done.

Vincent was, and, unexpectedly, now finding the transition from primary to senior school difficult. With the teaching and overall academic side of things, he had no problems adjusting at all. Still, for his subject teachers, Vincent wasn't quite ready for the self-responsibility that was now expected of him. But this was hardly surprising. For a start, Vincent was now at a school with many more pupils than had been enrolled at his primary school, meaning, at once, he was the proverbial 'small fish in a big pond'.

So, for someone who liked to lead from the front and be very visible with it, Vincent was finding the size of his new school was making everyday life very impersonal and, as a result, he felt totally anonymous to begin with. At his primary school, everyone knew who he was; this included the teachers who, as we have seen, knew precisely how to handle him, which was a long way from being repeated at the Maria-Boodschaplyceum. He now had lots of different teachers who didn't know him or seem to want to make an effort to get to know him. He felt lost and entirely alone. With that, his self-esteem initially dropped to a hither-to-unknown level, something the coaches at Anderlecht soon noticed.

But some of his teachers *had* noticed him. And remember him to this day. Simonne Pollet, a Mathematics teacher, remembers Vincent as a '...well proportioned and rather striking young man who was always stylishly dressed'. She felt, at the time, that Vincent knew that he looked good and, despite his still tender years, was already something of a charmer.

During our conversation, she imitated a performer, bestriding the stage with their chest stuck out and shoulders pushed back.

'He was an actor; he could play on the stage. He'd try to bluff you with an explanation that you'd always end up believing; he had all the necessary facial expressions and could, if he needed to, become the very epitome of innocence itself'.

These memories are very clearly good ones as far as Ms Pollet is concerned, as she revisits them with a warm smile on her face.

By the time Vincent had reached his third year at senior school, things were very different. He now cut a very commanding physical character, one who stood head and shoulders above all his classmates. Rita Moors, who taught Dutch during Vincent's third and fourth years at the school, commented on how Vincent used his height to show how confident he now was within himself and the way he moved about the classroom.

Unlike some tall children, she says, Vincent never felt self-conscious or tried to hide away, even if he did sit at the back of the classroom. She saw him as very much the 'top dog' in his class, this being best illustrated by how confident he was during any classroom discussion.

Vincent's Chemistry teacher, Griet Blondiau, recalls that Vincent '...liked to argue, to be correct. And to be interesting. Of course, he wanted to stand out occasionally; he was a man among children. On the playground, he reigned supreme. The whole school now knew him, and everyone saw that he was much better as a footballer than the other pupils.'

'Vincent was not a follower but a personality: sensible, polite, respectful and direct. If something was on his mind, he said so. If there was a maths test scheduled on Monday, then he was the first to say that his weekend activities required more time for him to prepare properly. With that, students voted on which day they preferred.'

Vincent was turning out to be an adolescent unlike any that his teachers might previously have taught. As for his fellow pupils, they all grew to like him '...because of his presence and mannerisms,' claims Johan De Donder, a Dutch teacher in Vincent's first two years and History in Vincent's first three years.

Simonne Pollet: 'In class, even in the early years, you had to force him to pay close attention because he was not self-motivated and did not do what was required. When he had to answer, he could beat around the bush because he didn't know the answer properly. But sometimes he'd put on a show and was funny because he wanted to be in the limelight.'

Pollet recollects how Vincent's class was one of the most challenging that she had to deal with. Yet, at her last lesson before her retirement, she received flowers from Vincent's class, who, under his leadership, went one step further by bringing her cakes, biscuits and drinks as well as decorating her classroom.

In Vincent's class, she remembers almost shaking her head in trepidation at what might lie ahead before she stepped through the classroom door. 'I always took a deep breath before stepping in. I could never teach without worry and always had to use all my strength.'

She was not alone: a Dutch teacher warned her that Vincent and his little group would sometimes hide behind curtains or in cupboards. But Vincent did work hard in Maths and rarely acted up. Pollet would keep the academic pressure on him and his classmates by giving them assignments they had to complete at home, with their parents acknowledging they had done the work by signing a form confirming so.

With Dutch and History teacher Johan De Donder, someone with a stricter approach to teaching, pupils found they had less chance to stir things up within the classroom. But this didn't stop Vincent from being assertive or wanting to stand out; he resorted to doing so without misbehaving in the process by showing, very emphatically, that he understood what the teacher was trying to explain. He'd do this by repeatedly sitting on the edge of his seat, ready to answer any question that was asked, either giving the correct answer himself or by following that up by testing the teacher with a question of his own.

If, on a rare occasion, another student answered a question before Vincent could do so himself, he'd still publicly speak up by agreeing with the answer given, commenting that he also knew what the answer was.

De Donder remembers Vincent's enthusiasm well.

'If his arm went up, I thought: there he is again!'

Vincent might then ask a long and thoughtfully worded supplementary question, which De Donder would duly answer, mindful that, as well as responding to Vincent with the sort of detailed response that he'd expect, she also had to keep, at the same time, the other thirty or so pupils there quiet and interested. De Donder was also aware that the class needed to be pushed as much as possible.

As Vincent's football career continued to develop, with him now playing at higher levels, his promising classroom performances inevitably began to drop off. In his Chemistry class, for example, his teacher often noticed that Vincent would sit with his head resting on his arms – and this was not the only subject where that happened. In Rita Moors's Dutch class, he was the only student she'd ever had in forty years of teaching who fell asleep during a lesson.

'He was sometimes overtired, but I woke him up: with me, they have to pay attention.'

Sometimes, he slept; sometimes, he cooperated. He was not embarrassed if he got a comment about it, he'd apologise and said he was tired. Characteristic honesty. Moors felt powerless to do much about it, other than to accept his apology, be it for falling asleep or general tardiness.

'When there were problems, we talked to him,' she says, 'what else could we do?'

Despite Vincent's tendency to nod off during her lessons, Moors liked him and often asked how his football was going after class, understanding, as Vincent spoke of all the training and playing commitments he had at Anderlecht, why he was struggling to sometimes even pay attention, much less stay awake. For example, during Vincent's fourth year, he spent a week with the youth national team after the Christmas break in Turkey. 'There...', she said, '...he was almost considered an adult; here he was an ordinary teenager again. Mentally, that was not easy for him, and it showed. On top of that came the divorce of his parents. What do you expect then?'

The teachers knew that Vincent's parents did not live together at the end of his second year. That helped explain why his behaviour at the time was initially met with some tolerance on their part. They realised that the divorce and the combination of school and football, along with the onset of puberty, were causing him some problems but they also recognised that his football offered a way out, with one teacher telling me, 'He wanted to stand out, but didn't know what to do with himself, so he was very moody.'

Yet, as Vincent was evolving into a leader on the football field in the early years of his time at senior school, he also wanted to be a leader there. According to his Maths teacher, Vincent wanted to be in charge. But he went too far in the wrong direction, so keen was he to make a good impression.

One of the things he ended up doing was encouraging some of the other pupils to have a negative outlook. He had, for example, something of a 'fan club', a group of four other boys who adored him and would, keen to curry favour with Vincent, pretty much do whatever he told them to do. Because of his influence over them, the other students became very wary, even afraid of them. One teacher took that little group to task, telling them not to let themselves be ordered around so quickly and to '...dare to be yourselves.'

The clearest example of Vincent's having 'gone off the rails' at school occurred at the annual sports weekend. This took place over the third weekend of September and involved the younger students heading out to the sports centre at Tongerlo to play sports and become better acquainted with one another – you might, were they all ten years or so older, have called it a team building exercise. Not long after they'd arrived, a staff member discovered that all the fruit juices they'd been allocated had disappeared. They were soon found under Vincent's mattress in his dormitory. Caught red-handed, Vincent admitted that he and some of his friends had taken the drinks, adding that they hadn't drunk any of them and had merely done so 'for sport'. This was, on reflection, Vincent all over. He was pushing the boundaries as far as he could to reinforce his status as the leader, the alpha-male in the group. This

Continued on page 117

It's lonely at the top. A three-year-old Vincent stands next to teacher Miss Inge. It won't be his last sky blue shirt. (Inge Devos)

Ten-year-old Vincent pictured during the annual school Day of Sports with his arm around his friend Murtaza, who Vincent liked to play football with. (Jaklien Deliens)

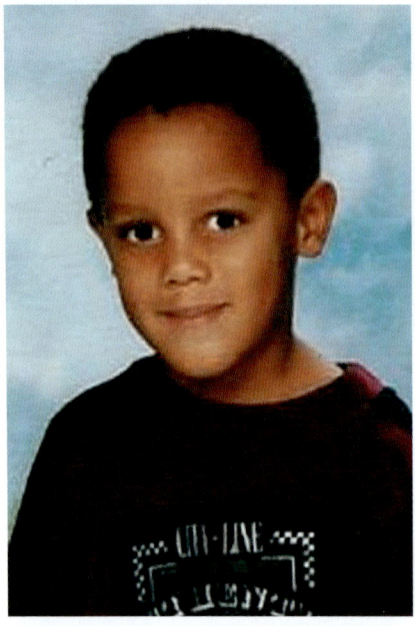

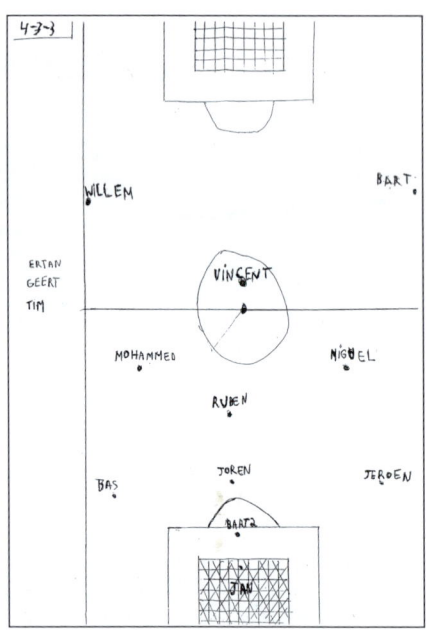

Six-year-old Vincent in the last class of kindergarten. (Joske Gezels)

Young coach VK decides the tactics, 4-3-3, with himself of course as the number 10. (Marleen Metens)

The famous two Vincents, Kompany and Petit, brothers in arms, during the annual school party in their first year at primary school. (Johan Vanhooren)

During the Javelin Festival in Boechout. Because the javelins were too heavy for his age, Vincent threw a field hockey ball. He waits for the result. (Francis De Buyst)

[Left] After winning the Flemish school championship volleyball playing for his school, The Maria-Boodschaplyceum, aged thirteen. (Marleen Metens)

[Below] Aged twelve, Vincent and his sixth grade classmates pose with Master Joost. (Joost Meskens)

[Above] Vincent, fifth from the left on the back row, playing for RSC Anderlecht U15 at the NAC Breda tournament in the Netherlands. (Peter Mommaert)
[Below] Playing for RSC Anderlecht's youth team in 2002. (www.rsca.be)

[Above] Vincent with his classmates during the last year at the Athenaeum in Anderlecht. (Viviane Smekens) [Below] Vincent reads coursework in the school playground at the Athenaeum in Anderlecht. (Viviane Smekens)

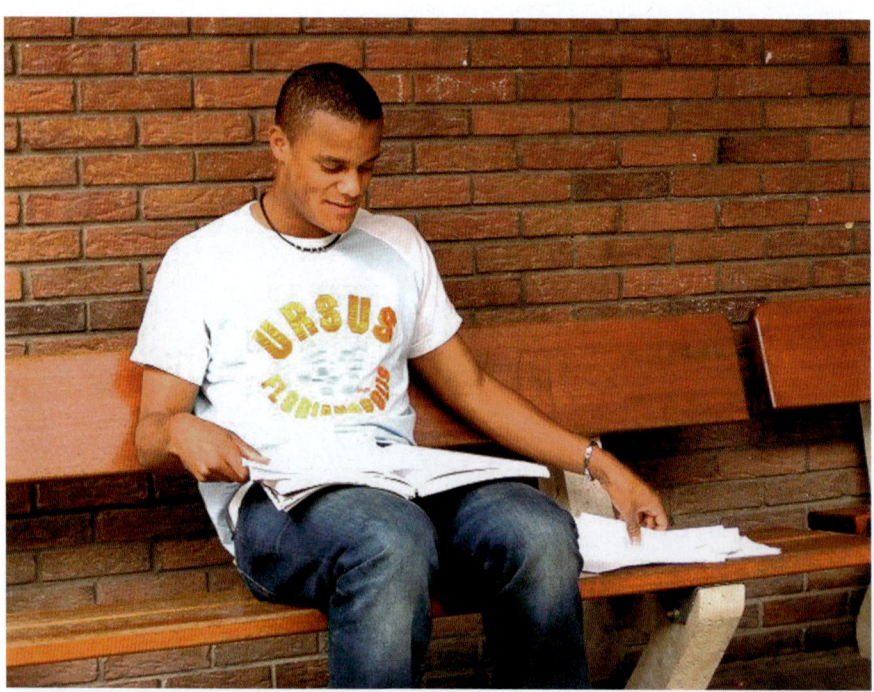

[Above] Still an adolescent, Vincent becomes a member of the Anderlecht A-team. (www.rsca.be) [Below Left] September 2002, playing for Anderlecht's youth team. (www.rsca.be) [Right] A short massage during training at Anderlecht. (www.rsca.be)

[Above] Kompany and his team mate Anthony Vanden Borre watching Chelsea's Eidur Gudjohnsen. (www.rsca.be) [Below] Vincent with a member of Anderlecht's Ketjesclub, 'Little Fellows Club'. (www.rsca.be)

Vincent Kompany – Don't get dribbled: protect yourself! One goal: all together against AIDS! Vincent is the face of a public health campaign in 2005.

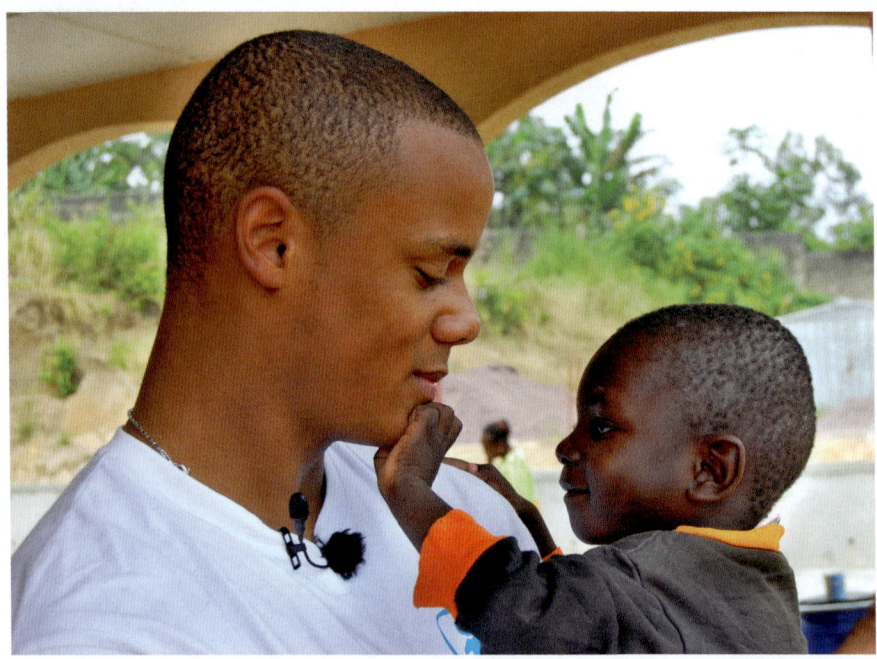

[Above] Vincent visiting an SOS Children's Village in the Democratic Republic of Congo.(SOS Children's Villages) [Below] Having fun and getting sweaty during a friendly football game in the SOS Children's Village of Bukavu, Democratic Republic of Congo. (SOS Children's Villages)

Vincent Kompany during the press conference which unveiled him as a Hamburg player in June 2006. (DPA / Alamy)

Stuttgart's Ricardo Osorio and Hamburg's Vincent Kompany fight for the ball in the Bundesliga match at the Gottlieb Daimler Stadium, Stuttgart, in April 2008. (Bernd Weissbrod / Alamy)

Vincent celebrates at Wembley Stadium after Manchester City beat Stoke City 1-0 to clinch the 2011 FA Cup final. (Neal Simpson / Alamy)

Manchester City captain Vincent Kompany celebrates with the Barclays Premier League trophy in May 2012. (Mike Egerton / Alamy)

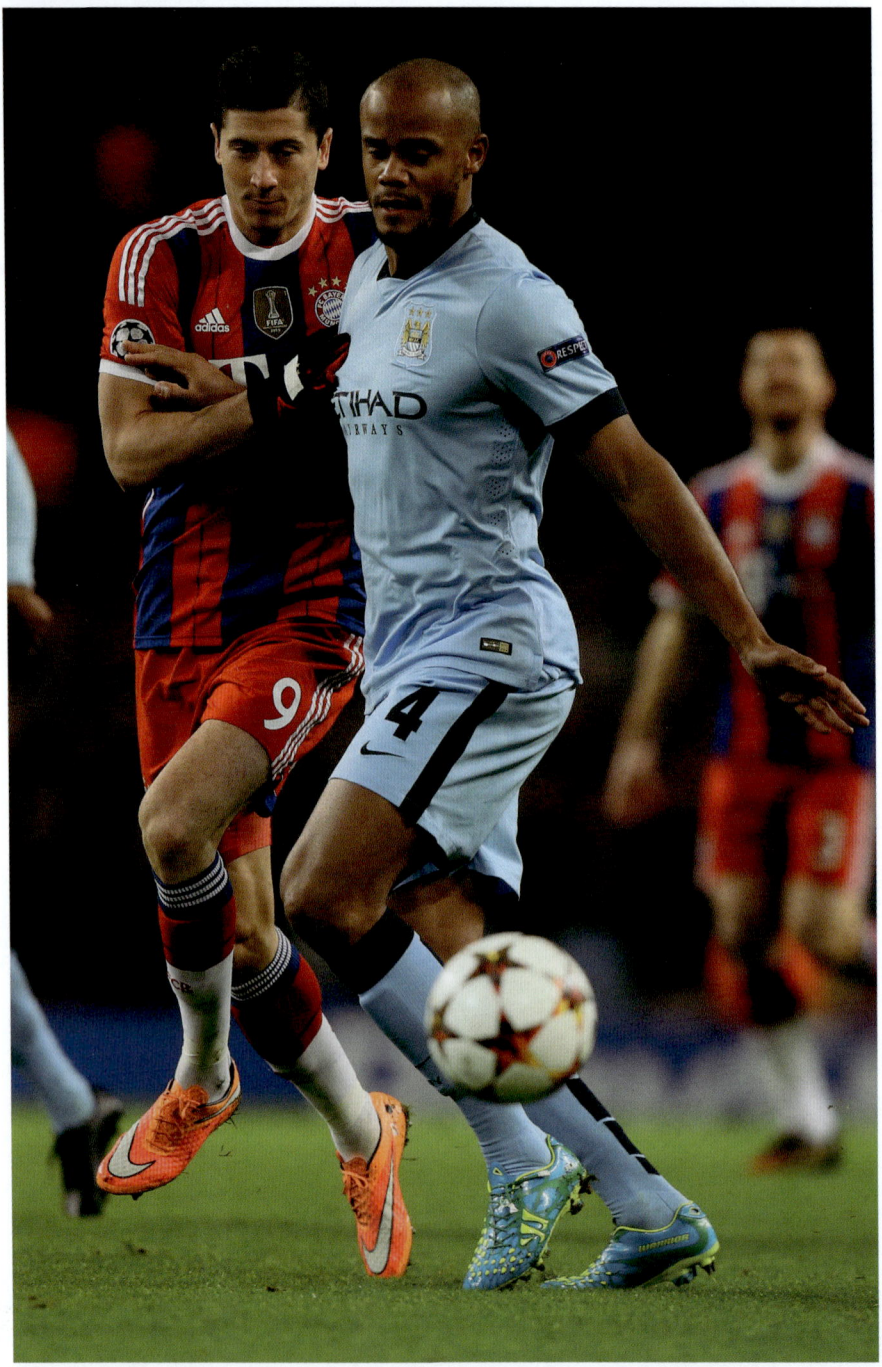

Robert Lewandowski puts Vincent Kompany under pressure during Manchester City's 3-2 Champions League victory over Bayern Munich at the Etihad Stadium in November 2014. (Simon Bellis / Alamy)

Christian Benteke celebrates with Vincent Kompany after scoring the opening goal against Scotland during Belgium's World Cup qualifier in October 2012 at the King Baudouin Stadium. (Bruno Fahy / Alamy)

Vincent Kompany challenges Lionel Messi during a quarter-finals match between Argentina and Belgium at the 2014 FIFA World Cup played in the Estadio Nacional Stadium, Brasilia. (Xinhua / Alamy)

A giant tifo of Vincent is unveiled before the Jupiler Pro League match between Anderlecht and KV Oostende in July 2019 (Stanley Gontha / Alamy)

Vincent Kompany coaches his team during a match between RSC Anderlecht and Cercle Brugge KSV in September 2020. (Virginie Lefour / Alamy)

Burnley manager Vincent Kompany and captain Jack Cork celebrate promotion to the Premier League following the Sky Bet Championship match at Middlesbrough in April 2023. (Richard Sellers / Alamy)

Burnley manager Vincent Kompany and Manchester City manager Pep Guardiola during the Premier League match at the Etihad Stadium in January 2024. (Martin Rickett / Alamy)

Vincent signs a deal to become new head coach of Bayern Munich and will now be competing for Bundesliga and Champions League honours rather than scrapping for promotion again in the Championship with Burnley.

might, you would perhaps think, have been enough, a one-off. But it wasn't. Later that day, all the students took part in an exercise in the nearby forest, using only torches and their wits to find some balloons, onto which the teachers had written instructions that would help the children find some treasure. But all to no avail, as Vincent and his group had burst all the balloons before the exercise could begin properly.

As far as Simone Pollet was concerned, Vincent had gone too far. So, on the Saturday, when the children were all down to play a sport, she took a table and chair out into a courtyard, set them up and asked Vincent to sit down and write about what he thought of his attitude and behaviour at Tongerlo so far. He wrote down an answer, occasionally looking up at all the other students as he did so with an expression of disbelief on his face before, after an hour, getting up and saying to his teacher, 'Mrs Pollet, I am cold. Can I play sports now? I have written my answer.' She replied that he was to carry on with what he was doing for the rest of the morning, but conceded that, if he was cold, he could go and put a sweater on. So Vincent missed out on a morning of sport although he was, once his punishment was complete, able to take part in the afternoon.

He later confided to another teacher that he had the utmost respect for Mrs Pollet because she was 'strict but fair'.

This didn't stop him from putting her to the test whenever he felt inclined. On one occasion, everyone had arrived and was sat down, ready and waiting for her lesson to begin. Everyone, that is, except for Vincent. A short time after the class had started, he walked in, as proud as ever, standing tall with his shoulders back, showing, as Mrs Pollet said, a touch of arrogance in the process. 'I have come from the gymnastics class', explained Vincent, only for Mrs Pollet to reply, 'So have all the other pupils – and they are here already, whereas you are late. And you only need as much time as they do to get changed and ready because you are not that slow'. She then let Vincent simmer in the corridor for a while, albeit with the classroom door open.

For her next lesson, Vincent arrived on time.

Another example of his questioning the authority of his teachers came when he began to realise that his market value as a footballer was on the up and up, and he said to Mr De Donder, 'Sir, one day I will earn more than you.' He felt able to do things or say things and then get away with it, something that came from the teachers never doing enough to keep him in check from day one. Looking back at when Vincent had said that to him, De Donder says, 'He liked to argue and wanted to be proved right... if you didn't have any authority as a teacher, he'd walk all over you in no time.'

Vincent was once made to sit in the school office as a mild punishment after he had mislaid something. As he sat there, De Donder walked past. 'I'm not going to make any more promises' said Vincent as he did so. De Donder replied by saying that he should not promise anything, but do what he was asked to do. But this only sometimes worked out, as proved to be the case on a school visit to the nature reserve known as the Drowned Land of Saaftinghe. Walking in the mud was not to Vincent's liking – so he wasn't in the most cooperative of moods. As the coach headed back, it became clear that they were running late, so the students asked for a toilet break... they were told that was all they were to do at the service station the bus had stopped at, nothing else.

Nevertheless, their teacher still looked inside the service station shop as they were about to head off again, and who was standing at the till buying sweets, contrary to what they had all been told? It was Vincent, of course. Once he'd got back on the coach, De Donder took all the sweets from him, only for Vincent to say, 'But Sir, I have already paid for them.'

By the time he was twelve years old, Vincent was already a master of time management – when he needed to be. He attended classes in Brussels, played football intensively in Anderlecht and kept up other hobbies such as athletics and the scouts. The result was an overcrowded existence that often left him too exhausted to perform at the top of his game at school, typified by his going to sleep in his lessons. He tried his utmost to cope with his extraordinary workload, but he had little time for independent study now and, as a result, his marks, whilst satisfactory, still needed to reach the high levels they had done previously. But he was relatively unconcerned about this; Vincent knew that his school work didn't need to be perfect and was, as a result, happy to attain good rather than exceptional marks.

He still particularly enjoyed Maths, a trait common within his family that included some who have gone on to have careers as engineers or scientists. Vincent later admitted that he regretted not getting better results in some subjects, attributing some of his shortcomings to simply not having enough time to memorise some of the complicated formulas in the more science-related disciplines. Maybe that is one of the reasons that he ended up struggling in Chemistry, although, as his teacher would have said, it might have been more about Vincent's attitude to the subject, as '...when he applies himself to it, he can do it.'

The same applied to Vincent's lessons in Dutch. He spoke French at home and to all his friends, as it was the dominant language spoken at Anderlecht. As Dutch wasn't his mother tongue, he didn't feel motivated to excel at it. Yet he was competent enough in the language to express himself in Dutch if he needed to, and, as time passed, was shown to have a more than decent understanding of the language compared to many others who had attempted to learn it.

By the time he'd got to the third year at senior school, Vincent was beginning to find the combination of both academic and footballing demands almost impossible to meet. This situation became all the more difficult as he approached his sixteenth birthday. His burgeoning talents were then, as we have already discovered, known to all of the top clubs around Europe, and he was very much in demand with talent scouts from just about every major footballing nation on the continent desperate to meet with and talk to him. Vincent knew that he was already earning more money than his teachers – what he had previously told Mr De Donder was never a boast but a statement of cold, hard fact – who were trying their best to encourage him in the classroom whilst his future was already assured with one teacher admitting, 'He knew that as a 16-year-old, he was already better off than us teachers, and said so. He told them Ajax wanted him and knew the amounts they were offering.'

Johan De Donder briefly played football with the youth of RWD Molenbeek and, more than any of his teaching peers, realised what it was all about, especially as Vincent had already played three to four times a week by then.

'From the third year, you felt he was cruising. Understandably, his interest in school waned in that third year.'

Vincent's mother views this opinion slightly sceptically, but was finding it challenging to impose her will because she no longer lived under the same roof as Vincent and his father. Pierre Kompany, in turn, was actively encouraging Vincent to push on as much as he could with his football career – although he also wanted him to do well at school and knew, like his wife, that Vincent's academic progress had stalled due to the demands of his football.

Pierre also demanded high standards from Vincent in all aspects of his life, not just his education or football. When, for example, his class had arrived back from their field trip to the Drowned Land of Saaftinghe, his teacher handed the sweets that Vincent had bought, contrary to what he and everyone else had been explicitly instructed, to Pierre Kompany.

Pierre's response was to look Vincent in the eye and tell him he had to obey all instructions given to him by his teachers without question.

Pierre later told Rita Moors during a parents' evening that he was 'disappointed' with the latest set of results attained by his two eldest children – but blamed his children rather than the teachers or school.

'Here in Belgium, they have everything they need, and education is free. What I experienced in Congo was a different matter. They have to realise how lucky they were to be able to study.' Vincent's parents fervently believed that, despite where his football career was likely to take him, they should still not glorify him as a footballer and ensure that his feet were always on the ground, which included encouraging him to keep up with his studies.

As for Vincent's siblings, Christel was somewhat quieter in class than her brother, with one teacher commenting that, with Christel, you didn't have to 'brace yourself'. Christel worked hard, although she had to put in a lot of effort to get the sort of grades she wanted, but, over time, even she changed and ended up having issues with authority herself. Yet, for all that, she was still the only Kompany to graduate from the school, whilst François, quiet and timid, was hardly noticed and ended up leaving that school to attend one in Laken, a suburb in the northwest of Brussels that is famous for its Japanese tower and Chinese pavilion.

Despite the encouragement he was still getting from all sides, not least from his parents and teachers, to push on with his education, Vincent's standards continued to fall away at the expense of his football. His Maths teacher from his first two years at the school had seen it coming, even then, but felt that her hands were tied as some of her teaching colleagues were, perhaps, not quite as concerned about this as she was.

'In his first two years, I was strict and talked to him a lot about the importance of his studies, but once he, and that group as a whole, reached the higher years, that is done less. They must learn to study in those first two years; there is much work and discussion. But, after that, you are expected to leave them to make their own way and pull yourself out of their battles. We should have done all we could to keep working with Vincent, however, that didn't happen…'

A long pause follows.

'…a pity, given his capabilities'.

Patience with Vincent, always generous, was beginning to run out.

Pollet: 'Some teachers felt he was annoying and made a negative impression on the class, especially in his third and fourth years.'

Rita Moors robustly defends him at this point.

'Was he totally derailed? No, I don't think so. It was better that he went to a school with more facilities. With his football career, he could no longer stay here in the fifth and sixth years. Not because he wasn't sensible enough, but because of that school-football combination and because we also set the bar very high.'

The chemistry teacher agrees with this argument. 'In primary school, you hardly have to study, but in senior, you do, which became a problem. He started falling behind, missing classes, and the ball didn't stop rolling from there.'

Things were going to come to a head. And they did.

In the February of his fourth year, Vincent Kompany received a harsh verdict: he had to find another school, and do so immediately, with the school's teaching staff standing by that decision; Principal Blondiau pointing out that her school emphasised intellectual ability over everything and suspects that, despite what happened, Vincent had no hard feelings over what amounted to an expulsion.

'In his new school, he connected with boys who also played football. And the facilities he had there allowed him to combine sport and studies much better than he could ever have done with us.'

What exactly took place in Vincent's fourth year at the school to precipitate his sudden removal from their ranks is now shrouded in the mists of time. One story alleges that Vincent 'escaped' from the school by climbing out of a school window, whilst another claims that he was, by now, driving his teachers to a very genuine point of despair.

'You don't surely believe that he changed schools just by chance,' claims one teacher who believes that Kompany was badly overstepping the line but has remained silent about it '...out of respect for Vincent's privacy'.

What does Vincent himself think? As far as we know, he has never publicly blamed the school for anything untoward in his life. He did say, however, that he suffered a lot there with 'force majeure', being subject to the whims of the higher forces, that is, his teachers and the school management, whilst he went on to tell *Het Laatste Nieuws* that, whilst other pupils never raised general issues that still concerned him with regard to the running of the school and everyday life there, he regularly did. This approach ultimately led to him having some very intense discussions with his teachers that, sometimes, saw him being sent to the headmaster's office.

'I can imagine they found me pretentious. I was occasionally wrong, sometimes I was also right,' he now claims.

Vincent was finding certain aspects of life challenging at that time. He knew that a career as a professional footballer lay before him, but that didn't mean he was entirely without personal pain too.

'My parents divorced when I was fourteen, a week before I had to take some exams. I didn't understand quite what was going on, and it hurt. Fortunately, I knew plenty of other kids with divorced parents, so I didn't feel alone. And I was able to take refuge in football.'

He is grateful to his parents for at least parting 'without a fight'.

Their divorce was one of many setbacks he experienced at that time.

'Between my twelfth and fifteenth birthdays, I went through a tough period,' he told the newspaper *De Tijd* and the weekly *Humo*.

'I don't *want* to be pretentious, but I was a kid who was pretty much good at everything. I did well at school, was good at football and had lots of friends – but I was thrown out of my school and quit the Belgian national youth squad. I had problems with teachers and coaches. I hung out on the streets more and made friends with people who sometimes did things they shouldn't have done. My father wanted to market the wind turbine he had designed at this time, but there was no money to do so. He took out a loan, and then it all started. Rent arrears, bills, reminders. We got into debt, a spiral from which we might never have escaped.'

As part of the downsizing, Vincent's father swapped their Ford for the smallest Honda he could find.

'I then became really independent. I had to make choices; I learned to see money's value and put things into perspective. Our life only fell back into the fold when I got my very first salary. Things got a lot better with that extra €300 or €400 a month. Fortunately, when I was sixteen, I'd signed my first professional contract with Anderlecht for a thousand Euros a month; with that, I started to pay off my parents' debts. Two years later, I bought a house for the family.'

When I asked Pierre how he'd found day-to-day life during that period, he made every effort not to make a drama out of it. His wife had left the house, but the children, mainly for practical reasons, continued to live with him while he, of all people, was out of work and struggling to market his windmill.

'You should never give up. I've been leading since I was a kid. In the humanities, I was a class leader; at University, I helped organise things; in Kitona, I had responsibilities and always took responsibility for the children.'

'When Vincent started earning money at sixteen, and a world suddenly opened up for him, he always had to keep his appointments. Not that I constantly controlled him – you shouldn't become your children's policeman. The fact that Vincent and his friends sometimes drove faster than permitted was not a problem for me, but using a bank card to withdraw money was unacceptable,' he told *De Standaard*.

Vincent now had to look for another school, which he found in the Anderlecht municipality, five minutes by car from the youth centre at Neerpede, so he travelled to his new school by Metro and was able to walk to training from there. He did so feeling very chastised on that first day as he'd received the scolding of his life from both parents, who felt indignant and ashamed because their son had been expelled from school.

It was a critical time in his life. Would he manage at his new school, the Municipal Athenaeum of Anderlecht? Would he change at all or remain the same cocky young man who'd been seen off the premises of the Maria-Boodschaplyceum?

And, perhaps most importantly of all, would he be able to combine school and football more easily?

Once again, his former teachers, this time from the Maria-Boodschaplyceum can give us some unique insights.

Yves Wiels taught him English in the fourth year whilst Nathalie Verbist was his class teacher in the fifth and sixth year, teaching Vincent Mathematics. She also gave him catch-up lessons at her home in Zaventem. Serge Yernaux was his Economics teacher in the fourth, fifth and sixth years whilst, although another Economics teacher, Mark Aelen, did not teach Vincent he knew a few anecdotes about him. Viviane Smekens, as his Headmistress, could also reflect on Vincent's time at his new school.

The philosophy of the Athenaeum is similar to that of the Lyceum, but also differed markedly from it. According to Vincent's class teacher, Nathalie Verbist, pupils need not be afraid to ask anything. Communication was open, and the atmosphere much more amicable than elsewhere. She calls this typical of Brussels schools because the teacher-pupil ratio is often smaller than usual where teachers show a holistic understanding of their pupils. However, she insists both stick to the rules with the school management sometimes intervening in the event of unresolved problems between the teachers and pupils.

The Athenaeum might have been a more relaxed hub of education. But the lines drawn in the sand between student and teacher were very clear.

Viviane Smekens says: 'One time, I was so dissatisfied with the behaviour of a young football player that I phoned the club and asked them not to field that pupil that weekend. That happened, and since then, they had all understood the consequences of poor behaviour – including Vincent.'

The Athenaeum had a tradition of 'producing' Anderlecht footballers. In the Sixties, the famous François Van der Elst, who would also play for West Ham United and New York Cosmos, was one of many who attended the school which was, tellingly, one of the first in Belgium to amend its timetable to ensure that all of its promising footballers got as much time with their coaches at the school as possible.

Smekens: 'The school philosophy did not deviate from the principle that someone should be able to develop his talent and be given every opportunity to do so. We once had a pupil who won a beauty pageant and wanted to go abroad for three days to gain international exposure. That was possible.'

Tutoring was a godsend for the footballers: teachers gave them private tuition voluntarily, without remuneration. They did it out of idealism and because they saw that it helped.

Nathalie Verbist gave him catch-up lessons at her home about eight times. She and Kompany quickly reviewed the year's learning schedule in April or May. She explained the theory and then had Vincent do one or two exercises before completing the rest at home.

She had no problem at all with helping him in her own time. Why?

'You want your students to succeed.'

Because of his football, Vincent couldn't now attend all his scheduled classes at school, so he would visit her during any spare time he found at weekends or between his training sessions. Thus, when Belgium trained at their practice centre in the village of Kraainem, he'd sometimes be able to take part for an hour or two. So yes, he now had teachers who'd make an effort for the budding footballers in their ranks. But there was also some jealousy in the teaching ranks. A teacher may earn a good living in Belgium, but a footballer's salary can rise to ridiculously high levels in the eyes of many. And that is not always easy for some teachers to accept. Think about it. You are a teacher with a student footballer in your class. They come in late, are excused from lessons, or are allowed to hand in their homework later than their peers. It may have been accepted within the school as how they 'did things', but it didn't always mean that every teacher supported it.

As a school principal, Viviane Smekens has always assumed that everyone is entitled to borrow a footballing analogy, a 'clean sheet'. She knew why Vincent came to the Athenaeum but chose to keep it to herself.

'Since I have forgotten the reasons, they couldn't have been that serious.'

Shortly after his enrolment by his father and himself, his mother visited Smekens.

'A beautiful, intelligent woman,' says Smekens.

She'd pressed her to ensure her son got his degree, adding that whilst she accepted that sport was very important to him, his studies were still critical. Smekens promised to do her best. That effort on the part of the school Principal would have been more than necessary, too, because even at the Athenaeum, Vincent Kompany still occasionally came in late, was punished for doing so, and had to stay behind after school. But he accepted this, admitting to Smekens that she was 'right' and that he should be punished.

Even during his sixth-year maths catch-up class with his teacher, Vincent still arrived late.

Nathalie Verbist: 'For example, we agreed to meet at ten o'clock, but Vincent did not show up. So I called him. He replied that I shouldn't worry. Coming on time? Never. He always had an excuse and could also explain it nicely. At school, he deliberately showed up later, explaining that he was seen as a 'God' to the young pupils, and to avoid all the attention that they gave him, he'd arrive by ten past eight when the bell rang, but only when everyone was already in class. Being on time was not his thing anyway.'

Even at the Athenaeum, he'd still fall asleep during classes, as he was frequently tired. Principal Smekens admits that certainly, when he first arrived at the school, Vincent was '...still a bit playful'. In a newspaper, she once called him 'a restless pedigree dog who bit everything', but she now thinks that was exaggerated. He did play truant, albeit to train, which 'caused quite a fuss' until she told him to ask for permission if the football club wanted him to attend a training session. After which, Vincent did so every time the club needed him.

The Athenaeum also took the opportunity to work out a tailor-made timetable for Vincent. Smekens asked the Education Minister of the Flemish government, Marleen Vanderpoorten, for special permission for him to leave for training at 10.30 a.m. The club then picked him up with a van then, after training, dropped him back off at the school gate.

Vincent was, by then, training in the mornings and afternoons, which meant Vanderpoorten had to be asked to extend the special permissions granted to him.

At least that meant the smouldering fuse had been removed from the powder keg, and everyone was now satisfied. As a consequence, complaints made about Vincent by his teachers rapidly declined.

However, when the English teacher arrived for the first lesson in the fourth year, he saw eight students, seven of them sitting near the front of the class, with a much taller than average student slumped at the back, clad in his training gear and a particularly expensive, flashy, looking pair of trainers… and a face that seemed ready for mischief. Did he want to introduce himself to the rest of the class? He did and, as he proceeded to tell everyone that he was Vincent Kompany, his teacher looked again at the trainers, their laces left so loose they had almost come out of the shoes altogether and said, 'Well, my dear friend, I'll give you one hundred and twenty seconds to take off that baseball cap, move two benches forward, then put your trainers on properly.'

Vincent promptly obeyed.

Teacher Verbist once asked Vincent why he was walking around in sweatpants rather than wearing jeans. Vincent replied that his thighs were so muscular that regular trousers were too tight and restrictive and, therefore, uncomfortable. That growing stature and confidence was now impressing others. Jonas Maes, in turn, looked up when Vincent came to visit him at the end of his sixth year for a tutoring session in Economics.

'I was impressed by his stature. I measure 1.88 metres, but by then, he was already a few centimetres taller and twice as wide as me.'

Vincent would often express himself in a very generous manner says Wiels, who once asked Vincent for two tickets to an Anderlecht match, but he also wanted to go to the post-match reception, 'was this possible?' 'Come but…,' Vincent replied, '…tell them at the entrance I invited you.' Wiels did this but admitted to being shocked at later being charged five Euros for a glass of white wine. Clearly, Vincent's largesse only went so far, but, for all that, Wiels now saw him as a good man of modest disposition who was not genuinely 'flash', even if he sometimes played up to that image.

Nathalie Verbist got to know Vincent better when she taught him Maths at her home. She recalls that he could act '…very silly" with her children of three and four, with Vincent playing with them in the garden and at their basketball hoop. He'd further impressed her with his broad general knowledge: he could talk about many things, including topics his peers hadn't even thought about yet, much less discussed. He liked to know about other people but kept information about himself and his family under wraps.

'I think you will never fully fathom him…', she now says, '…there is much that he keeps to himself, perhaps out of self-protection. Although I don't think he has any secrets, a part of his personality we don't know about.'

But then, she asks who had ever seen his wife before he proposed to her? She also never knew that he had a girlfriend during his latter school days as he could be very discreet. But they got on well together. She dared to tease him when his favourite basketball club, Charleroi, had lost, and he did the same when her team, Leuven, lost a match. He was, she summarises, a pleasant student '…who could be funny'.

He was charming and always presented himself well and, according to Verbist, he had the flair to use his charms. Her economics colleague meanwhile called him a '…sweet boy who never acted exuberantly but was calm and wise' whilst Headmistress Smekens recalls that '…you couldn't get him angry and, at school, he never created real mischief.'

Vincent, therefore, underwent something of a metamorphosis at the Athenaeum.

'I did not like going to school at all,' he told Sport-Voetbalmagazine. 'Everyone told me I had everything in me to be a brilliant student if only I put in a little effort – but that was not my priority. Only when I changed schools and was close to a professional contract did I want to succeed at school. That was also a reason why I didn't make an earlier switch: I wanted to finish school. I came from a neighbourhood where people are always unlucky. I didn't want to leave anything to chance. If I struggled, I would talk to one of my parents or with a teacher. Those were the pats on the back I needed to get myself motivated again.'

Despite his incredibly hectic schedule, Vincent had now found himself and was in balance with everything and everyone around him. His tailor-made class schedule gave him particular satisfaction because it showed him respect, but also expected him to still study as much as he could, despite his football.

Principal Viviane Smekens: 'His classmates came home, ate, studied and had a free evening. But Vincent had to perform constantly: but his studies were not optional.'

He became, nevertheless, a person whose company was always enjoyable to share, someone who was generous and a young man who was not only concerned solely with himself, he had become a 'gentleman'.

On one occasion, teacher Mark Aelen remembers he was doing some photocopies in a room just opposite the school entrance, noticing, as he did so, that Vincent had, once again, arrived for school late. A window cleaner was working on the glass at the front door of the school, so, as Aelen observed, Vincent stood and waited for a few minutes until the man had finished his work, not asking, or expecting him to move aside and interrupt what he was doing so that Vincent could walk past him. This made quite an impression on Aelen, who noted that although Vincent was seventeen and earning a lot of money, he was definitely able to keep his feet on the ground.

One trait that reappeared at this time was his shyness, something which had very much been part of Vincent's character during his childhood.

'My first impression?' asks Jonas Maes, who tutored him in Economics in Ganshoren. 'He was modest, a bit shy. Although I did have the feeling that, of the three children, he was the central figure in the house. You could tell by how he interacted with brother and sister, there was a natural authority, he was allowed to call the shots but did not act overbearingly. Polite, pleasant and correct, if somewhat calm and mature for his age.'

Maes was convinced that Vincent would, if he took the test, prove to have a very high IQ, something he said he sensed just by talking to him – ensuring that whenever they did meet and have a conversation, he didn't get all starry-eyed from being in the presence of a budding superstar footballer, but just treated Vincent as an 'ordinary' person.

Nathalie Verbist, whom Vincent stayed in touch with long after he had left the school in 2005, recalls getting a text from Vincent five years later which announced, "Carla and I are proud to announce the birth of our daughter'. Who are they, I thought, Carla and I, and why are they texting me in the middle of the night? She then realised it was, of course, Vincent, who was now playing for Manchester City and that he had wanted to pass on to her the news of the birth of his first daughter.

By the time he finished his education, Vincent had grown up a lot, something that was, undoubtedly, influenced by those he was working with – all grown men, many of whom were married and enjoying successful careers. However, according to Verbist, Vincent still showed himself to be occasionally indifferent at times and gave the impression he no longer wanted to be regarded as a talismanic figure in and around the school. By then he'd become 100% a footballer, which reflected in his final weeks at school where, she said, 'he just looked tired nearly all of the time'.

Even if Vincent sat back in class and looked half asleep, his mind would still be alert. Verbist would try to catch him out by asking a question that he, far more often than not, still knew the answer to. It was clear that, even if he was now more withdrawn and felt compelled to stay in the background more than ever before, he still picked up a lot in class, even if he didn't seem to be paying much attention. Maes felt the same way; he had to give Vincent extra tutoring in Economics prior to the exams and comments on how his concentration levels didn't always seem to be that high, even though he still asked questions and knew what he was doing.

Maes: 'He didn't say much in class, but when he did, it made sense. You had to watch your step with him though'. On one occasion, having realised that his new school were using the same Economics textbook that he'd been using at Maria-Boodschap, his previous school, Vincent brought that book in for his lessons, showing, in the process, that he had already completed it and was therefore ahead of everyone else in the class. Undeterred, his teacher immediately asked Vincent to hand the book over to him, and although that was met with mild protest, Vincent did as he was asked, remaining thoroughly composed and polite throughout the incident.

Yves Wiels, one of Vincent's English teachers, as well as an author, believes that Vincent had little real sense of language, suggesting that, 'When he spoke English, it was a kind of Franglais, a nonsense. His Dutch was filled with influences from French and Brussels dialect'.

Because of his sporting commitments, Vincent was, during his latter months at the school, spending more time away from the classroom than he was inside it, only coming in, it seemed, when it suited him, for example, on days when he had no training or if the Anderlecht players were given some time off. At that stage, he might have been accused of taking advantage of both the situation and the school, but he vehemently denied this.

'My privileges are also a disadvantage. I realise now that with teachers, it is easier to follow what I need to do, education-wise. But actually, I can't complain. I am lucky to have people at the Athenaeum who tutor me.'

Another advantage for the footballers at the Athenaeum was that their time in the class took place from ten past eight through to three in the afternoon, with the morning sessions only lasting until twelve thirty – plus an afternoon break. Therefore, the lessons in the main subjects usually took place in the morning whilst, in the afternoon, there was room for the peripheral subjects like religion, moral studies and gymnastics. Vincent was 'well in' with the backroom staff at the school by now, who always kept track of his needs. 'These are copies for Vincent,' was a standing phrase in the school secretaries office.

Copies for Vincent were never a problem.

The support for Vincent went so far that Yves Wiels occasionally watched him play for the Anderlecht youth team at Neerpede. Wiels was interested in football and wanted to know how his sporting pupils progressed. He'd played the game until his early forties, a central defender in a minor division.

'I'd sometimes chat to my students after one of their matches, then, back at school when I entered the classroom, they would say that they liked that I'd gone to watch them.'

He watched Vincent play several times, finding that, after the game, Vincent was always amiable and ready to have a chat about the match. Yves Wiels noticed, after more than twenty years in the game himself, that, besides his footballing talent, Vincent also stood out for just how calm and collected he was during games. For that reason, Wiels did not consider him an effective man-marker as Vincent always played three or four metres behind, or alongside, the opponent – so he could never effectively neutralise any threat that player might be to his side as, to do that, you had to stick much closer to them. He also felt that, despite his height, Vincent was still 'quite weak' in the air at that stage.

Vincent was very well looked after as a student, with, as we have seen, all manner of concessions made to enable him to combine his studies with football, but, with regard to the latter, he was also taken care of there, primarily by Pierre, a former footballer himself, but also by Anderlecht. Yvon Verhoeven, who looked after the player's social affairs at the club, became something of a mentor to him and, in the process, almost a second father to Vincent, Nathalie Verbist believes.

Verhoeven had to shuffle between what was best at school as far as Vincent was concerned and what was also best for Anderlecht. Verbist feels that Verhoeven was an exception to the general rule that football employees tended to show less sympathy towards the school, whilst Verhoeven made sure Kompany could still attend the school despite Vincent's football career always seeming to take precedence over everything else.

For example, if the club called him on his mobile phone during his lessons, Vincent would take the call. Then there was the time when, whilst he was taking his Economics exam, the club rang him. Vincent would not turn his mobile phone off, even during an exam, so an interruption was always possible, no matter what he was doing at school. Anderlecht, who must have been aware of this, simply wanted him to know he was due to take some physical tests at Neerpede later that day.

A compromise was reached when his teacher insisted that if he took the first part of the exam, he could go off and take the tests at Anderlecht before returning later that day to finish his exam.

This story raises an interesting question: surely a football club cannot legislate for how a school manages itself? What does the Headmistress think?

'The club (*Anderlecht*) invests in young footballers, and training costs money. If the player still wants to go to school, that is their business but not the club's business'.

But Anderlecht still had a say in what Vincent could or couldn't do at school.

For example, they wouldn't permit him to go on school trips any longer, in case it meant he missed a training session. And any form of gymnastics was now also forbidden, in case the player got injured. But, above everything else, they had to be at every training session and on time.

However, the relationship between Anderlecht and the school was good, and the Headmistress liked that the football club were happy to invest in it. For example, someone from the club would come along to parents meetings and would always make sure their footballers took enough time out to study as well as carry out their training commitments, with Smekens concluding, 'I am pleased that Anderlecht has since realised the importance of education for promising footballers.'

Regardless of whether he, the school and his teachers desired it or not, Vincent Kompany was, from the age of seventeen, a genuine star when, just before the start of his fifth year at school, he made his debut for Anderlecht's first-team. From that moment onwards, he secured his place in the team's strongest starting XI, and in doing so, introduced the wider world to his remarkable levels of flair and self-confidence as well as his tendency, only too well known at the school, to make cutting statements if provoked. With that came new pressures and the kind of attention that seemingly comes as standard for anyone decreed to be 'a star', with TV cameramen, assorted journalists, and photographers stalking the school gates at the end of the day, eager to catch a glimpse, and maybe get a few words from Anderlecht's latest sensation.

Privacy became ever-more important and, with those watchful hoards in mind, Vincent would often find himself being advised of their presence fifteen minutes or so before the end of the school day, which gave him the opportunity to make his way home via another exit.

Despite the vast changes this amplified stardom brought to his life, Vincent still seemed to enjoy himself whenever he was at school, with one teacher from his final year commenting, 'What I appreciated in him was that he wanted to be normal. He lived at Anderlecht among grown-up men with a completely different mentality and in a different world. If he then occasionally came to school, he could enjoy being with his peers again.'

But even at school, he was often accosted.

Headmistress Smekens: 'Vincent was a star at school. He would sneak into the school early in the morning, hidden under his hoodie to avoid people on the street accosting him. However, he was fantastic to the little ones in the first and second years. As soon as he entered the playground, they behaved like supporters, shouting "Vincent! Vincent!" and asking for his picture. He always said 'yes', and handed out autographs.'

The school's younger pupils would even stand by a classroom window if Vincent was in that room, staring at him as if he were some sort of exotic creature at a zoo. At the school's sports day in his final year, Vincent resorted to walking around the playing field in a hooded coat that had a fur lining. He wasn't cold by any means, but that hood gave him the level of protection and anonymity he wanted, as he didn't always want to be recognised and have to sign autographs.

When Vincent won the Golden Shoe (awarded to the best footballer in Belgium every year), the media almost besieged the school. Along with his classmates, he was on the front page of *Het Laatste Nieuws,* whilst television channels *VTM* and *VRT* dropped by to film a piece about him. 'Vincent was a showpiece and *our* showpiece', admits the English teacher. That Vincent had to pay the price of fame and genuinely thought about avoiding it at times was made clear to his class teacher of the fifth and sixth form at least three times. When Vincent had left her car after their catch-up lessons, she'd drive away, usually for another appointment, but she would sometimes look back and see Vincent standing on the street nearby with lots of people looking at him, their faces fixed and eyes wide open.

'Like they'd seen the American president.'

'When he arrived at the gate of my house, he always called me', Verbist says. 'The first time, it went like this.'

'Madam, I am here.'

'Vincent, in future, get out, ring the entrance gate buzzer then it'll open and you can park in the driveway'.

'Yes, but ma'am, if I phone, you can open the gate, and I can drive straight in. Then I have to get out fewer times, and there is less chance that the people on the street will recognise me and bother you about it.'

One particular moment stayed in that teacher's mind for a long time. Verbist does not like, she freely admits, football much, preferring to go and watch basketball as she is a big fan of the Leuven team. Vincent knew that, and they once agreed to go to the Leuven versus Charleroi game together.

Verbist: 'He was overwhelmed there, especially by the girls approaching him for a photo or autograph. When he took a seat in the stands later, I teasingly said I would charge money for every autograph, photo or kiss while it lasted. He replied that I mustn't say that. He thought it was part of his life now. Vincent thinks about everything; every step is reasoned. He weighs and estimates the consequences of what he does.'

Vincent admitted as much in *Humo*. 'I always want to be one step ahead of the facts, so I am not surprised. I don't see things negatively; I try to think of as many future scenarios as possible.'

The school year in which Vincent had switched to the Athenaeum was unsalvageable in terms of results. He had achieved very poor grades in his previous school and needed more time to turn those grades around. He retook the fourth year of economics and modern languages at his new school and, this time, he passed and continued to do the same in his other subjects.

Verbist: 'The catch-up lessons were an encouragement. I urged him to do his best one more time.'

Vincent had to pull out all the stops, though.

'I had a hard time combining school and football, but it has become almost unfeasible this year. When I struggle, I sometimes ask myself whether I really need to put all that effort into that piece of paper. Sometimes, I am so tired that it affects my mood and interaction with the people around me. I really want that degree, but maybe it will take me more than one year to get it... that or I'll look for alternatives,' Vincent admitted to *Het Laatste Nieuws*.

A diploma is something tangible, and despite his upwardly mobile status, the school insisted that he obtained it. Vincent agreed that was for the best too. But whether he completed his studies in one, two or four years' time did not matter to him.

Vincent applied himself to his schoolwork as much as he could, given the circumstances with his mother who was unimpressed, you will recall, with the whole concept of professional football, constantly encouraging him to do so whilst Pierre, his father, still believed that excelling at both would be impossible.

English teacher Yves Wiels believes that Vincent 'received his diploma gift-wrapped' in that he certainly worked for it but was, in the process, accompanied in his endeavours by about five personal tutors.

'He filled in the exam forms himself, but here and there, someone whispered something to him.'

Wiels is honest enough to admit his role at the time. 'I stood next to him to see what he had filled in and asked if he was sure of his answer?'

Principal Smekens retorts such claims, however.

'Vincent did not get the diploma as a gift; he worked for it.'

He was relieved when he passed his final two exams, in Economics and German. Vincent had his diploma, hugging his teachers in thanks before he finally left the school, writing a note to his German teacher saying he was glad he didn't have to worry about learning German anymore. Ironically, when he joined the Bundesliga club Hamburger SV a little while later, he certainly needed to draw upon his schoolboy knowledge of German again, with his teacher admitting '...we had a hearty laugh about that.'

At the end of June 2005, Vincent Kompany was presented with his school diploma at a solemn award ceremony, commenting that he got '...surprisingly good marks'. He was now nineteen and, as well as his diploma certificate, was given a book about Economics and a fresh rose. In addition, Smekens also handed him a drawing that her husband, the internationally renowned illustrator Ever Meulen, had made in his typical style. It depicts a cartoon-like Vincent, juggling with his eyes closed, his football boots on and wearing an Anderlecht shirt, whilst the ball he is juggling has the initials of the school on it. He is also holding several books, onto which the names of all his teachers have been added.

In a separate drawing, Vincent is seen tipping his head towards a much smaller woman who is holding open a book entitled 'Proclamation'. She looks like Viviane Smekens, who, in turn, has placed her right foot on a globe. At the bottom of the drawing is written: *All happiness for the future! Viviane Smekens, director G.A.A., 28 June 2005.*

You can imagine Smekens' surprise when one evening later in 2005, at the Passa Porta International House of Literature event in Brussels she was attending, along with her husband, who was promoting his new book *Verve,* Pierre Kompany turned up with a camera crew who were following his progress in the build-up to municipal elections in which he was standing as a candidate for Ganshoren, one of the nineteen municipalities in Brussels. He had an Anderlecht shirt from Vincent as a gift for her and had also arranged for the book to be promoted on a French-language TV station.

In her new office in Evere, where she has started a new job, stands a giant, wide-spreading Ficus plant, another gift to her from Pierre Kompany that she was given whilst she was at the Athenaeum. Not wanting to leave it behind when she left the school, Smekens has taken it to her new job and is now forever reminding her staff, 'Don't forget to water the Vincent!'

Smekens: '...I used to drag that plant home in the summer holidays... but now I come here during the holidays to water him!'

The office also contains a picture of Vincent in a tracksuit, with a signed personal message which reads; 'Thanks to all the teachers who have supported me over the past few years and made it possible for me to enter a new world of opportunities.'

Viviane Smekens has continued to follow Kompany closely and has watched him blossom as a footballer and a human being: 'Without his intelligence, he would never do the things he does. And everything he does is spot on. He summarises a social situation in a few words or sentences, a skill that is the envy of many a copywriter. The fact that he has remained down-to-earth and modest and that he knows how to convey a universal message. I appreciate him. Just as he was an example at school, he is now an example for all the young people in Brussels and beyond. I think of his socio-sports project, BX Brussels, a football team that welcomes all footballers from the capital. You have to pay to become a member, but you get the registration fee back if you attend all the training sessions and don't play truant at school.'

Vincent had become a happy man, for more than one reason.

At the end of October 2004, almost a year before he graduated, he moved, along with his father, sister and brother, from the Brussels North Quarter to Georges Simpson street in Ganshoren, a Brussels' borough in the northwest of the city. Vincent said of the move: 'Now that I am playing at Anderlecht, I can finally give my family something back and improve their standard of living.'

'Anyone who grows up in social housing in the North Quarter wants to leave there. But I'm not moving because I no longer feel connected to the people who live there,' he notes in *Humo.*

Jonas Maes was tutoring him in Vincent's new house in May 2005.

'It was a quiet side street in a nice, residential neighbourhood. I remember a gate with a bell and a videophone. When I was let in, I had to walk through the front garden to get to a modern house – it was very well appointed with a nicely equipped kitchen, a large living room with sofas and a flat-screen television, which, for that time was very different to the bulky televisions people usually owned. Sleek, minimalist furnished, with some subtle African sculptures and other pieces that created a stylish impression'.

'I also remember there being lots of football boots from Vincent's sponsor, *Adidas*. "I get those for free" he once said, "and a lot of them". Every week, he could wear a new pair.'

133

Maes: 'At my first appointment with Vincent, Christel and François were also present, and his sister greeted me. I was waiting for Vincent, who was still on his way – which was usually the case. The contact with all the Kompany family members was jovial and friendly. The children looked up to their father with great respect, although he was more the calm, silent type. Pierre was smaller and leaner than Vincent but clearly a controlling figure who kept the family in check and everyone's feet on the ground.'

'With the children, I spoke Dutch, with the father, French – the children spoke French and Dutch interchangeably, as you often see in Brussels. If the tutoring session ran late, I was allowed to join them at the table. Then, for example, we ate a home-delivered meal from *Les Petits Os*, a well-known restaurant in Jette. There wasn't much cooking: they usually didn't have time for that'.

Meanwhile, the children's contact with their mother had also improved, as Mrs Kompany explains.

'Although Christel, Vincent and François live with their father in Brussels and I work in the province of Hainaut, we are in regular contact and call each other a few times a day.'

Vincent enjoyed the breathing space, privacy and peace the new house offered.

'I relax mainly by staying at home. I play *PlayStation* with my brother, read a book or study.'

He used to read just for school, but since he was seventeen, he also read '...to get away from things'. He found it an excellent way to unwind before going to sleep, a much better method than watching television. He also started to dress more stylishly. 'My son is not changed by his success, except for one aspect: his clothes,' his mother observed.

'Before, he only used to wear ripped jeans. These days, he has changed his style.'

So, all's well that ends well... thanks to the new school's facilities, the total commitment from teachers and management, along with the school's philosophy to offer tailor-made solutions running in parallel with top sports coaching. That combination played a vital part, as did Vincent's own commitment to transformation.

He'd chosen to be a professional footballer, but Yernaux, his Economics teacher, still encouraged him to continue studying and proudly admits; 'That he eventually opted for Economics did give me pleasure: apparently, I didn't turn him off the subject!'

At the end of September 2005, Vincent enrolled at the *Vrije Universiteit* Brussels as a credit student at the Faculty of Economics and Sociology.

In truth, he had little or no time to go to University, so, in the end, Vincent hired a lecturer from the University as his private tutor, someone who could fully explain and teach the courses to him at home, with Vincent's motivation being to acquire knowledge that he could apply throughout his sporting career, then expand upon when that came to an end.

Caroline De Roose was once captain of the female Belgian basketball team and the American University of New Jersey Rutgers team. As a then sports manager at Randstad, she guided top athletes in combining sports with their studies and recognised his special qualities.

'He was still young but very ambitious and already a leader in the making with a great sense of responsibility. He knew very well what he wanted and could assess his capabilities. He didn't just want to reach the top... but the top of the top.'

De Roose added; 'He exuded charisma and commanded respect. His distinct communication style also stood out: he translated information smoothly, was hands-on and always adapted it to the person he was talking to, whether that was a child, player or manager. I also found his thinking skills and foresight striking at his age. You felt that he had all the scenarios in mind beforehand. Typical of leaders.'

Kompany started his university studies in good spirits, enjoying being taught at home, but ultimately sat no examinations as, during a lengthy spell out due to injury in the early part of 2006, he decided to put his studies on hold so he could focus on regaining his fitness without any distractions whatsoever.

'I put everything on football because I knew it was a defining moment in my career and that I would never get out otherwise,' he told *Sport-Voetbalmagazine*.

In July 2006, he'd informed *Le Soir* newspaper he was counting on becoming a commercial engineer when his football career was over, adding that he was torn between continuing his studies at the VUB via distance learning or via English-language courses at the University in Hamburg, where he was then playing.

But, playing top football at an elite level for both his club and the national team, enjoying a private life... plus finding the time and space to study, was all too much in the end. That is until Vincent joined Manchester City, when he took up his studies again by embarking on an MBA in Economics in which he eventually achieved a merit grade along with a distinction for his final project, receiving the award in 2018.

Christel, Vincent's sister, also studied at the *Vrije Universiteit Brussels*, initially taking Commercial Engineering studies but ultimately being awarded a BA in Communication Science. She'd fought and won a fight against Hodgkin's Disease, attending her first chemotherapy treatment on her 23rd birthday. Happily, she was completely cured of the condition and has since married Zouhaier Chihaoui, a Dutch-speaking lawyer from Tunisia who specialises in human rights at the *Just Rights* firm which he founded, with Christel keeping up the family connection with football via her role as the President of BX Brussels FC.

Vincent was maturing fast. He had more or less worked his way through his parent's divorce, coming to accept it and, after remaining somewhat precocious up until reaching his seventeenth birthday, started to make the considerable step up from being an occasionally cocky adolescent into a maturing young adult. Vincent had become a self-assured man on a mission, both on and off the pitch.

CHAPTER SEVEN
BREAKOUT AT ANDERLECHT

It was something of a lucky day for Vincent Kompany when Frankie Vercauteren arrived back at Anderlecht in 1998. He'd previously worked as a youth team coach at CS Braine and KV Mechelen – where he'd been first team coach for the 1997/98 season – before accepting an offer to return to Anderlecht as Assistant Manager.

Vercauteren had an established track record working with, and improving, young players, which was one of the main reasons Anderlecht had sought his return in the first place. It was hoped that under his leadership, Vincent's overall game would develop and move forward from its already well placed position, which is exactly what happened.

Upon his return, Vercauteren had noted that many of Anderlecht's youth team players were technically excellent and possessed a great turn of pace. But they also tended to be rather slight of stature and lacked the physicality needed to prosper in senior football. He'd also noted that the players' mentality was sometimes a little on the negative side. He knew he would have his work cut out at the club he'd first joined as an eight-year-old in 1963.

According to Vercauteren, a good footballer needs to possess four qualities in abundance. Of those, talent is the most obvious and important but, on top of that, he cites the need for an appreciation and understanding of tactics, in-game vision and both physical and mental strength. Working alongside another former Anderlecht player, Jean Dockx, Vercauteren made enough of an impression upon the club hierarchy to eventually be appointed as Head Coach, taking time out at that moment to sit down with the club's then youth team Chairman, Philippe Collin.

Vercauteren: 'Collin and I were looking for solutions to improve Anderlecht's youth. The club did not have powerful, firmly rooted, youth players, even for strategic positions, and often had to make do with relatively small players who were physically not up to the task.'

There were, as Vercauteren quickly discovered, two exceptions to the rule: Vincent Kompany and Zaire-born right sided defender/midfielder Anthony Vanden Borre, both of whom were, at twelve and eleven years old respectively, much more physically well developed than their peers. This was, for Vercauteren, a welcome exception to the perceived rule, but, even so, he knew he just couldn't coach the other players until their own strengths matched those of Vincent and Anthony, a point expanded upon by another coach at the club, Eddy Van Daele.

'The problem is that you cannot force a physical breakthrough. Some were just ready quicker than others.' Collin admitted, adding, 'We decided to make training more difficult. The volume of work was drastically adjusted: made heavier and more intense.'

Vercauteren also decided that the talented youngsters should move into the B-squad, alongside players just below the A-team with additional individual training sessions arranged to help ease their transition to that level. Vercauteren became the link between the club's Head Coach and the emerging youngsters, who he trained himself. He therefore had a quick appreciation of who the real talents were at the club and when they would be ready to step up to the A-squad, emphasising that, as soon as the B-squad players had proved themselves capable, they'd win that promotion, regardless of their age.

Vincent Kompany was, of course, one of those players who had proven himself to be exceptional. Vercauteren noted that he already possessed a lot of positive attributes – not just his physical fitness and overall strength for his age but also his overall footballing ability, pace and his outgoing personality. Yes, there were elements of his game that needed to be worked upon. For example, he could be inconsistent to an even nonchalant level at times, either in a game or during training, whilst he also found it a challenge to stick to the accepted rules and agreements laid down at the club. Kompany also needed to work on his left foot. He trained well but needed structure to his day and game.

Vercauteren: 'In the youth, Vincent could compensate for a mistake in positional play through his physical strength and maturity but that approach doesn't last at the top level. His heading game was also work in progress: that was not his speciality.'

Vincent got a lot of attention and was usually to be found in the spotlight – he was always ready to express an opinion on something, which were not always the same as Vercauteren's... however the differences were not so extreme that the coach felt he needed to question them.

'Vincent has his nature and you have to respect that...' Vercauteren says, adding 'he was temperamental and he didn't always have to agree with me. But, importantly, on a disciplinarily level, he did know what to adhere to.'

Not arriving late in other words.

'He learned his lesson quickly. In the beginning, Vincent and I didn't do too much chatting. I was a man of doing, not talking, although I have evolved in that since. On a few occasions, we talked as a group a bit more elaborately, like at the evaluations mid and post-season, which the parents also attended. But I was not one who liked to sit with someone every week.'

Vincent was very keen on communication and would invariably always speak up if something was on his mind. Vercauteren: 'In the beginning, he didn't always have an easy time with me. But then I sometimes did annoying things to make him better. If I only said what he did well, I wasn't doing him any favours.' Vercauteren tells the same story as Eddy Van Daele, who says, 'That was initially a problem because he was surrounded by people who'd constantly told him he was the best and the strongest.'

Vincent was good. Everyone knew it, not least Vincent himself. But no-one was going to allow him to become complacent about his talent.

Vercauteren won two European Cups as a player and, like Kompany, was born in Brussels. Both joined Anderlecht when they were six, attended school there, ended up winning a Golden Shoe as well as national titles with the club and made their international debuts for Belgium whilst they were still at Anderlecht. So, other than the very obvious difference in age, the two had a lot in common.

Vercauteren: 'I don't think Vincent was too aware of my list of honours. He did respect tradition though and knew I was a former Anderlecht player. The players might, if they didn't know you too well, ask "…who is he to say this?" when you asked them to do something in a training session but, as soon as they realised that what you said or did was right, you then have their respect.'

So it was very much a case of Vincent and his peers respecting a coach for who they were in the present, rather than the past.

Although Kompany was already on his way to earning a starting place for Anderlecht as a central defender at the age of fifteen, Vercauteren would still allow him to play in a variety of different positions in other matches.

'I don't like players telling me where they will play: that's the first team coach's job. If I listened to those young players, I'd have five number tens! I have to form a squad.'

In Vercauteren's training sessions, a player has to be flexible to start with, no matter where he feels he should be playing, he will only find out the position that the club deems best after some time has passed. Because of that, Vincent found himself playing in some games as a right-back as well as taking up a defensive midfielder role in front of his back four. In the last game he played in that position for Vercauteren, Anderlecht lost, which ended that particular tactical experiment. But it still served a purpose, the need for Vincent to master different systems and scenarios within a game and, in doing so, to receive as broad a footballing education as possible.

It was ultimately decided that his best position was playing as a central defender. But Vincent was not quite ready to give up his dream of playing in midfield, and Vercauteren gave him many chances to impress in that position. But, as with the likes of coaches Deraeve, Van Daele, Martens and Klinkenberg, Vercauteren realised that Vincent was not the type of hard running player best suited to perform there.

'With me he mostly played in defence,' Vercauteren remembers. 'I could use him better there and he is at his best there. In midfield, he sometimes had problems with pure ball sense. You might play much higher, but he is not a playmaker. You can afford more freedom there and play out of position because you have cover from the defenders. But in his younger days he had a harder time to play in his position and keep that discipline.'

Yet even Vercauteren did not totally write off Kompany as a midfielder.

'I'm not saying he couldn't play there, just that he had less mastery of the different facets of that position. Vincent could pass a ball over twenty or thirty metres and drop it at the feet of a teammate, but he sometimes didn't succeed at that, and the final through-ball failed to materialise. In modern football, that is absolutely necessary... His average passes in midfield were not good enough.'

The coach was delighted with his attitude though: Vincent had shown himself, from day one working with Vercauteren, that he was eager to learn and did so quickly, was constantly evolving and always keen to demonstrate his progress. His youthful 'sins' were fast disappearing.

During the 1999-2000 season, Aimé Anthuenis was appointed as the new head coach of Anderlecht, replacing their previous managerial duo of Dockx and Vercauteren. Anthuenis arrived at the club via a round-about route that had taken in roles at Lokeren (two spells), Charleroi, Germinal Ekeren, Waregem and Genk with whom he'd won the Belgian Cup, and then the Belgian League Championship (Jupiler Pro League) in consecutive seasons.

With Anderlecht increasingly desperate to win a championship again for themselves, their previous triumph being in 1995, Anthuenis was expected to follow up his success there by bringing some silverware back to Anderlecht as well as making a credible effort at doing well in European competition. He did both, winning the Jupiler Pro League in his first season before excelling in Champions League fixtures against Manchester United, PSV Eindhoven, Dynamo Kiev, Real Madrid and Lazio; his team and style of play epitomised by the hard working and clinical strike pairing of Jan Koller and Tomasz Radzinski.

Vincent was, at this stage, the club's most promising teenager, one of whom big things were expected. And he was involved on some of those Champions League evenings, taking part in the pre-match rituals of running onto the pitch at the Vanden Stock stadium along with his peers holding the Champions League flag, then rushing off home immediately after the match (one of which was a 1-4 defeat to Leeds United) to see if he could spot himself on the television.

Anthuenis left Anderlecht at the end of the 2001/02 season – eventually taking over as coach of the Belgian national team – and was succeeded by Hugo Broos, another former Anderlecht player. It wasn't long before he became aware of just what an outstanding prospect the club had in the young Vincent Kompany who was, at sixteen, not so much knocking on the door of the first team as running straight through it.

Broos spoke to Vercauteren, a former team mate, with the latter recommending that Vincent should be promoted to the the the first team squad for the start of the 2003/04 season, with Vincent commencing training with that elite group in June 2003. His old youth team coach, Albert Martens, saying, 'Vincent came to me after his first training with the first team and said: "It's not that exceptional, I can fit in here. I didn't expect that, but I am worthy of my place and am even one of the best."'

'Indeed, he was very good during training.'

On April 10th 2003, Vincent celebrated his seventeenth birthday. A little less than three months later, on July 4th, he took part in the first team's opening match of pre-season at lower league club Knokke as member of the starting XI. Anderlecht won with ease and, despite leaving the pitch with a slight limp after a duel with an opposing player who, perhaps, didn't like to be made to look second best by a precocious seventeen-year-old, Vincent was the proudest man in the whole of Flanders. And even more so after he was given the first team squad number 27, with Broos saying, 'When you have someone with so much talent, you shouldn't wait too long to give him opportunities.'

Broos went onto admit that he couldn't understand why Werner Deraeve wanted to hide Vincent so that he would be less obvious to foreign talent scouts.

'What kind of explanation is that? Letting players have it easy because you fear that another club will come and take him away? Then you are holding back his development. Vincent's problem in the beginning was that he wanted to solve everything football-wise. That's why Frankie (Vercauteren) said he *should* play with us, then he will develop even more. Yes, I do think we could have got Vincent even earlier. That didn't happen because they wanted to keep him in the youth team. Frankie had disagreements about that with the youth coaches because he wanted to take Vincent out of that level much sooner.'

The reasoning was that if Vincent stopped learning, laziness or frustration could set in. Vercauteren tutored him intensively so he was able to make the step up to the A-squad. It didn't take long for Vincent to show that he was ready as, according to Broos, he simply stood out at every opportunity.

Vincent had been training with the A-squad for no more than a couple of weeks when, in late July 2003, he was picked for the starting XI for a vital European match against Rapid Bucharest as club Captain Glen De Boeck was unavailable for selection due to a knee injury, in addition to several other first team players. It might have been seen as a moment of triumph, the day he could say he had officially 'arrived'. But Vincent was keeping his feet on the ground, at least publicly, saying, in a feature with *Het Nieuwsblad*, 'You won't hear me say I'm already there. I still have a lot of work to do. This season I'm not with the A-squad to play but to learn, although I want to take every opportunity.'

In hindsight, he was underestimating the value that Broos was already placing on his young shoulders, with the chief coach admitting, 'Journalists didn't declare me crazy but still asked me if I knew what risk I was taking. A seventeen-year-old boy in the Champions League? But if you see he has talent, why hesitate? His physique was his advantage: big, strong and he is also definitely not slow.'

It had been twenty years since Anderlecht had selected such a young player to debut with the first team.

Anderlecht scrapped out a 0-0 draw in Bucharest, earning themselves a favourable position for the return leg in Brussels. But in truth the team were, perhaps, a little fortunate not to lose as, just before the end of the game, a misunderstanding between the Anderlecht goalkeeper, Daniel Zitka, and Vincent almost led to a goal. Vincent had already been yellow-carded midway through the first half after a typically rumbustious tackle so, all in all, it hadn't been a quiet debut at this level, with *Het Nieuwsblad* reporting that, '...after a hesitant start, he played as if he had been around for a while'.

Vincent had his say as well, admitting in a newspaper feature the following day that he'd set out to play '...as soberly as possible and did now want to reflect on what he did wrong' with the club's general manager, Michel Verschueren, no doubt rubbing his hands together as he did so, claiming that, 'If you see how he plays his football here, you know he will be a very big player.'

In the return leg Anderlecht started poorly and went 2-0 down, before fighting back to win 3-2 to progress to the final qualifying round of that season's Champions League, where they were drawn to play against Polish champions Wisla Kraków. Nothing less than a convincing victory was expected from Vincent and his teammates, and that turned out to be exactly what happened, with Anderlecht winning the tie 4-1 on aggregate and, in doing so, qualifying for the lucrative group stages of the competition. Now the quality of opponent would unquestionably be higher, a challenge that Vincent would have been relishing, especially when the draw saw Anderlecht placed in Group A along with Bayern Munich, Celtic and Lyon.

Vincent played a part in all but one of the those matches (missing the game at Lyon) but, although Anderlecht subsequently finished bottom of the group, with just two wins, both of them at home (against Lyon and Celtic), he made a good overall impression in the games, especially in the home win over Celtic where he had to marshal the defence for much of the match after his central defensive partner, Glen De Boeck, was sent off. Club chairman Roger Vanden Stock commented after the game that he hoped Vincent would '...sign on for twenty years'.

He didn't, however, impress quite as much in the game in Munich where Kompany's error led to a goal being scored. Yet, overall, he'd done exceptionally well, even if Anderlecht's campaign had, ultimately, been something of a disappointment.

After the game against Lyon, French legend Michel Platini commented that Vincent '...had a great future' whilst the prestigious French sports newspaper *L'Equipe* reported that he had shown '...incredible class, because of his speed, technique and offensive qualities'. Yet the away match against Celtic in early November, a 3-1 loss, was a different matter. 'What a hellish night,' said Kompany afterwards to *Het Laatste Nieuws*. 'We had good intentions but it turned out differently. We left too much space, played too far from the man. I too made that mistake. We were put to shame and we all have to blame ourselves for that.'

Footage from all the Champions League matches quickly circulate around Europe so it wasn't long before clubs from all over the continent were aware of the young rock at the centre of Anderlecht's defence. He was not, as many commentators on the game would have observed, anything like the finished product yet, but he was most certainly a raw diamond, with Ajax, Arsenal, Bayern Munich and Juventus all claimed to be amongst his admirers.

Despite this growing interest, Vincent made the most of the plaudits he was constantly receiving by agreeing, before that season's winter break, to extend his contract at Anderlecht until 2008... in exchange for a hefty rise in his salary. It was quite an achievement for the seventeen-year-old, who was still not legally an adult. However, any fan-led celebrations that his decision to sign a longer contract might have provoked were severely tempered by Vincent's agent, Jacques Lichtenstein, who announced that his client would, new contract or not, be leaving Anderlecht the following summer. England, Italy or Spain were his favoured destination at the time, although, as it turned out, this claim that was never backed up by Vincent who was more focused on his football rather than speculating about a premature departure.

Football generates gossip like few other industries though, and it seemed that rarely a day went past without another new club being linked with Vincent Kompany. Arsenal, for example, were said to be preparing a bid of €3.5 million for his services with Vincent's childhood friend, Yves Ma-Kalambay, who was at that time a goalkeeper at Chelsea, said to be amongst those urging Vincent to come to England. The rumours and gossip intensified further after it was claimed that, following Arsenal's supposed interest, Manchester United were prepared to pay €4.5 million for him, eager, perhaps, to team him up with Rio Ferdinand in the centre of their defence – it would have been an enticing prospect for any fan of the 'other' Red Devils.

Yet, for all the adulation and the speculation that went with it, Vincent Kompany still had a lot to learn about football as he discovered in a league game against Standard de Liège shortly after the defeat at Celtic – Anderlecht stumbled to a heavy 4-1 defeat with Vincent very much culpable for the first goal after an uncharacteristic error. Ever keen to defend his young protégé, Hugo Broos spoke after the match, saying that people needed to '...remember that Kompany is still only seventeen' whilst Vincent himself spoke about that particularly chastening period at the end of the season, saying, 'Suddenly it all became too much for me...the news that Alex Ferguson (then manager of Manchester United) was coming to scout me was the straw that broke the camel's back and I couldn't keep up for a while.'

Kompany had played in a lot of matches following Glen De Boeck's knee injury, but he was not missing from the team purely for that reason, with Broos stating, 'I had to eventually tell Glen "Sorry, but Vincent is just better."

De Boeck was naturally fiercely disappointed to receive that news, pointing out that he was the club captain and had always had a good relationship with his head coach, with Broos defending his decision further by saying, 'I couldn't justify picking Glen given Vincent's level of play.'

De Boeck was fifteen years older than Kompany. He was a leader and one of the few Belgian players with flair and style to his game. Captain of the team plus, on top of that, an inspirational figure in the dressing room and anything but silent. De Boeck could play a fair bit too; he wasn't the traditional 'stopper' type of centre-half by any mean. So he gritted his teeth, accepted his new status in the squad and tried to pass on some well meaning advice to his successor, words that Vincent took onboard but gently dismissed, not that this apparent snub bothered De Boeck, who said, 'I can only point things out, I am far too old to get frustrated about such matters.'

Anderlecht's midfielder Yves Vanderhaeghe experienced all of that first-hand.

'A regular who has to give up his place, that's not pleasant. Glen struggled for a while, he didn't handle it well. It was a painful episode. Vincent was also immediately proclaimed as the star of the future. He also played several times in my place as a defensive midfielder... and I struggled with that too.'

Vincent was being given the opportunity to shine and he was not only seizing it with both hands but grasping it tightly. He had been asked by Broos to play a sweeper-type role in the centre of the Anderlecht defence, with Finnish international Hannu Tihinen playing alongside him as a more traditional centre-back – the two of them integral to a back four with full-backs on either side – Vincent on the right hand side of their central pairing with Tihinen charged with stopping opposing centre forwards with Vincent left to win the ball and get things moving.

He was more than happy, in training and during games, to take onboard the advice Tihinen always gave him whilst the Finn had absolutely no issues at all with Vincent's drive and determination, even at that age, to demonstrate just what a good player he was. They made a good pairing with Broos, himself a central defender at the club in the Seventies and Eighties, easily appreciated, possibly because he saw a lot of himself in the way that Tihinen played.

Broos: 'Even during training Vincent and Hannu always played together, I never pulled them apart and so we created robots'.

Yves Vanderhaeghe was unstinting in his praise of the young Vincent Kompany.

'Every time he played he was on edge, always physically and mentally sharp, from the first to the last minute.'

He had to be. At Anderlecht, even a drawn match is sometimes regarded as a sign of a club in crisis. As Belgium's number one club side they were constantly under close scrutiny throughout the country, befitting their status. So Vincent was going to be under the spotlight at all times, whether he liked it or not.

If anyone needed reminding just how young Vincent Kompany was, despite his rising prominence, then they needed to consider this: he was not allowed to even enter the dressing room with the other first team players at first. Anderlecht's young talents all had to change in the dressing room next door, which was normally used for visiting teams.

'But...', says Broos, '...Vincent stood out, and he quickly got a locker alongside the seniors. From the first minute, you could see he had flair, wanted to show himself to everyone, was assertive. He was sharp, quick and had a serious physique for someone of his age.'

'Impressive.'

Did Hugo Broos consider playing Kompany as a defensive midfielder, the position he had always thought his best and the position he wanted to play in from a very early age?

'The board insisted on fielding him in midfield. But I ended up *not* agreeing to that because Vincent is *not* a midfielder. He can cope with playing there, especially in emergencies. But he should actually have the game in front of him. In the midfield you are under pressure very quickly and that's a very different way of playing.'

Collin, the Anderlecht chairman, used the argument that the club would get at least two million euros more on a transfer fee if Vincent excelled as a midfielder, rather than a centre back, but Broos was insistent.

"Sorry..." I said, "...then you're going to get two million less."

Broos was now caught between the proverbial rock and a hard place. If he antagonised Kompany too much about what his best position was, then Vincent might feel the urge to leave for a club that *did* want to use him in that role.

But, if Broos consistently ignored the suggestions that came from Collin and his fellow board members too much, it might have ended up weakening his position as a head coach because, at the time, it was Collin and chairman Roger Vanden Stock who decided who was head coach — and they wouldn't have hesitated to remove someone from the role if their opinions on certain matters, including football related ones, directly opposed those of their coach.

Broos did not completely dismiss the possibilities that Vincent might bring to the team if he was to regularly feature in midfield and, every now and again, Broos played Vincent in midfield before sitting back to assess what happened. On one particular occasion, when Anderlecht were competing in a tournament held over the winter break that season, he did just that, with Vincent ending up playing well and scoring two goals, something that engendered a little excitement in the Belgian press: was this the future playing position of Vincent Kompany?

'No, not at that stage', responded Broos, adding that he '...hadn't yet completely ruled the possibility out'.

He may well have meant that. But, despite those thoughts, Broos still saw Vincent as a central defender, end of story. He'd tried him one more time in midfield that season, and in a game where silverware was at stake, namely the Belgian Super Cup against Club Brugge (the Jupiler Pro League's equivalent of England's Community Shield) but Vincent had a quiet game and Anderlecht lost the match.

Collin's suggestion about Vincent being more valuable to the club, potentially, as a midfielder, could have been made partly tongue-in-cheek but Yves Vanderhaeghe shared his chairman's observation about just how valuable an asset Vincent already was to the club.

'Not only was he catapulted skywards by the press, Anderlecht themselves also placed him centre-stage; he was, for example, the face of club sponsor *Adidas*. They knew what his potential was and what that attention was worth to the club's portfolio. They could sell him for a lot of money.'

But when the time came, as it seemed it inevitably would before Vincent was out of his teens, it would be as a central defender with Broos now content to point out that other coaches had seen Vincent as a centre half just as he had done.

'Even my successors rarely, if ever, put Kompany in midfield.'

In the end, Kompany did not make much of a fuss about it, although he never hid his opinion on the matter whenever the Belgian press asked him about it.

Yves Vanderhaeghe was able to offer further justification for playing Vincent in the back four.

'Playing at the back is his best position because he is very precise there and can use his solid body. In midfield he was too eager to keep the ball, especially when he was a youngster. Now he is much more disciplined. As a young player, he overdid it and sometimes dwelled on the ball. This caused Vincent to sometimes lose possession which caused dangerous counterattacks because he had ventured out of position.'

But he was at least capable of playing in midfield, certainly according to one of his senior colleagues, namely Vanderhaeghe when Vincent once stood in for him whilst he recovered from injury, with Vanderhaeghe commenting, post match, 'He did a fantastic job.' Tihinen, Vincent's partner in the back four, also saw opportunities for his young team mate to be pushed further forward.

'He is good on the ball and quick. It doesn't happen that often that a defensive midfielder is fast. With his long legs, he can take the ball away from someone well. What he does need to watch out for is staying in position well and not getting too involved in the offensive plays.'

Head coach Hugo Broos had a reputation for being strict. Eleven years after Kompany's debut with Anderlecht, Broos has no intention of changing his initial thoughts about his then young star. But he does put things into perspective, especially in terms of Vincent's professionalism and punctuality, something that may have been slightly disregarded at the time, given the apparent furore about what his best position was.

'Vincent was someone who always got his way within the youngsters' group and had been pampered. Youth chairman Collin once told me that Vincent no longer wanted to come if he was not allowed to play in midfield. And he stopped coming altogether at one point. Then I thought: a teenager doing something like that, and the club allows it!'

'Then suddenly he came into the first team and he had to be on time, dressed in a suit and had to have his passport with him when we travelled abroad. That didn't always work out. Little things he did back then did annoy me on occasions, but they were never a major drama. My satisfaction will always be that he showed on the pitch exactly what I believed he was capable of doing.'

Vincent's defensive duties had to, according to then assistant coach Vercauteren, take priority over his offensive ability... as well as his innate desire to bring the ball forward from his defensive position. He had some licence to attack but it had to be part of his overall game and the tactical plan that Broos and Vercauteren were playing, with Broos pointing out that there was a big difference between Vincent dominating youth team games, as he had, and adapting to playing for the first team.

Vanderhaeghe elaborates. 'In the youth team, he was used to dribbling out from the defence, dribbling past seven opponents and then scoring. He wanted to try that with us too, and he failed'. But that's a phase every youngster experiences.'

Broos said Vincent would realise he would not always be able to solve things the way he used to do. Also, Tihinen was not a fast player and Vincent had to take that into account: it was an extra reason to be careful. Vincent had to cover and remember that he couldn't catch up with the striker who passed Tihinen by sprinting back from the oppositions penalty area. 'You can play on a line...', says Broos, '...but if twice in ten minutes you have an opposition striker pop up in front of your goalkeeper alone, you have to conclude that your defender doesn't have that game intelligence he displayed originally.'

A simpler truth might have been that it seemed as if Vincent had been in and around the first team long enough to be considered one of Anderlecht's more seasoned players. But he was still just seventeen and desperate to impress.

He had been such an outstanding player in the Anderlecht youth teams because he never really had to think too hard about his game because in-match solutions came to him naturally in terms of his great strength, power and technique on the ball. So opponents were often almost completely incapable of living with him. But now, at the higher level, he was coming up against older players who matched him in terms of their strength and physique. As a result of that, Vincent now had to think about the positional aspect of his play a lot more rather than just roam at will, safe in the knowledge that he'd be able to make up for any gaps his temporary absence from the centre of his defence might create for their opponents.

Broos: 'Even though we were angry at times, he was allowed to learn it while playing on the pitch and again the following week, because I had given him a starting place. It's not like De Boeck got another chance if Vincent made two mistakes. I never for a moment even thought about replacing Vincent with Glen. Vincent had convinced me immediately.'

'I had never worked with such a young person with so much talent.'

'His big advantage was that we now had someone in defence who could pass long and could change the game very quickly. If you drew his attention to any weaknesses he might still have, or errors he made and you can see him improving as a result, then you are satisfied. He can't do everything at once. He was open to my comments. Take a league match at Ostend where he made a couple of errors. That's when I did have to lecture him afterwards.'

'Because he challenged the crowd, he played up to them – although I don't think that was his intention. He just wanted to show how good he was. You can't do that and he accepted this. A coach should not give in to that, especially with a young footballer. No dribbling all over the place. That is a learning process; these were youth mistakes.'

'I never had any problems with Vincent. Look, until I was thirty-six, I was a central defender at some of the top Belgian clubs. I played in three European finals and in the World Cup in Mexico 1986. With that sort of experience you are more than able to help someone, to pass your knowledge on. But honestly, we didn't have to coach him that much. In terms of basic qualities, he already had everything you need to have as a young player to become a top footballer'.

'The rest he could only learn from doing it on the pitch.'

Tellingly, the young Vincent Kompany sometimes asked his coaches if he could train for longer to practise a skill, such as his long passing.

Broos: 'Things progressed very quickly. Withing six months of the initial plaudits, he had got to the very top at Anderlecht, including games in the Champions League. That is very fast. But for a boy of seventeen, in modern football, he was always strong. If you can't stand your ground, you go down. He stood his ground. I will admit that, in terms of technique I am not fit to even tie Vincent's laces. I was a pure defender. But the fierceness and doggedness I had, he didn't always show. He had lots of flair to go with his traditional qualities, the sort of indiscipline you can never get rid of completely. But we were able to reduce it a little!'

Hugo Broos's coaching qualities eventually transferred themselves to international level when, in 2017, he led Cameroon to victory in the Africa Cup of Nations. In 2023, Broos also won the bronze medal at this tournament as head coach of South Africa.

Vincent remained hugely ambitious. He wanted to be the best. The coaches kept that ambition in mind to keep him on target and found a measure of success in doing so by occasionally giving him something of a mental prod.

'Vincent, your heading game still needs work.'

'Vincent, the way that striker dribbled past you…'

'Did that ball go between your legs, Vincent?'

Comments like this would wind Vincent up and he would then want to prove that, whatever had happened, whatever little negative that they had picked out in his game, was nothing more than a fluke, a one off, a piece of luck that went the opposition's way. He couldn't be questioned in the way a headmaster might chastise an unruly pupil. So it did work, this more informal, even part joking approach. Vincent would go along with that approach because he was so ambitious, ambitious enough to constantly know what parts of his game needed to be improved upon.

It was just a matter of how you approached him about it. His coaches were learning quickly too, finding that, in turn, he would now constantly be asking them for feedback with one example (of many) being, according to Broos, the fact that he was regularly asking the fitness coach what the results of his training sessions were – runs, distances covered, heart rate, recovery time, you name it. He'd want to improve on all of them.

'A real up and coming professional' says Broos, proudly.

Vincent was, according to Broos, '…first and foremost a jovial guy. He did not say or do stupid things, but did what was needed to be done with a smile on his face. Vincent is not someone who gets drunk and causes car accidents. And if you have the awareness and qualities to take charge without offending anyone, you are a leader.'

His jovial behaviour did not get on the team's nerves much (yet!).

'Vincent was fairly self-conscious when he joined the A-squad and did not ignore the advice he was given by the senior players. Tihinen and others saw that he was listening. He was not someone who said he knew it all already, even if he was aware of his qualities. But he was not arrogant. So he was quickly accepted in the first team player group.'

'It's like that in football', continues Broos. 'If you perform, you are quickly accepted. Vincent also participated in group activities.

'Of course we sometimes went out after a good result, especially away games in European competition. To relax and have a drink. Vincent was open to that,' says Yves Vanderhaeghe.

Vincent Kompany was not yet a leader at this time but all the signs were there and everyone around him knew that he would soon become one, either at Anderlecht or elsewhere. He didn't shout at and cajole his teammates during games which is, perhaps, something you do expect of a central defender. But you could see how that responsibility suited him perfectly and that he was already beginning to lead simply by the way he was playing – actions speaking louder than words.

One thing that Vincent and Hugo Broos did occasionally clash over was the subject of club discipline. For example, the players having to dress smartly, including a tie, when on club duties.

'Wearing a tie, he did not agree with that...', says Broos. "...why do I have to wear a tie now?"

'Because everyone wears a tie, that's the policy, to represent the club stylishly," Broos would reply.

'He also wondered why he wasn't allowed in at five past nine when the training started at nine. And he also disagreed during half-time of a practice game against West Ham United with the position errors I was accusing him of. He needed to cover better because a couple of opponents had turned up alone in front of *(goalkeeper)* Zitka. That was typical, he could seriously argue. I read him the riot act in response and quite vociferously. Fellow player Pär Zetterberg even told him, "Will you shut up now?" The following day, he had to apologise. He was allowed to disagree with me in my office, between four walls, between him and me, but not in front of the whole player group.'

'Yes, Vincent was stubborn...', says Yves Vanderhaeghe, '...but so he should be. He did pick up comments from others and was always up for talking about his game'.

Whatever the other players were telling Vincent and however much he was taking in what they were saying, his late arrivals for training continued. Doing so is considered a cardinal sin, arriving on time is seen as a core value in being professional. But it wasn't as if Vincent was defying anyone in repeatedly arriving late when older and far more experienced players than him always arrived on time, he simply couldn't comprehend that five minutes past nine wasn't acceptable... what, after all, was five minutes?

He also found himself getting into his coaches' bad books for using his mobile phone when he shouldn't have done but, again, couldn't see why that was a problem. That meant a fine, something that, according to Hugo Boss, he didn't agree with either. The club were, by now, starting to work out how best to respond to the misdemeanours of their prodigious young talent and ended up not always fining him for those and other offences, something, you have to assume, his teammates didn't protest about.

Vincent had, in order to ease some of the criticism he was in receipt of, started to add a little more of a cunning edge to his game plan. He could have come in on time of course but, to him, that wasn't the point. So he carried on arriving five or ten minutes later than he should have done, but went out of his way to make sure Broos didn't know this. Broos may well have known anyway but chose to cut Vincent a little slack. If, after all, you have a seventeen year old gem featuring in your first team, one who is already earning covetous glances from leading clubs all over Europe, you don't always want to complicate their development by throwing in the occasional curveball, with Broos saying, 'You obviously don't play any better, or worse, depending on whether you've been wearing a tie or not. But we insisted that the players did. And he had problems with that, they were, Vincent felt, rules that had nothing to do with playing football'.

Broos also understood that young people use their appearance to shape and demonstrate their identity. And, as part of that, they often like to rebel. For teenagers like Vincent Kompany and his peers, the tie was a symbol of the bourgeoisie and that if you chose not to wear one, it wasn't that big a deal. But, to Broos it was.

'You had to convince him that the unimportant still had an importance.'

But was Vincent being allowed to get away with too much? During the following season, Broos found himself being criticised for being too lax in his approach to him. This had been precipitated by Vincent oversleeping the night before a training match and finally arriving not five or ten minutes late but two and a half hours after he should have been there and, of course, two and a half hours after all of the other players had arrived. But there were no repercussions, no punishment and, in Anderlecht's next league game against Genk, Vincent was selected to start as if nothing had happened.

He had become indispensable to both the club and Broos, so it was now very difficult for the coach to leave his jewel out of the side when it was clearly better for him being in it. Broos also did not want to be the man who was seen to come down hard on such an immense talent.

Vincent's excuse was that he had been in for training '...fairly early' the previous day before, that same evening, attending Belgium's Sports Personality of the Year TV show.

'It became much later than I had thought. The sequence of those things caused me to oversleep. That is no excuse: I understand that I was not allowed to be late and that I was fined. I would have accepted any penalty because not coming to training on time is bad. You can see it as a lack of respect. Next time I will think twice if I am asked out on a Sunday evening.'

A symbolic fine of one hundred and fifty euros was eventually handed out to Vincent although, according to *Het Laatste Nieuws,* the club did everything that it possibly could (unsuccessfully, as it turns out) to keep the incident out of the news.

Yet it wasn't a one-off that *might* have been forgivable as Yves Vanderhaeghe recalls that Vincent also arrived last at tactics meetings with, on occasion, a cutting remark or two made to him about it, but, ultimately, and as Broos had always believed, all that really mattered with regard to Vincent was his performance on the pitch.

Both Broos and Vercauteren chose not to single Vincent out for any sort of extra coaching, even though he was a very young player to have in a first team squad.

'I told him what I expected from him,' Broos admits. 'That the A-squad was not an end but a beginning and that he would still have to work a lot. And that he had to listen very carefully to experienced people. But actually you didn't have to tell him that. He did it by himself. I thought his attitude was brilliant and I knew he would reach the top of European football and even the top of world football. Because mentally he was well put together. And because the things that did go wrong at times were mainly due to his youthfulness and not his intellect'.

'He had everything lined up well'.

'Besides, he comes from a warm family. When Vincent joined the A-squad, I talked to his father because I want to know what sort of family background my young players have. His father was fairly principled, he thought it was important Vincent still continued to work hard at school for example. So I immediately had a good feeling about things. Vincent came from a good family, although they didn't have loads of money. But there was a good foundation.'

Yet a danger surfaced very quickly. In a country like Belgium anyone who performs at a young age is immediately portrayed as a star, someone the media are constantly chasing for new stories – and not being particularly subtle about it either. Vincent therefore found himself under a lot of pressure and having to work twice as hard as some players on his media requests as both the Dutch and French language media were claiming him. And those requests were now putting him in the spotlight much more than the comparatively humble ones he'd felt more comfortable about previously (eg) the shop openings or appearances on behalf of a charity. He was now, as far as the media were concerned, much more than the young Brussels' boy who excelled at sport, took school seriously and was happy to chat about the story of his family background in Congo and in Brussels' North Quarter.

Much, much more.

Vercauteren: 'You had to keep an eye on him both in terms of his sporting commitments and his non-sporting commitments. He was asked to do anything and everything and felt he could hardly say no. It wasn't easy: he had to find the right middle ground between paying attention to sport and those personal issues'.

'But training came first, even if it had to come above something very important in his private life.'

Both Anderlecht and Vincent had made a superb start to the 2003/04 season, so much so that, when the Jupiler League stopped for its winter break, Vincent could look back at his breakthrough into the first team with satisfaction. He'd played in thirteen league games, nine more in the Champions League and, on top of all that, had been selected for the national team. He had also, and significantly, learnt how to handle the criticism that was sent his way whilst, at the same time, remaining highly self critical of some of his own performances. He didn't, however, like his weaknesses to be picked out by others, preferring to analyse his game, identify what he might have done wrong and work out how to ensure it didn't happen again.

Outside 'interference', as he might have seen it, was still something that he didn't find easy to accept.

'Sometimes I was so angry with myself that I couldn't tolerate others stating the same things. The drive home from the match is a moment for me when I go over everything again and analyse my performance. Having to then hear that same analysis again from someone else is something I found hard.'

One thing that had sunk in with him was that, life-wise, he'd won the lottery and that everything was laid out in front of him now if he wanted it enough.

'We live in our little cocoons, get an education and go onto play football... and, perhaps, succeed at doing that. The best would one day play football elsewhere and, who knows, probably succeed. That sums it up best: you play football at Anderlecht to hopefully advance in your career elsewhere.'

He knew he had to work hard. The success and acclaim he was now in receipt of hadn't really changed him as a person, he still had the same friends as he'd always had and did pretty much the same things with them. But the 'cocoon' he talked about wasn't going to protect him from the wider world forever.

In February 2004, with Vincent still under eighteen, he was awarded another salary increase as more transfer speculation began to grow around him with Chelsea (who'd now pursue their interest in him for the rest of his time at Anderlecht) and AC Milan the latest clubs rumoured to be preparing a bid.

Two months later, with Chelsea still being linked with Vincent, Anderlecht's newly appointed General Manager, fed up with hearing the constant speculation about him, felt obliged to comment, if only, you assume, to put a stop to it.

'Kompany may leave... for no less than twenty million euros.'

That sum was, at the time, roughly the same as Anderlecht's entire annual budget.

But quoting it had a clear objective. Firstly, the accepted price for Vincent was now a lot higher than it had previously been. And by quite some considerable distance. Secondly, it had, at a stroke, reduced the number of clubs who could either afford him or even be prepared to pay that amount to a very small number indeed, and, finally, was a not so subtle way of telling everyone, Roman Abramovich and Chelsea included, that Vincent Kompany was not for sale.

Because no-one was going to pay that amount for a seventeen year old back then.

For all of Vincent's potential, twenty million Euros was, at that stage, a completely unrealistic asking price for him. The amount that had been more readily quoted in stories and footballing gossip pages had usually been five million Euros, a quarter of that amount. Any clubs thinking that might be enough now had to think again. It was certainly enough to keep Vincent where he was, for the time being at least. But the Anderlecht hierarchy knew they wouldn't be able to retain his services for much longer. They also knew that if he continued to stand out, particularly in Champions League matches and games for the Belgian national sides, it would, eventually, not seem such a high amount after all, especially if a cash rich English, Spanish or Italian side decided to make a sudden offer of, say, ten million Euros.

With Vincent Kompany anything now seemed possible.

Vincent was already becoming worldly wise as to how football worked, telling *Het Laatste Nieuws*, after his eighteenth birthday, 'Football is theatre and I know that all the gossip and rumours are part of it.' He'd celebrated his eighteenth birthday on April 10th 2004 with nothing more ostentatious than a small cake, choosing to spend his day with his family as he had always done. He also gave the newspaper a couple of quotes that reflected the man he was turning into, one being 'Getting presents is not important, I prefer to give.'

Then, when he was asked what his big dream was, he replied, 'It takes place after my career. Then I want to spend a lot of time with all the people who are dear to me, time I definitely don't have now.' He went onto explain that even walking down the street was now next to impossible and that, although he did his best to do as many of the 'ordinary' things as he used to, simply going shopping or visiting the cinema had become very difficult.

Anderlecht's form in the second half of the 2003/04 season was maybe not quite as convincing as it had been in the period leading up to the winter break, but they still did more than enough to end the campaign by winning their twenty-seventh national title, with Vincent celebrating by having his hair coloured purple. He didn't drink much, certainly not like some of his teammates might have done, as he didn't particularly like the taste of beer or wine. In the *Carré* discotheque in Willebroek however, he was in his element. He was also, perhaps, a little taken aback by having success at such an early age, saying that he'd never dared to expect that his dream of becoming a champion would come true in his first year playing for the first team and that although in his youth, he'd already won four titles, this particular achievement felt '...completely different.'

The title win was more than welcome as far as Anderlecht were concerned, having missed out at the end of the previous two seasons. And, at the end of that one, Vincent's stats looked impressive. He'd made twenty nine first team appearances and been substituted only twice. Of the three league games that he had missed it was either because of injury or because Broos had decided to give him a rest, the same logic applying for the other games he played in that season, nine in Europe, five in the Belgian Cup plus the Super Cup match played at the start of the season.

Excellent figures for a very young player, especially one who was playing in central defence.

The interest, far and wide, in Vincent Kompany's life grew bigger and bigger. And it wasn't just football that people want to ask him about.

In *Het Nieuwsblad*, he answered some readers' questions, including about his personal life.

One thing he revealed is that he was currently single although he did recently '...have a girlfriend'. He goes onto admit that he is 'quite shy' (which might have come as a surprise to some), was very fond of spare ribs with fries and Greek salad as well as the jam that his grandfather made.

When the questions did get around to football, he said that England's Premier League is '...fun to watch and must also be to play football in' but that La Liga in Spain is the most fun whilst Italy's Serie A looks the hardest. He follows this up adding, with an ambassadorial quality that, when it comes to where he, or anyone might end up playing their football, that '...there are no bad choices.'

He also ended the season being voted Belgium's Young Professional Footballer of the Year.

Much excitement surrounded Vincent. But that was tempered by Frankie Vercauteren, one of the few people in the game who judged Vincent's first season in a more sober light. Talking to *Sport-Voetbalmagazine*, he said, 'He is someone with a lot of potential, who is still making mistakes. In the beginning they weren't punished, now they are. I may see more of them than others, but still do. It has to do with nonchalance and position. Ask him in training to make five passes over twenty metres and there may be four bad ones today and five perfect ones tomorrow. This is the case in matches as well. In terms of positional play, he has not mastered a number of things: where to run, where to cover, when to distance himself.'

Harsh words? Maybe. But Vercauteren, who made 63 appearances for Belgium and played in two World Cups, likes to argue from an international perspective. He is setting the bar high. A club like Anderlecht owes it to itself to aim for constantly top performances from international footballers. There is no room for mediocrity at the club. Vincent certainly finds nothing to argue about with regard to Vercauteren's words, saying, 'Is Vercauteren too strict? Certainly not. I demand from my coaches that they are hard on me. They have to say what they think of me.'

Vincent Kompany's second season (2004/05) with Anderlecht in the Jupiler League ends with him being awarded a number of prizes for himself as an individual in what was a disastrous campaign for the club, which saw them finish bottom of their Champions' League group with zero points from their six games and only four goals scored. Anderlecht also surrendered their status as Belgian Champions to Club Brugge by three points as well as losing to the same opponents in the Belgian Super Cup. Coach Hugo Broos wasn't even given until the end of the season however, with Anderlecht sacking him in February 2005 and Vercauteren taking over alongside De Boeck as his assistant.

Amidst the malaise, Vincent Kompany's performances repeatedly stood out. He had become a far more mature player and was progressing as fast as anyone might have hoped, although he ran into trouble for his behaviour in August 2004 with Broos admitting that Vincent '...already had a clash with his teammates as well as an altercation with me and received some criticism'. By 'criticism', Broos is probably referring to a quote from Belgian national team coach Aimé Anthuenis, who'd said 'Kompany was sharper last season'. Broos didn't react too strongly to those words but they clearly resonated with the soon to be ex-Anderlecht coach, who, typically, defended Vincent in the wake of Anthuenis's comments, saying, 'It sounds harsh but it's fine for him to be knocked back a few times. That's normal in a learning process.'

In *Sport-Voetbalmagazine*, Kompany expanded on the more difficult start to his second season. 'What I do is far from perfect, in terms of positional play and so on. Perfection does not exist. I am absolutely willing to learn, even if I sometimes dare to argue.'

And yes, he did agree with others... sometimes at least.

'I may not like to show that I agree with someone but I think about it anyway. Objectively, I then try to make a judgement. I really don't look at everything from my point of view.'

And of his game, he noted certain progressions. 'I no longer commit youthful sins, but make mistakes that a full-fledged first-team player makes.'

His positional play was indeed getting better. 'What I could never do before is control things because of my position. Last year, I had to make up for a lot of mistakes because of my speed. I still do that, but have less need for it.'

There was a perception among some that Vincent was an easy target and that there was little understanding of his personality and obstinacy. *Sporza* journalist Frank Raes stood up for him in a column in *De Standaard*. 'The most notable victim these days to accuse of a "lack of experience" is Vincent Kompany, because he is only eighteen, stands twice as far from his opponents as he should and doesn't just chuck every ball away. That Kompany has superb timing in direct duels, positions his body perfectly and usually plays hard and precisely, apparently no longer stands out. It's strange that every time we make a fuss when a super talent emerges such as the new Vieira, Desailly or Rijkaard, but can't have a new star also showing some personality and even wilfulness.'

'In the end, we opt for good workers, an ideal son-in-law who always wear their tie,' he concluded ironically.

At *Het Nieuwsblad*, Ludo Vandewalle asked Kompany about the 'six principles' that help him to feel good as a professional footballer and he happily listed them.

Top of the list was 'Don't read newspapers'.

The second is 'Ignore pressure'.

Vincent's remarkable third observation was 'Keep studying'. This, he said, helps him to stay out of the stress that surrounds football for as long as possible. Music and books help the senses, because ...reading broadens your mind and enriches your vocabulary... so does school'.

Number four was 'Discuss to learn'.

'If you always nod yes but don't know why, you won't progress', he explains. 'Discussing is not synonymous with arguing', he adds, mentioning that he has learnt to stop his one-to-one 'discussions' with Hugo Broos when the whole group is there.

This is something that the older players made very clear to him that he had to do.

His fifth insight was to 'Go on holiday alone'. He'd visited Marbella and enjoyed spending a few days of living without an agenda and walking around and interacting with people there virtually anonymously.

Finally, he listed a desire to 'Radiate positivity'... by that he means that people '... should be able to pull themselves up when faced with all manner of difficulties, through using positive behaviour'.

For many, it seemed almost unbelievable that an eighteen year old possessed so much life wisdom. Vincent had placed his football career and life in a broader framework and saw himself not as the centre of the world but as a leader who reflects on his actions and wants to inspire others. He avoids, as much as he can, any negative influences whilst embracing those that are positive and beneficial to him.

It's perhaps important to point out here that these six points never made Vincent Kompany a guru or even a philosopher. But his six commandments for a footballer's life are still an interesting guide.

By the autumn of 2004, there was talk that Barcelona were also actively watching him and that Inter Milan were even going as far as preparing to make a bid of fifteen million Euros for him. Soon afterwards and, perhaps, not wanting to be usurped by their biggest rivals, Real Madrid were said to be interested again.

It's hardly surprising and, maybe, the man who says he did not read newspapers, may have ended up picking one up that claimed that, of all of Anderlecht's players, he was the only one capable of playing at Champions League level.

Whilst all the speculation and tentative interest was flying around his ears, Vincent became convinced he would be better off staying at Anderlecht for a while longer.

'If I stay, it is because I realise that I still have to develop as a footballer and want to invest in my future. Among other things, my positional play, head game and left foot are not yet what they should be,' he admitted. At Anderlecht, he will be given the time and space to hone that.

'Then, in two, three or five years, as a better and more mature footballer, I can make the step to a bigger club.'

New Year started with good news for all those who support Anderlecht when, after a season and a half playing in the Belgian Premier League, Vincent was awarded, by *Het Laatste Nieuws*, the Golden Shoe as the best footballer in Belgium for 2004. He was still just eighteen but had received 507 points in total, over four hundred more than the runner up, Luigi Pieroni of R.E.Mouscron. It was not only a record winning margin for the competition but the second highest points total won since the trophy was first awarded in 1954.

One of Kompany's best statements about the trophy win was made in the organiser's newspaper.

'I even wonder why such an award was invented for a collective sport like football.'

Hugo Broos had long seen the award coming.

'We had to guide Vincent because he would be dragged from place to place. And then we would have a problem. We had to make sure his peripheral activities didn't become more important than the football itself, and make sure he got his humanities degree in the best conditions. We wanted him to have a normal life, not a king's life.'

The club asked Vincent if he thought media coaching was a good idea and, with Yvon Verhoeven, who worked in social affairs at Anderlecht, the club found the right man to help him. For Vincent, that was a very good thing. Dealing with fame is never natural, especially at eighteen. One of the first things he learnt at that stage in his career was to have two mobile phones in his pocket... one for his private life and employer, and one for journalists.

By then, Anderlecht's general manager Michel Verschueren had already given way to his successor Herman Van Holsbeeck. Mister Michel, as he liked to call himself, acknowledged that what was not an issue in his playing days was now something that had to be both acknowledged and dealt with.

'I thought the social and media coaching of our youth players was a good evolution. If you don't have that, sometimes those young players break down. Freedom is about accepting boundaries, otherwise you end up with anarchy. Especially with young people, who still have to learn everything. If you give them too much freedom, things sometimes go wrong: at night they don't know what to do, end up on the streets and in cafés and then things go wrong. I never saw Vincent make any mistakes. I have never seen him drunk. He really led an exemplary life with us.'

Team mate Vanderhaeghe: 'With his Golden Shoe, he had built up a lot of credit. Of course he still made mistakes but he never strayed too far. What also helped was that under Vercauteren we were secluded before every match. This also allowed the youngsters to concentrate fully. That was necessary, because someone like Kompany is very social. Vincent is clever and an intellectual but cannot say no quickly. That takes strength and fitness. Because of these seclusions, he was not seen in the city.'

According to Vanderhaeghe, Vercauteren handled Vincent very well, regularly motivating him and, in the process, always keeping him sharp. In addition to that, Vincent had team mates who wanted to fight and wanted to win. Amongst them were a lot of midfielders, some of whom were nothing more than, as Didier Deschamps was once memorably labelled by Eric Cantona, 'water carriers', content with their status at the club, however, several others felt that Anderlecht would not be the pinnacle of their playing careers – players who intended to move onto bigger and better things.

Vercauteren kept things strict but pleasant enough – so not exactly a 'my way or the highway' mentality. Broos had assumed his squad of Anderlecht players had the core qualities required to play for the club but could, when necessary, adapt to different roles or responsibilities, he wanted them to be flexible. Vercauteren, on the other hand, was more rigid, tactically, he wanted to introduce more patterns of play, in both training and matches, until he got the result he envisaged and however long it took.

Winning the Golden Shoe in a relatively limited league like the Belgian Pro League is so often a springboard for a professional footballer, the starting point for a winner, an accolade that inspires them to go on to greater things overseas. Previous winners to Vincent had been Jan Koller in 2000 (one of a select few non-Belgians to have won the award); Franky Van der Elst (1996), and Philippe Albert (1992). All three were players who became well known outside of Belgium, with, for example, Albert shining as an integral playing member of the Newcastle United team that came so close to winning the English Premier League in 1996 and 1997. Did Vincent Kompany want to use the recognition he now had to advance his career elsewhere, whether that be in England, Spain, Italy or Germany?

Vanderhaeghe thought he would.

'If Kompany wants to push his limits, he is left with nothing more to do than make a move abroad next season. He can now afford to be two-and-a-half hours late for training without losing his place in the team. Knowing that he will not be punished means he is getting complacent. He needs more. He needs a tough hand to further develop his career. He should resolutely opt for the top and the best working conditions.'

Kompany disagreed with accusations of complacency, telling *Het Laatste Nieuws* that every tall player looked nonchalant, adding, 'My attitude hangs between nonchalance and composure? I don't like that word. It is starting to become synonymous with laziness. I sometimes take it a little too easily, but lazy is really the last thing you can accuse me of.'

Speaking to *Het Nieuwsblad*, he said, 'This Golden Shoe is not a crowning achievement for me. I see the recognition more as a new beginning.'

He thanked Anderlecht and said: 'Furthermore, I want to dedicate this award to the friends of the North Quarter. That's where I learned my specific, playful way of playing football. That's where I perhaps also picked up my lifestyle. Anderlecht's youth school added efficiency to it.'

Although he had thanked his friends from the North Quarter in his acceptance speech, he claimed there was no deeper social message. 'It may well be that as a bilingual Congolese Belgian, I will be taken as an example of the multicultural society that Belgium should be within Europe, but when I dedicated my Golden Shoe to the North Quarter there was no politically correct message in it'.

'I have no ambition to make the world a better place.'

Perhaps inevitably, his higher profile in the game was now inviting comparisons. Vincent had no time for them and was dismissive.

'The new Beckenbauer, the new Desailly, the new Rijkaard: who will it be? None of the three. I am Vincent Kompany.' He revealed that he would decide on his future at the end of the season.

'I want to be like everyone else higher up, my goal is everything that might not be achievable for a Belgian footballer.'

In *Le Soir*, an anonymous senior Anderlecht player whinged about Vincent, saying, 'He no longer listens to anyone and just does what he wants. He thinks he's always right and doesn't even listen to the coach anymore. Vincent is not a bad boy, but he is making himself impossible. Even if from now until the end of the season, I will not have paid as many fines as he has already'.

Was Vincent getting above himself as suggested? He certainly didn't think so, for, as part of that acceptance speech for his award, he also said, 'Rest assured, I will not get carried away. As you can see, my head is still firmly on my shoulders.'

This was taken as a sign he was, contrary to what a lot of people were expecting, staying at Anderlecht.

Which is exactly what he did, thanks, in part, to Yvon Verhoeven, who'd taken him under his wing and given him the social and media training he'd needed to cope with all the added expectation and demands on his time. It's not surprising that Vincent ended up responding so well to Verhoeven, who was the kind of man you tended to come across in managerial positions at Anderlecht at that time, someone who was a little older, bilingual, engaging and classy in all that he did... a man who could relate to both the ordinary supporter as well as the CEO of a multinational company. Or, for that matter, a budding eighteen year old superstar footballer.

Verhoeven had certainly lived a full professional life. He'd spent some time working in asset management, was an international hockey referee as well as, amongst many other things, a member of the executive committee of the Belgian hockey federation. He was bringing all of that rich experience in life and business to Anderlecht and, in particular, Vincent Kompany.

Verhoeven: 'Someone had to look after the young players and, if necessary, take care of all their extracurricular demands and offer them some agenda management. With Vincent it clicked between us from the very first moment.'

The former bank manager had discussed his approach with his wife beforehand. She was a former hockey international, whilst her nephews Jérémy and Grégory Gucasoff were, at that time, both current Belgian hockey internationals. She advised him to adapt to Vincent and not vice versa, because, after all, it was Vincent who had won the Golden Shoe. Verhoeven certainly did not want to become a schoolmaster and tell Kompany what to do and what not to do. He did, however, often go along to Vincent's social activities, sometimes as his driver, although he did not always attend.

'I was not a babysitter!'

'During the first months after the Golden Shoe award, it was about one or two activities a week, then a few less. But Vincent remained very active, partly because everyone wanted to invite him. He was more than happy, for the most part, to attend'.

Verhoeven dealt with Vincent's diary management, becoming more of a secretary than a social facilitator. In the beginning, about a dozen charity requests per week were coming in and working through them became almost a full-time occupation for him.

'That was a tsunami. I did the pre-selection, I weeded them out. Let's forget this one and that one, I suggested things to Vincent when we sat around the table, but I always let him decide for himself what he would do.'

'He was still going to school then, so there wasn't much time for those visits.'

Vincent managed purely commercial requests, such as sponsorship along with his agent Jacques Lichtenstein whilst Verhoeven did the social initiatives (eg) visiting hospitals (especially the Queen Fabiola Hospital in Brussels which treats children with cancer); non-profit organisations and non-governmental organisations. So, for example, more high profile activities like appearing at charity football matches, or making a special appearance at a charitable event that had been organised, for example, by the Red Cross. So there were individual meet and greets with sick children with Vincent giving them a signed jersey or donating a ball. The only criterion for getting involved in any activity of this kind was whether Vincent considered it interesting and practically feasible.

Vincent always made the effort to talk to sick children but also to their parents, with Yvon Verhoeven remembering one visit particularly well.

160

'I remember a little boy of seven or eight who was playing football at Union Namur. He broke a leg and in the treatment process it was discovered that he had cancer. Vincent played with and talked to that boy, but also showed compassion to his parents. He'd then tell the people in the hospital that the kids could play at being a journalist and ask him questions. Then they would all sit at a big table with him at the head.'

'When you see something like that, you may see a boy of eighteen, but you think that's a real gentleman'.

Vincent felt these social activities were almost a moral duty for the Golden Shoe winner to carry out. But he did not see them as an obligation. He saw it as part of an ambassadorial role he was carrying out on behalf of Anderlecht and Belgian football.

Something he was more than happy to do.

Yvon Verhoeven certainly looked up to Kompany.

'In terms of intelligence, charisma and personality, I have never met such a footballer. Vincent was an adult at seventeen or eighteen, that made it easier for the senior players to accept him, they even looked up to him themselves at times for what he was... not just as a footballer, but a human being.'

Werner Deraeve already saw Vincent as an established leader.

'A leader is not necessarily the best player in the team. Vincent did keep the group together and happily came forward to voice his opinion. He worked people out well and was able to influence them. Of course, he also learnt a lot, because there were always small verbal fights, right up to the first team level. He'd already had a fight with De Boeck who'd told him to do something in a certain way... with Vincent disagreeing. De Boeck then tried to justify his approach by saying, "I have the experience", to which Vincent replied, "I can play good football and you can't."'

Verhoeven: 'Vincent was a figurehead and role model, he was no longer the raw teenager but someone with sense, common sense too. We became close and he appreciated me. Of course, I never interfered. Nor was that the intention. His private life was a closed book and I felt it was best that way for me and the club.'

'Vincent is a killer on and off the pitch. He always goes to extremes. And he knew it was his job to be there for good causes and to make a contribution. He is task-sensitive. He learned a lot from them and was happy to be able to be there. Vincent is not someone who lives in a cocoon of people bathed in affluence or just lives for himself and his family'.

'He sometimes just seeks out people who are struggling.'

Verhoeven thinks Vincent would definitely have obtained a University degree without football.

'He strives for perfection. With that same mentality as he has, you become a civil engineer or a lawyer or a tax expert.'

He vividly recalls Vincent's rehabilitation period in Lyon when he was injured during the 2005-06 season, when things were not looking good with his shoulder injury.

Verhoeven: 'That was a long project. Vincent was in a specialist hospital in the mountains. Jacques Lichtenstein, Pierre and I encouraged him at that time as well as during his rehabilitation in France. The impact of serious injuries on the morale of a footballer is underestimated: they are in physical pain, suffer mentally, are socially isolated from their teammates and wonder if they will reach their former level again.'

Verhoeven will never claim that Vincent, or indeed any young footballer, will ever be perfect. But as a human being, there was little to add to Vincent's character that wasn't already there.

'I can't say I tried to change anything. He was not yet eighteen, but was already an adult of twenty-five, even verbally.' He then refers to a press conference at the Conrad hotel in Brussels during which Kompany replied in French, Dutch and English.

'That was a game for him, theatre. Yes, athletes like to be in the spotlight. Vincent feels at home there'.

Vincent's mother admitted to *Sport-Voetbalmagazine*: 'I am glad the club has appointed someone to help him in these matters, because Vincent cannot ever say no.' She also talked about his attitude. 'There are those who claim he is intimidating because of the way he looks and plays. Maybe, but he is putting on a mask, to hide his reserve, because my son is, first and foremost, shy'.

'Whether he wants to or not, he will find himself integrating into a very different world from the one he knows over the next few years. He must not be naive by any means; not everyone has good intentions,' added Joseline.

The golden triangle to succeed is parent-school-football, believes Yvon Verhoeven. If the parents support the project then their offspring have a chance of reaching the top. And the Athenaeum had done everything possible for him.

'School must not be underestimated. They get a certificate at the club and are free to train and stay away from school and so can miss many classes. So at least just stay motivated enough to get your school certificate.'

Vincent once said his mother asked head coach Hugo Broos not to take him on a European trip as she preferred to see him sat at his school desk.

Verhoeven: 'There was only one aspect I was disappointed about, and that was that he kept turning up late to his charity activities. "We'll get there", he said. But in some cases, plans were changed quickly. I remember a friendly match for a charity in Barcelona. He had boarded last and the doors of the plane closed immediately. Before our departure for Brussels airport, he was already late for the appointment and then he had forgotten something so we had to return to Ganshoren'.

'Pierre Leroy, the team manager at the time, had warned me: "You will have some experiences with Vincent because he is never, ever, on time." So I always added an hour whenever I made an appointment with him. And even then we were sometimes late. I remember a broadcast on TV channel *VTM,* barely a few minutes before it started we finally turned up.'

'Yes, a bit of coolness was needed when you had to go somewhere with Vincent.'

Kompany was also seen as the bright spot in the otherwise bleak season that Anderlecht were enduring, one saw him winning more individual awards – Young Professional Footballer and Professional Footballer of the Year – amongst other accolades. Yet he was aware that the best thing for his career remained to be in a successful Anderlecht team. If the club was standing still then, by definition, so was he.

Anderlecht, naturally, always put the overall interests of the club first and above that of any individual player, including Vincent Kompany. But that didn't mean he wasn't central to their strategic thinking as they attempted to bounce back after their disappointing 2004/05 campaign. Vincent would, the club made it perfectly clear, be staying put, despite the growing interest and ever higher transfer fees that numerous teams were supposedly ready to pay for him.

Anderlecht were realistic. Everyone at the club knew that, for all their posturing, Vincent would eventually be sold to the highest bidder. But, for now at least, there was a good reason why he had chosen to stay at the club beyond the summer of 2005, which was in addition to the loyalty he felt he owed them. That was the influence of Pierre Kompany, his father, who always wanted family interests to come first and foremost, something that was understandable at the time, given he had not long been divorced from Vincent's mother.

If Vincent left Anderlecht and went to play for a foreign club, the family would, once again, be separated. Vincent would be in a new city and country whilst Pierre would be left in Brussels with his two other children. It wasn't as if the family wouldn't be able to cope if Vincent moved onto pastures new but perhaps it didn't feel right for such a close-knit family to to be further fragmented at that time. Yes, Vincent had long seen himself as something of an 'adventurer' but he was very closely attached to his friends, family and familiar surroundings in Brussels.

Pierre Kompany had previously told *Het Laatste Nieuws,* 'My children's happiness is most important. All three of them get equal attention. You can't do that if you let a boy of seventeen years old play abroad.'

Michel Verschueren, the general manager at Anderlecht until January 2004, spoke about the speculation about Vincent saying, 'By adjusting his contract step by step, we still managed to keep him until 2006. His father played a big role in that. And yes, in the negotiations, the Kompany's made the most of it. They are very good negotiators, especially the father. They were very correct but these were not easy discussions. They knew what they were talking about and where they wanted to go, but also always how far they could go.'

In the run-up to the new 2005-06 football season, Anderlecht made some big changes at the club, the end result of which was that whilst Vercauteren was set to stay on as Head Coach, striker Aruna Dindane would be amongst those leaving with the then 24-year-old Ivory Coast international joining RC Lens in Frances's Ligue One. Also leaving were Nenad Jestrovic, who joined Al Ain FC in the United Arab Emirates, Anatoli Gerk (Twente FC) and Christophe Grégoire (KAA Gent) whilst, during the season, six more players left Anderlecht on free transfers and a further four left on loan deals. The most significant of several new arrivals was Club Atlético Independiente striker Nicolás Frutos.

Vincent was, as ever, wildly ambitious and had gone into the 2005/06 season with initial high hopes, including, as he saw it, the chance to finally play in midfield for the club, admitting as such to *Het Laatste Nieuws*, 'If the coach thinks I can contribute in midfield, then something like that could influence my decision to stay in Belgium.'

So, at the beginning of July 2005, nineteen-years-old Vincent Kompany was ready for his third season in the starting eleven – he had also finally left school and could fill more of his schedule attending the events that Verhoeven accompanied him to.

Yet anyone worrying that he'd let his commercial interests come above his commitment to the club would have been mistaken, Vincent's intention was, very much, to regain the Belgian title with Anderlecht, with him telling *Het Laatste Nieuws*, 'Not winning the league again would hit harder than last season. Then we were coming from a title year and we were too confident. Losing twice in a row would be a huge disappointment.'

New season and another new Anderlecht contract for Vincent Kompany with, as early as May 24th 2005, *Het Nieuwsblad* boldly announcing 'Monster deal – golden five-year contract for Vincent Kompany'.

If their claims were correct, then he was now in receipt of the biggest salary ever paid by the club. A little over a month later, the same newspaper announced that Vincent had not only signed the new contract but that it ran until the summer of 2010.

But nobody really expected him to still be at the club then.

The longer the duration of a contract is, of course, the higher a potential transfer fee for the player in question becomes. That is something that softens the blow of losing a prized talent for the selling club. For the player it meant both job and financial security, including, crucially, if they suffered a career threatening injury. *Het Laatste Nieuws* claimed Vincent's new deal was worth at least €750,000 a year, although Anderlecht did not, at any time, confirm that (or any) figure. As for Vincent himself, a man who now knew his value to the club and, by definition, Belgian domestic football, all he'd asked for was to be the highest earner at the club, which he managed by asking for the symbolic sum of €1 a year more than his second highest earning teammate.

In Kompany's third season as a first team player, Anderlecht reached the group stage of the Champions League after eliminating Baku and Slavia Prague in the qualifying rounds. After that, however, their (2006) Champions League campaign was once again a huge disappointment, with Chelsea, Liverpool and Real Betis proving to be predictably difficult opponents. Anderlecht lost their first five group matches without even scoring a goal, a 3-0 defeat to Liverpool at Anfield proving to be a particularly chastening experience, a game that Vincent, who might have made a difference, didn't play in.

Honour was, at least, partially restored in their last group game against Real Betis in Spain when Anderlecht recorded an impressive 1-0 victory, the goal coming courtesy of Vincent a minute before half time. That victory, pyrrhic as it might have later been considered, brought with it a huge sense of relief to everyone at the club. Finishing bottom of the group again (and, as a result, not even qualifying for the UEFA Cup's latter stages, the 'reward' for clubs finishing in third place) was bad enough. But to have done so without winning any points, scoring a goal or keeping a clean sheet would have been anathema to a club that, whilst it would never be one of Europe's elite footballing institutions, certainly considered itself good enough to occupy the tier directly below that occupied by the likes of Real Madrid, Barcelona, Chelsea and Bayern Munich.

Vincent's goal in Seville had therefore spared some blushes, but it didn't prevent *Het Nieuwsblad* pointing out the deficiencies of the club at that level, citing that Anderlecht had played (including the previous season's tournament) nearly eleven hours of Champions League football without scoring a goal, a statistic that was impossible to gloss over.

Domestically, Vincent didn't have the best of starts to the 2005/06 Jupiler League campaign either. He played in all of Anderlecht's first four matches, impressing in victories over R.A.A Louvièroise (6-0); Club Brugge (0-2); Beerschot AC (3-1) and in a 3-3 draw with Genk on August 28th, before playing for Belgium against San Marino in a World Cup qualifying match a little over a week later, in which he had to come off after just twelve minutes suffering from back pain.

Vincent wasn't, at least initially, too concerned about what he saw as a niggle that had been exasapated by his having to sleep in an uncomfortable bed prior to Belgium's match against Bosnia-Herzegovina a few days earlier. San Marino were not exactly the most taxing of opponents for Belgium (who won the game 8-0, with Vincent's replacement, Koen Daerden scoring one of the goals), and he was declared fit for Anderlecht's next league game, against R.E. Mouscron on September 10th, three days after the San Marino match. He didn't, however, last the full ninety minutes and was substituted with a little over ten minutes to go with a recurrence of the problem that had forced him off against San Marino.

Vincent's injury was immediately assessed and diagnosed as the bulging of an intervertebral disc – a painful and potentially debilitating injury that necessitated Vincent taking three days of rest, during which time, he was instructed, he was only to move if he needed to visit the bathroom.

So a little more than just a 'tweak' then.

It was an injury that turned out to be far more serious than originally thought.

The Belgian press soon picked up on the story and started to print ominous articles of the '...once a back patient, always a back patient' variety, suggesting that, even now, Vincent would never be the same player he was. There was also talk about how his still young and developing body was paying the price for playing so much football from a very early age – the demands of regularly playing at the highest level of the game and, apparently, how unhealthy it was. The stories also spuriously claimed that Vincent was further disadvantaged because of his height (1.93m or 6' 4") which meant he was allegedly more prone to back injuries.

The pessimists initially seemed to be wrong. On November 10th, Vincent appeared for Anderlecht in a Belgian Cup match against Geel, a relatively low profile and undemanding fixture for his reintegration back into the team. He also played in two Champions League matches (a 0-2 home defeat to Chelsea as well as the win against Real Betis) and then a further five league matches that took the Jupiler League up to its Christmas break.

But this run of games didn't last and, after 67 minutes of the league game against Club Brugge on January 21st, Vincent had to be substituted once more because of back pain.

Rest and recuperation seem to rectify the problem but, at the end of the month, whilst taking part in a training match, Vincent dislocated his right shoulder, tearing the ligaments in the process.

That was certainly not an injury that could be dealt with by merely putting his feet up and resting. Vincent needed to undergo surgery, which meant he would almost certainly not play again that season. What was of equal, or perhaps even greater, concern to Anderlecht was whether a long term injury would adversely affect Vincent's value in the transfer market. Would those clubs purportedly interested in signing him think twice about signing a player emerging from surgery with months of rehabilitation ahead? But, at that point, any possible future transfer was the least of Vincent's worries. His main thoughts were to get fully fit again, and, once he had done so, to start playing football again as soon as possible.

On February 23rd, Vincent was operated on by orthopaedic surgeon Gilles Walch at the Clinique Sainte-Anne de Lumière of Lyon in France. He'd chosen not to take the usual footballer's option of taking a long haul flight to the USA for his treatment but had looked around for the best relatively local solution. The operation was deemed a success, with Vincent going on to rehabilitate, along with several other recovering footballers, at the Centre Européen de Rééducation du Sportif in Saint-Raphaël, with attending doctor Robert Cohen telling *Het Laatste Nieuws* that Vincent's shoulder '...was dislocated so a piece of bone was brought down to prevent it from dislocating again. Like a stopper holding the joint in place.'

Vincent recovered well and was able to recommence training with Anderlecht on May 2nd 2006.

At around that time, the respective club presidents of Anderlecht and French Ligue One club Lyon struck up a conversation. The two men knew each other fairly well and, as they chatted, Jean-Michel Aulas mentioned Kompany and how much his opposite number's club might be expecting to get for him in the transfer market? 'Fifteen million Euros', was the reply, an amount that Lyon could certainly afford to pay if they really wanted to bring Vincent to France. Interest in him, injury record or not, seemed to be about to intensify again, with Lyon seemingly now leading the way.

Whilst all of that was happening, Vincent was purely focused on his continuing rehabilitation. Summer was fast approaching but he would have no time to chill on a beach. Physically, at least, he was prospering, able to work through the exercises that had been set as part of his recovery programme and, day by day, he could feel his strength and fitness improving. Mentally, however, he was finding this prolonged period out of the game increasingly difficult. He was missing his family and friends, as well as his teammates and, perhaps most of all, he felt homesick. Yet, he also knew he 'only' had a relatively straightforward football injury to concern himself with and there were many things far worse being experienced by countless people on a day to day basis.

For all that, he welcomed the chance to unburden himself of his worries within the pages of *Humo* magazine. Despite the inury, the last few months, he says, have done him a lot of good.

'I prefer football of course, but my mind and body needed the break. My body was not quite ready for top level sport when I made my Anderlecht debut, I should, maybe, have both rested and trained more at that time. However, the *(then)* demands of school ruled that out. Now I have finally had the time to work on some of my weaknesses and have, as a result, become stronger and fitter.'

Reassurance for would be suitors?

Possibly.

'The human body protests when the load is too high.'

Vincent had become very philosophical about his injury, it was, he has seemingly concluded, inevitable.

'My rhythm was too high.' Not football *per se*, but the combination of all Vincent's activities: football, school, press and sponsorship obligations.'

KOMPANY THE MAKING OF THE MAN

He further reveals that his shoulder no longer dislocated so easily (more reassurances to would-be interested parties?) because the shoulder socket had been tightened.

But has he struggled during his lay-off?

'How can I mind where I am right now? I'm in a nice hotel on the Côte d'Azur, it's beautiful. Walk into a hospital and you'll find dozens of people who are ten times worse off than me.'

Perhaps what surprises readers most of all is that, at twenty, he feels he does not need a steady girlfriend. But he doesn't cite lack of time as an excuse for this (which would seem most reasonable) but goes onto explain, 'The relationship I have with my family and friends is strong enough. I don't need anyone else.'

Admirable sentiments, undoubtedly, but Vincent was a charmer and a magnet to women – a young man who effortlessly radiated affection and warmth – who you would imagine saw the need for someone in his life to support him.

It's a very surprising revelation. But perhaps nothing about Vincent Kompany should surprise anyone by now.

In early April, *Het Laatste Nieuws* caused something of a furore in Brussels by claiming that 'Kompany will play at Lyon next season, two sources have formally confirmed.' The newspaper went onto say that Lyon were prepared to pay sixteen million Euros to secure Vincent's transfer, one which, if it went ahead, would make him the most expensive transfer in Belgian football history.

The story was almost immediately rebuffed by both Anderlecht and Jacques Lichtenstein, whilst the club's general manager, Herman Van Holsbeeck, went as far as to 'emphatically' deny there is any truth in the story through a hastily put together press release.

A day later, Lyon president Aulas was featured in *Het Nieuwsblad* claiming that the story was 'nonsense' and the quoted fee of sixteen million Euros was '...far too much', adding that six to eight million Euros would be a far more realistic price for Vincent. In response to that, Van Holsbeeck called that amount 'a joke', and continues to quote sixteen million Euros as the sort of figure required in order for any interested club to sign Vincent Kompany.

A game had started, one in which the supporters of both clubs never knew who was telling the truth and who was not.

Anderlecht eventually regained their Belgian title, crowned for the 28th time, by beating Zulte-Waregem 3-0 on the last day of the season. Vincent was there, albeit as a spectator only and responded to post-match claims that Anderlecht were only 'minor champions' (as they'd done so by winning only 20 of their 34 league games), by saying that, as with the previous season, Anderlecht had shown themselves to have two faces, '...almost unbeatable at home, too often a wet mop in away games'.

168

What, at that point, did assistant coach De Boeck think of Vincent?

'A difficult season for him. He was not at the top of his game at any point. He suffered for a long time with back injuries and often couldn't train when he needed to. The lack of training was not conducive to this level and it was a lost year in his development.'

Vincent was being questioned at every turn where he saw his future. A club like Lyon is indeed a 'logical intermediate step' in his career, he admitted to a suggestive question in *Het Laatste Nieuws* about the Ligue One club's interest, adding that, 'I understand that Barcelona and Chelsea do not want to pay huge sums for someone who was injured for five months.'

That he even mentions Barcelona and Chelsea indicates his ambitions at this point.

In mid-May, new rumours surfaced that Bundesliga club Hamburger Sport-Verein want to sign Kompany, with the leading newspaper in Brussels and Wallonia, *Le Soir*, believing Kompany would take the place of his former teammate Daniel Van Buyten at Hamburg SV, as he was moving to Bayern Munich.

It had also been an 'intermediate step' for Van Buyten's career at the time he'd joined Hamburg, so maybe Vincent would look at what compatriot 'Big Dan' had done and would think along similar lines?

Initially, nobody had suggested Hamburg SV, or even the Bundesliga, as a likely destination for Vincent when the myriad rumours about what club he might join were at their fiercest. Chelsea and Real Madrid, yes. But Hamburg were a club that Anderlecht may have argued were, size and aspirations wise, one of their peers.

They'd never been a consideration. Up until then, anyway.

On June 8th 2006, Anderlecht's General Manager Herman Van Holsbeeck revealed to *Het Laatste Nieuws* that Hamburg were now showing the most concrete interest. Pierre Kompany then revealed that, for him, it didn't matter whether the interest was coming from France, Italy, Spain or Germany. All that mattered was that it was a club with ambition.

Hamburg clearly were. But Lyon still remained the favourites for Kompany's signature.

Yet the coup de théâtre was Hamburg's for, on June 9th, the local newspapers reported that Hamburger Sport-Verein (HSV) had won '...the battle for the golden boy' with the deal being signed late the previous evening, with Vincent expected to arrive in Germany imminently as Hamburg SV's replacement for Van Buyten, with the fee paid to Anderlecht believed to be in the region of around €10 million.

Vincent's choice of next club came as a surprise to a *lot* of people. And not all of the reaction and comments were particularly complimentary.

Hamburg SV? A club that was living on its past glories? A Bundesliga team? Surely, some critics said, the Bundesliga was the league for men who did little but 'run all day', one where fighting spirit and hard work overshadowed, were prioritised even, over the technical qualities of the players? Although physically strong, would Vincent Kompany be ready to be the rock solid defensive unit at the heart of a team that played in a league where power and pace (as well as punctuality) reigned supreme?

But there were counter arguments. Other observers of the game could see why Hamburg might have been an attractive option for Vincent.

They had, after all, just finished the 2005/06 season third in the Bundesliga, so Vincent would be playing in the following season's Champions League. Furthermore, they'd had the best defensive record in the league that season, conceding just 30 goals in their 34 matches. So Vincent hadn't been signed to improve a poor defence, but to make a good one even better. Their AOL Arena (now the Volksparkstadion) had a capacity of 57,000 and regularly attracted attendances that weren't far off capacity... almost double the number Anderlecht attracted for their home matches.

Then there was Kevin Keegan. His move to Hamburg SV from Liverpool in 1977 came as something of a surprise to the European footballing community as well. Yet, during his time at the club, Keegan won a Bundesliga title, played in a European Cup final and won the coveted *Ballon d'Or* title twice.

Kompany had no fears about thriving in the Bundesliga, saying, 'Things have changed. My new team mates Rafael Van der Vaart and Nigel de Jong are technically skilled players.'

Het Nieuwsblad remained cool about the transfer. Ludo Vandewalle, usually level-headed in his analysis, wrote, a tad spitefully, that it was '...only Hamburg'. Was that fair? Vincent was, remember, still just twenty. Surely, if he had, as many expected, signed for a club like Barcelona, then critics like Vandewalle would maybe have claimed he was 'too young' for such a big move. As for Vincent, his retort to all the criticism his choice had provoked was to tell *Le Soir*, that 'I want to continue my career calmly and seriously.'

That should have been that. But *Het Laatste Nieuws* also found Hamburg SV a puzzling choice. They'd already looked foolish after their 'scoop' about Kompany heading for a much more glamorous destination was shown to be wrong, now they were questioning the move he had made whilst, over at *Sport-Voetbalmagazine*, Jacques Sys was, refreshingly, a little bit more pragmatic, saying, 'Initially Kompany was linked with Real Madrid and Barcelona and a fee of twenty million euros was put on his head. Now Anderlecht has to do with half that amount. But Kompany can grow up in Germany, he knows the mentality there. A player can only push boundaries if the competition gets sharper and the discipline increases.'

Sports manager and former football player Dietmar Beiersdorfer said Vincent '...is a football player who has something very special', adding that HSV had been following his progress for a long time, long enough for him to constantly have shown his class in not only the Belgian league but both Champions League and the international stage. Kompany would later confirm to *Le Soir* that Hamburg had indeed wanted to recruit him as early as the winter break prior to his eventual summer move and to sign him as a defensive midfielder.

It was no coincidence that Kompany and Daniel Van Buyten, the player he was replacing at Hamburg, were physically similar, something that had been immediately recognised by the German newspaper *Morgenpost,* which acknowledged the comparison and said of Kompany, 'You immediately recognise his power and elegance.'

On June 10th Hamburg's new signing made his first public appearance when – clad in a black suit and a purple shirt – Vincent was officially introduced at a chic boutique hotel in the city. Fourteen years at Anderlecht, that had included three seasons in first team, had now come to an end. His 73 league appearances, plus seven cup matches and twenty more in European competition, gave Vincent a grand total of exactly 100 appearances, during which he had scored six goals. It was undoubtedly an impressive tally for one so young.

He had become the most expensive purchase in Hamburg SV's history. The contract term was for six years, with his gross annual salary estimated to be around €1.8 million a year.

'I earn more for Hamburg than Lyon had offered me...', admitted Vincent, With *Le Soir* adding, '...that was not decisive but *(perhaps)* an extra argument in Hamburg's favour'. Kompany, meanwhile, sung the praises of Hamburg as '...a beautiful city where you don't see big buildings, but where there are lots of greenery and lakes.'

'It is a city with a human face and the mentality from the south, an open mentality,' he observes as if he is not talking about a football club, but on behalf of the city of Hamburg tourist board.

He stresses that he is ambitious and wants to help the club revive its past. Once HSV was a European great, but that dated back to the late 1970's and 80's. The club's Austrian manager, Ernst Happel, was one of the trailblazers, winning three league titles, a German Cup plus both a European and Cup Winners Cup final with right sided defender Manfred (Manny) Kaltz and Felix Magath amongst the other club legends at the time.

However, one burning question remained unanswered.

Why had Vincent snubbed Lyon?

Financially, Lyon hadn't offered as much to Vincent as Hamburg had, whilst HSV's chairman also said that they had been 'very quick on the ball' when dealing with Vincent whilst negotiations with Lyon had, according to him, dragged on and on without really getting anywhere. But, more crucially, Vincent had, in the end, been enticed to Germany by head coach and former player Thomas Doll, who, together with his chairman, had gone to Vincent's manager Lichtenstein's house in Brussels with a tactical plan that completely charmed Vincent.

Another reason was that Lyon were nearly always French champions (seven consecutive Ligue One titles between 2002 and 2008) at the time, so the challenge, for Vincent, didn't seem too appealing – the one at Hamburg (no Bundesliga triumphs since 1982) clearly was. As far as the Champions League was concerned, the same logic applied: Lyon almost always made it through to at least the quarter finals of the Champions League whilst Hamburg had done very little in the competition since their sole triumph in the competition in 1983. Indeed, in recent years, even Anderlecht had achieved more in the competition.

Vincent clearly wanted a challenge and he was clearly going to have one with Hamburg SV.

He'd also rejected Chelsea because he feared becoming just one of many players in their 'factory', believing that, as a consequence, he would struggle to get into their starting line up. He went on to say to *Le Soir* that Chelsea had advised him he would receive the twenty-fifth highest salary at the club, so it seemed only logical, to Vincent, that Jose Mourinho would therefore see him as the twenty-fifth choice for a place in the first team.

It was the second occasion Vincent had said no to Chelsea.

At eighteen he could have headed to London for a salary almost double what he was receiving at Anderlecht. It was one of the greatest Chelsea sides of all time, still managed by José Mourinho, which contained potential teammates that included Frank Lampard, Didier Drogba, Arjen Robben and Michael Ballack.

On reflection, therefore, it did seem as if Vincent had made a wise choice in opting for Hamburg SV as his next move, for that 'intermediate step'. A well respected club with great potential that paid excellent wages and which had managerial stability.

Most importantly, of course, he almost certainly had a starting place, which almost certainly wouldn't have been the case at a number of his other suitors.

The only real nagging doubt was whether, immediately after an injury-ravaged campaign, he was right to move to a league where physical strength was so vital.

Anderlecht received around €8m of the overall transfer fee of €10.5m – the rest of the money possibly went to Vincent and his agent as a signing-on fee. Added to that initial amount however, were bonuses that meant, if Hamburg became Bundesliga champions, or reached the Champions League in the next three years, Anderlecht would be entitled to more money from the sale. They also, it was reported, negotiated a 15% fee payable from any future sale, which meant that when Vincent moved to Manchester City in 2010, for between €7-8m, Anderlecht would receive a further €1m-plus in additional fees.

Anderlecht's accountants might, on reflection, have managed a wry smile at how things had eventually fallen into place from their point of view. Before Vincent had needed his operation, he might, reasonably, have fetched at least €17m from Valencia or Seville if they had made a concrete offer for him (with, you assume, add-ons), whilst during the winter break Lyon were set to offer €12m, plus a player in exchange, for his signature on a long term contract.

However, you can be certain that Chelsea, Barcelona, Real Madrid et al would have been watching his progress at Hamburg SV from day one with more than a passing interest. Vincent added to the 'what if' stories that were circulating at the time by confirming the four clubs that had previously taken a very proactive interest in signing to Le Soir magazine... 'Seville, Chelsea, Inter Milan and Lyon.'

That interest would not have faded away upon his signing for Hamburg SV either.

And so Vincent Kompany began an important new chapter in his life. For the very first time he was living away from home, distant from the four people who were the most important in his life... his father, mother, brother and sister. He might, at least, have had some consolation in knowing the 366 mile journey from his parental home in Brussels to the AOL Arena took, at least if you were behind the wheel of a powerful Mercedes, less than six hours.

However, up the E34, then along the A1, there was Hamburg, ready and waiting for its new prodigal son.

CHAPTER EIGHT
UPS AND DOWNS WITH THE RED DEVILS

Vincent Kompany had closed the door behind him at Anderlecht for the last time and had, a few weeks later, opened a new one at Hamburg SV.

It was a busy time as he also had some catching up to do with the Belgian national team, for whom he hadn't played since September 2005.

It hadn't been the best of times for the Red Devils, as the Belgian national team is referred to amongst their supporters. By the time Vincent was fit again, they'd slipped to fiftieth place in the FIFA world rankings, with less renowned footballing nations such as Egypt, Ghana, Switzerland and Togo all placed above them. This had been quite a dramatic fall from grace as, when Vincent had made his debut for Belgium against France in 2004, the Red Devils were in fourteenth place and above the likes of Portugal and Uruguay.

Strangely enough, for such a multi-talented group, Vincent's inclusion in the squad coincided with Belgium's fall down the world rankings, which seems, even now, incomprehensible for a national side then able to call upon the services of world-class players like Thibaut Courtois, Jan Vertonghen, Romelu Lukaku, Kevin De Bruyne and, of course, a certain Vincent Kompany. Back in 2013, that generation, along with Kompany, qualified for the final round of the following year's World Cup in Brazil and got as far as the last eight, narrowly losing 1-0 to Argentina, whilst, four years later, and after topping their group stage (one that included England), the Red Devils reached the semi-finals, losing 1-0 to France.

Good times. But it hadn't always been as enjoyable as that because Vincent's early years as a fledgling Red Devil were, from kick-off to the final whistle, much more about toil and sweat rather than success and recognition.

From both a physical and football perspective, Belgium is a small nation, however, it has a decent list of national honours to call its own. A gold medal for football at the 1920 Olympic Games (beating Spain, the Netherlands and Czechoslovakia) and qualifying for six consecutive World Cups from 1982 to 2002, including a fourth-place finish in 1986. It wasn't too dissimilar a story in the European Championships with a third-place finish in 1972 and, albeit surprisingly, ending the 1980 tournament as runners-up to West Germany.

Not that bad. But it's not a mediocre CV either.

Yet, for Belgium and all the promise that the Red Devils showed, little of note occurred for them in the first two decades of the twenty-first century as they failed to qualify for the World Cup in 2002, 2006, 2010 and 2014 as well as the 2004, 2008 and 2012 European Championships.

It feels, in retrospect, that whilst they were more than capable of qualifying for big tournaments and doing well when they played the role of underdogs, the better they got and the more accomplished and technically adept players they had to call up, the more difficult they found it to live up to expectations.

Much of the steady improvement in the Red Devils' fortunes came as more and more of their players started to play at Europe's top clubs. Vincent went from Hamburg to Manchester City, Eden Hazard shone at Chelsea, as did Kevin De Bruyne at Manchester City, whilst, after leaving Chelsea for Real Madrid in 2018, Thibaut Courtois became, in the eyes of many, one of the best goalkeepers in the world.

Vincent's first fourteen appearances for Belgium saw them win just five games – losing seven of them, with two ending in draws. He was substituted in four of these games, failed to score any goals and was booked in three of those matches.

Form wise, he was as patchy as the nation he was playing for.

Yet, for all that and his still tender age, Kompany was, slowly but surely, emerging as one of Belgium's key players, a leader in the making who, according to Belgium coach (from 2002-2005) Aimé Anthuenis, who'd previously been at Anderlecht, was a 'huge talent'.

Anthuenis: 'I coached Anderlecht from 1999 to 2002. Frankie Vercauteren was my assistant and provided the link between the A-team and the youth sides. He trained occasionally with the talented youth players. On weeks when there were few players about from the A-team, we added those youth players to our ranks during training. And one huge talent was already running around at Neerpede. Vincent Kompany. Vincent had already played with us in practice matches but was still too young for the A-team. I joined the national team as a head coach at the end of June 2002 and got to know Vincent and yes, I called him up for the national team while he had only just joined Anderlecht's A-team'.

On August 20, 2003, Vincent Kompany played in just six matches for Anderlecht's first team, three in the league and three in the preliminary round of the Champions

League. Yet Anthuenis says that, even then, he was not far away from being selected. He was impressed by the combination of Vincent's physical stature and pace, two qualities that rarely occur together in the average footballer.

Barely two months later, Anthuenis, talking again about Vincent, said that it was 'never too soon for those who are good enough', adding he thought Vincent was playing with the flair of someone who has been combining league and Champions League for a decade and was 'outstanding' in Anderlecht's match against Bayern Munich.

It was Anthuenis who selected Vincent, for a place in the squad, if not the match itself, for Belgium's match against Estonia in October 2003, explaining that it was 'To introduce him to the players and coaching staff. To get him used to life in the national team. In short, to give him a taste.'

Belgium won that final preliminary round match for the 2004 European Championships 2-0, but were still eliminated as they finished in third place, behind Bulgaria and Croatia.

But maybe their elimination at the group stage only served to hasten Vincent's international debut?

As things transpired, the match that saw Vincent make his international bow, a Brussels friendly against European champions France, who were second in the world rankings, was probably about as good as it gets. A high profile match against elite opposition but no real pressure to stand out. Thus, at 17 years and 314 days old, Vincent became the fifth youngest Red Devil in history.

But Belgium were outclassed from the start and lost 0-2.

One positive from the night was that Vincent looked more than capable against an opposition that included Desailly, Thuram, Vieira and Zidane, and made a strong case that he could handle the pressure and expectation at that level already. There were those who pinned at least partial blame on him for France's second goal, claiming that they hadn't expected Zinédine Zidane to outsmart him so effortlessly.

Vincent blamed that on a lack of experience.

'How could I have been so stupid? I knew he would pass me on the outside,' he told *Het Laatste Nieuws*.

For Vincent, there was more positional work to do. According to Anthuenis, he had stayed too much in his fixed position instead of putting more pressure on the French legend as he made his run. But, other than that, the Belgian coach was pleased with Vincent's performance, especially in the second half.

Years later and, talking to me for this book, Anthuenis looks back at that match.

'Why had I selected Vincent? Because we didn't have a surplus of talent. Average--to-good players, but not the very top players. Injuries sometimes messed it up, too.

Vincent was also very mature. And very worldly wise for one so young. But he knew what his duties were which translated to his football'.

On March 31 2004, another tricky international challenge was handed to a young Belgium team – a friendly against World Cup runners-up Germany – in which the Red Devils went down by three goals to nil. It had been a hopeless, but perhaps expected, defeat. But Vincent, again, did not disappoint.

His third appearance, on April 28 in Brussels against Turkey, saw another defeat, 2-3 this time, but Vincent made a costly error that led to a chance.

Anthuenis was, by now, aware that his team were conceding goals far too easily and were not particularly game savvy in that some of his players were, in his words, too 'well behaved' in their duels with the opposing attackers. He also thought Vincent was occasionally a little too relaxed, positionally, given his continued tendency to make positional errors.

The 18-year-old Kompany had played three international matches, during which the team had conceded eight goals. That wasn't be a good reference for a central defender.

Fortunately, friendly matches exist for national coaches to learn and to try out new players and experiment tactically; the results are less important. Moreover, it is to the Royal Belgian Football Association's credit that they always picked strong opponents. It is better to learn things, however unpalatable they may be, against opposition like France, Germany or Turkey rather than learn nothing against Luxembourg, Malta or San Marino.

On May 29 2005, Vincent experienced his first win with Belgium, a 1-0 success against a languid Netherlands in Eindhoven, the match settled by a Bart Goor penalty in the 78th minute. That was progress. The Netherlands were fifth in the FIFA world rankings, and Belgium were then 42nd. Plus, The Netherlands had not lost a friendly match in five years. In their post-match analysis, *Het Laatste Nieuws* were fulsome in their praise of Vincent.

'Van Nistelrooy, Makaay, Kluivert, Van Hooydonk: Kompany put them all in his back pocket. Apart from a few flaws, he was masterful alongside Timmy Simons.'

Kompany had no complaints.

'Organisationally, I played the perfect game. It's logical; I'm getting more experience, getting older, learning from my mistakes.'

He thinks it is excellent that Belgium practices against top countries.

'The higher the level, the harder it is, but the quicker you see things and pick them up'.

That excellent result against The Netherlands significantly boosted the Red Devils' collective confidence before they embarked on their qualification matches for the

2006 World Cup. Belgium had been drawn in Group Seven, along with Bosnia & Herzegovina, Lithuania, San Marino, Serbia & Montenegro and Spain, with the group winners qualifying automatically for the finals in Germany a little over two years later, with the second-placed team having to play a further play-off match against a runner-up from another group.

Spain were seen as the favourites, with either Belgium or Serbia & Montenegro more than capable of finishing in the runners-up spot. However, the FIFA World Rankings at the time favoured Belgium, with Spain ranked third in the world, Belgium 29th, Serbia & Montenegro 51st, Lithuania 60th and San Marino a very distant 169th.

Looking back at that group draw and the matches that followed, Anthuenis reflects, 'We had missed the final round of the European Championship by one point. But the opponents in the World Cup qualifying stage were of a different calibre than those for the European Championships.'

'We would have to be exceptional to qualify. Even finishing second, which entitled you to a play-off match, would have been very difficult to attain. Spain were clearly the favourites and, for second place, it was between us and Serbia & Montenegro.'

Belgium's final match prior to the qualifying campaign getting underway was a 2-2 draw against Norway, their two goals coming courtesy of Thomas Buffel, with Vincent starting the match in the centre of the Red Devils' defence, playing alongside Didier Dheedene, before being replaced by Daniel Van Buyten in the 66th minute. Anthuenis was unhappy at Vincent's level of performance in the match, claiming that he is 'too complacent' (that familiar accusation again), and that he could have done more to prevent Norway from scoring their first goal. Not the sort of feedback that Vincent, who thrived on self-confidence and praise from others, would have wanted to hear, especially as his national coach then spoke of how well Van Buyten had played when he'd replaced him.

This had given Anthuenis a dilemma prior to Belgium's first Group Seven game at home to Lithuania, one they were expected to win and do so comfortably. Would he start with Kompany, classy and composed but still prone to rushes of youthful blood to his head, or opt for the less elegant but somewhat more savvy Van Buyten? Or would he play them together?

In the end, he went with Van Buyten, with Vincent, who had acknowledged the error he'd made in the game against Norway, sat on the bench. The game ended in a 1-1 draw, with Vincent coming on at half-time in place of Eric Deflandre, who'd recently won his third consecutive Ligue One title at Lyon before returning to Belgian football to play for Standard de Liège. Vincent initially filled in for him at right-back before finishing the match playing in midfield.

Het Nieuwsblad were impressed enough with Vincent's cameo appearance to call his appearance 'rock solid' and added that Vincent is '...now also the booster in the midfield'. This was not hyperbole as he'd slotted into that position effortlessly, passing well, reading the game and acting as a focal point in driving his older and more experienced teammates forward, almost ending the game as the match-winner when his late shot went just over the crossbar.

Vincent's view of the match was '... it's a slip but not the end of the world' and that he thought (along with everyone else) that the Belgium team had the personnel to do a lot better, adding that the Red Devils hadn't, in his eyes, taken control of the game and had, as a result 'forgotten how to score.' He was also concerned that too many of the players that were regarded as automatic choices for the Belgium team were, for the most part, bench players at their clubs, a weakness which, he felt, made them vulnerable.

Strong views for one so young. But not many people were going to disagree with him.

The Belgian media largely agreed with Vincent. *Het Laatste Nieuws* singled him out as the one bright hope in an otherwise lacklustre team, saying, 'Kompany's rare talent should never be missing. Anthuenis should seriously consider using him in midfield.'

Belgium's poor start to their qualification campaign got even worse five months later when they lost 2-0 to group favourites Spain in Santander – second-half goals from Albert Luque and Raúl doing the damage. Vincent had started the match, replacing Timmy Simons of Club Brugge. But, rather than opting to play him in midfield, Anthuenis chose to play Vincent in defence, losing, in the process, the genuine opportunity of letting a forward-thinking and positionally aggressive Vincent drive forward with the ball, wholly un-intimidated by the fact that he was up against players like Carles Puyol, Raúl, Fernando Torres and Xavi.

It seemed, in hindsight, an opportunity missed, but, looking back at the decision he made at the time, Anthuenis seems certain it was the right one, claiming, '...it is important to consider the atmosphere at the game that night. We felt intimidated even before the match; the atmosphere was explosive.

Anthuenis further added, 'Milton Nielsen often refereed in the Champions League, and the Spanish players were regulars in that. He didn't know us at all. But they did.'

To add to Belgium's woes, they received two red cards on the night, with Eric Deflandre (29 minutes) and Bart Goor (68) the villains in their matching red shirts. Vincent, for his part, was booked; he'd been asked by Anthuenis prior to kick-off to try and stay calm in the face of possible intimidation and, to his credit, he was able to do that, despite the booking by the zealous Nielsen, who only yellow-carded one Spain player in the game. But did that affect Vincent's game and the effect he might have had on it? He certainly thought so, admitting his part in the build-up that led to the first Spain goal.

'I should have cleared that ball... it is logical and right that you should not take risks, and I am certainly not angry when people criticise me for that reason.'

He went on to explain his mistake.

'I could have kicked the ball away blindly, or I could try to get out while playing football and set up an attack. I was never taught in youth to kick a ball away wildly. Not that I want to put on a show; on the contrary, I try to play football as efficiently as possible. That also means that I not only try to defend but also try to build up.'

He did not call the second goal his fault; he'd thought, perfectly reasonably, that his teammates would have cleared the danger and had, therefore, left his position. But, even so, he was tough on himself.

'I will make mistakes and have no problem being judged with reference to my age. It is by not always being pleased with yourself that you progress,' he told *Het Laatste Nieuws*. Vincent was not a footballer who'd blame others, but someone who'd learnt to deal with criticism and the first to hold his hand up if he believed he had made a mistake.

One point from six for Belgium, then. That meant their next match, a home game against Serbia & Montenegro, was already being talked about as a 'must-win' encounter. And rightly so. If Belgium lost, it was likely that, given how the group was working out, they'd be in real danger of being as good as eliminated after just three matches. Unity was, therefore, essential. The players, coaches, fans and media needed to come together for the common good before such a critical game, but, typically, it didn't happen with Vincent, who was surprisingly the subject of criticism both before and during the match.

He'd undoubtedly drawn attention to himself in the build-up, turning up half an hour late for one training session, excusing himself to the lurking press by saying his stomach had been bothering him. Then, shortly afterwards, the real reason for his lateness was made public: he'd forgotten his boots. He tried to gloss over this by saying he hadn't wanted to disrupt the preparation of the other players, adding, as mitigation, that '...my school bag looks like my sports bag, and I took the wrong one.'

But things didn't stop there. When Vincent was eventually seen with the rest of the Belgium squad, he was the only one who wasn't wearing a tie, which proudly displayed the Belgian FA's logo. But he had an excuse for that too; apparently he'd moved to his new home in Ganshoren, and the tie was in a box that had not yet been unpacked.

Why he hadn't asked for a replacement remains a mystery.

He'd also upset *Nike*, who sponsored the Belgian team by walking around carrying a bag emblazoned with the *Adidas* logo. *Adidas* were his sponsor, and rather than cause any more anger, Vincent put his *Adidas* bag into a plain plastic bag, and everyone was, eventually, satisfied.

Anthuenis attempted to put the acrimony in its proper context.

'I got along well with younger players, and there were few problems with them. The older ones may have felt awkward when the youngsters got a bit over-excitable at times, or failed in what was expected of them, but I could, for the most part, empathise with them. I was seventeen once and can be lazy and forgetful sometimes too.'

'It happens to us all. Vincent included.'

Anthuenis recalls the incident with the boots in Koksijde. The players were all kitted out and ready for training, with Anthuenis prepared to start when one of his staff asked him to delay the session as Vincent was going to be late. In the former head coach's opinion it was simply a lack of attention, yet ended up causing a disproportionate fuss in the Belgian media. To this day, Anthuenis feels that it was wrong for Vincent forgetting his boots to have been treated as a big story when, in reality, it was just a minor, peripheral, issue that sometimes happens in all walks of life.

But despite Anthuenis's attempt to downplay the issue, disciplinary incidents, no matter what the scale, rarely escape media attention, and journalists worldwide are always swift to sound the alarm. Those same journalists would have universally agreed that Kompany was an exceptional footballer who was already technically and tactically mature. But they'd also point out his occasional failings regarding his disciplinary and mental skills. Vincent's perceived sloppy, absent-minded or rebellious behaviour off the pitch clashed with his professional attitude and ambition as a footballer on it. Although Vincent would say that it had nothing to do with being lazy or complacent, it was just a simple case of absent-mindedness.

On to the 'game of life and death'; match three in the World Cup qualifying group at home to Serbia & Montenegro. A win was vital. If Belgium lost, they would almost certainly be eliminated from the tournament, it would be the first time the country had failed to qualify for a World Cup since Argentina in 1978. A good start was therefore essential.

But it was Serbia & Montenegro who took the lead when Zvominir Vukic scored after just seven minutes, the Serbs having seized possession after a woeful pass from Walter Baseggio, a teammate of Vincent's at Anderlecht. Belgium offered little in response, and the game was as good as lost when Mateja Kezman doubled the advantage fifteen minutes into the second half. Strident and prolonged whistling from the Red Devils' supporters pierced the evening air at the end of the game, one which saw Vincent awarded a match rating of 6/10 from *Het Nieuwsblad*, a figure he shared with five of his teammates, with the publication commenting that, 'Vincent moved into the midfield. He was technically impeccable but didn't get the machine going.' *Het Laatste Nieuws*, meanwhile, talked about a team that combined '... hesitantly and inflexibly' and awarded only one Belgian player an eight, the highest mark. There are no prizes here for guessing the identity of that player.

'Kompany was by far the best Red Devil. He advanced to midfield after the team went a goal down and he was the only player with ideas and actions.'

The chances of Belgium competing for the world title in the summer of 2006 therefore became highly improbable. Having gained just one point from the nine on offer prompted a memorable quote from Vincent, who said, 'On behalf of the whole team I apologise.'

It had been a big gesture in defeat from the eighteen-year-old. To stand centre stage and take responsibility on such a bad day for the national team certainly demonstrated his leadership credentials.

Head coach Anthuenis had seen and done much during his playing and coaching career (including a Belgian league title win with Genk in 1999), but that was one of the most significant moments he had experienced so far. He knew, deep down, that Belgium had little to no chance of making the short journey to the German World Cup. But rather than apportion blame, or make excuses, he took nothing away from his team, saying they had done their best and had, at times, been in control of the game – they had been a little too impulsive when they were in possession – which could be seen as their desperation to win. Winning was something they all very much wanted to do, and, for him, there was no dishonour in that despite the clear disappointment and criticism he and his players were receiving. He also looked back on the previous game against Spain with more than a little honesty.

'The players knew there was a quality difference with Spain. But we came up short, that's the reality.'

So, the national teams ended 2004 with six defeats, one friendly win and two drawn games. The Red Devils' next match was in Cairo, for a friendly against Egypt, in which changes and signs of progress in the team were expected. Sadly, that would not be the case. Egypt, who were ranked eleven places above Belgium in FIFA's world rankings easily won 4-0. Vincent started the game in his preferred midfield position, but was replaced by Racing Genk's Koen Daerden early in the second half, having been unable to be influential against a technically excellent Egypt team who, a year later, won the Africa Cup of Nations.

They were a decent side who, on the night, had proved themselves a much better one. But the Belgian press didn't hold back post-match, giving the impression it had been somewhat of a shock result, with *Het Nieuwsblad* commenting about how the Red Devils had been '...totally ridiculed, have a rickety defence and were languid in defeat'.

Anthuenis had treated the game as something of an experiment from a tactical point of view, opting to select the Anderlecht midfield to start, with Walter Baseggio on the left and Kompany on the right. He hoped that would encourage (his words) 'spontaneity and enthusiasm', but that proved not to be the case. Again, Belgium were unfortunate when it came to refereeing decisions because, at 0-0, the Egyptian assistant referee had disallowed a Belgian goal – Kompany having 'scored' what looked to be a perfectly legitimate strike.

Vincent had initially been looking forward to playing in the centre-right position in midfield, but the success of that experiment is best gauged by the fact he was replaced after 58 minutes, with Anthuenis later saying, 'We played with Kompany on the right, but not against the right wing, more in the middle, with Vanderhaeghe centrally and two box-to-box players: Baseggio on the left and Vincent on the centre-right.'

He went on to explain: 'Vincent often had to run back to catch his opponent. I was criticised for allegedly sticking him wide. So why had I put him on the right? Because he had a good running ability, was technically strong and had a very good shot. So box-to-box, not on the outside, not central-centre.'

A similar role, Anthuenis stressed, to the one that Marouane Fellaini usually played, with his stature also making it easier for him to get in front of goal, but still having the energy to return and recover. In short, the classic box-to-box midfielder. Vincent had, he insists, all of the qualities to play in that position.

'Vincent could have given the team a lot of impetus as a midfielder. Getting up and down the pitch, playing the one-twos, that sense of purpose, that suited him better. But, it was stupid to try him as a right midfielder in the match against Egypt, who we'd underestimated. On the other hand, don't forget that we were looking to get our squad up to standard. Can I then experiment to make the squad more balanced and, therefore, better? I have to say that nobody was convinced about Vincent's role as a right midfielder. Including himself.'

During the Egypt match, Vincent suffered from an injury to his back that, according to him post-match, now felt as flexible '...as concrete', an injury that was perhaps provoked by the exceptionally hard pitch.

'But it should not be an excuse. I played badly, full stop. The president of the Royal Belgian Football Association is allowed to be angry, you journalists are allowed to be angry, and the fans are allowed to be too. I have never felt so powerless before and feel a tremendous urge to restore honour.'

He was certainly not *yet* the leader of the squad, but he was emerging as a player spokesman thanks to his sensible words and an aversion to use lazy clichés. Vincent was increasingly seen as a breath of fresh air in a team without an indisputable star player.

'We were second in all aspects; the Egyptians won many more duels,' Yves Vanderhaeghe recalls.

Vincent's Anderlecht teammate had played 48 times for his country as a defensive midfielder including at the World Cup in 2002.

'Yes, that was a bad one, but it wasn't because of the tactics or this or that player. If you don't have the right mentality, you don't succeed. In the national team, Kompany was exemplary. He wanted to show he could handle the level, was one of us, always sharp, always keen to prove himself. A defensive midfielder like me knows he has to take over and pick up a lost ball when Vincent advanced, but it's not like I panicked every time Vincent went forward. In fact, it didn't happen that much. He was better than any of us; it was as simple as that.'

Anthuenis was now under pressure, which he managed to increase by stating in a radio interview that he would resign if Belgium did not win their next two matches –

against Bosnia & Herzegovina and San Marino. There was, after all, still a chance, albeit a small one, of qualification, if his team got six points from six in those two games. The games were to be played over the Easter weekend, so *Het Nieuwsblad* opted for a topical headline which stated, *Crucifixion Or Resurrection?* However, they didn't go as far as proclaiming Anthuenis as the next Messiah.

Anthuenis could afford to smile again after an easy 4-1 victory against Bosnia & Herzegovina, one that came almost two years since the Red Devils had last won a match by a three-goal margin, and the first time under Anthuenis' leadership. Belgium's four goals came from Emile Mpenza (2), Koen Daerden and Thomas Buffel.

It had been an effective attacking display and, at the back, the start of a good centre-back pairing had emerged courtesy of Vincent and Daniel Van Buyten. It was the second time they had played together for their country and, after the disappointment against Spain, the two clicked. Kompany later told *Het Nieuwsblad* that he felt his game was maturing.

'I have found a balance between playing intuitively and rationally. A few months ago, I was perhaps still playing football too much on instinct, which sometimes proved detrimental to the team because I consumed useless energy. Now, I have more experience, and I know that everyone has to stick to their own role first and foremost. In my case, that is defending in an austere way.'

Austere? A new Kompany had undoubtedly arrived.

Anthuenis was very satisfied with the win and the result, believing that, although Bosnia-Herzegovina were nowhere near the level of Serbia and Montenegro, the performance '...had shown that much in the past was due to circumstances'.

Though he didn't elaborate too much on what those circumstances may have been.

Belgium now had four points out of twelve and were still in with a *slight* chance of qualifying for the World Cup. Four days later, the Red Devils played in San Marino and won 2-1 in a less-than-compelling game; not that anyone was worried about that; a win was a win. But, on the downside, Vincent was given a yellow card, meaning, having already been carded in the Spain match, he'd miss out on the crucial return game against Serbia & Montenegro. As things stood, Belgium had seven points from five matches, sitting fourth in the table.

The game in Belgrade ended in a 0-0 draw, a good enough performance by Belgium to secure both the point and clean sheet, but a result that would only have been worth celebrating had they won their home match against the Serbs. That point kept them in fourth place and meant they now had to win their remaining four matches, as well as hoping their rivals tripped up in some of their final games. Anthuenis optimistically observing of the situation that, 'As long as there is life, there is hope.'

Footballing logic now dictated that if Belgium were able to get a point in Serbia, they should certainly be able to go one step further at the Bilino Polje stadium in

Zenica by winning the return match against Bosnia & Herzegovina. But that turned out not to be the case as the Red Devils lost 1-0, on a pitch that Anthuenis had called a '...provincial potato field'. Although he went onto add that Bosnia had deserved their win in a match that saw Vincent receive his third yellow card of the qualifying tournament. Mathematically, at least, Belgium could still qualify, but their coach had ruled them out of contention, saying, 'Over and out. It's done.'

Vincent, disappointed at the result, knew he would have more opportunities to play in World Cups, despite his team missing out on the 2006 tournament.

'There will be World Cups to come. Our start ruined our chances because, back then, many players didn't get games at their clubs. Many of them will soon be playing regularly in European competitions. That says something about our progress.'

About himself? He was not yet satisfied.

'I have not yet fulfilled the role I would like to play. I have become stronger but still need to have the influence I had at Anderlecht.'

After the Bosnia match, he was 'speechless' but, once again, he strikes a *mea culpa*.

'We have ourselves to blame for everything. When playing, things often went wrong. I feel guilty towards Anthuenis. It is not his fault: he has put together the best possible group. I was ready to perform at this World Cup.'

Unbeknown to Vincent at the time, on a personal level, he would spend more time in the doldrums after the match as he started to suffer from renewed back pain, which was traced back to the Serbia and Montenegro game.

Four days later, back home against the part-time footballers of San Marino, Belgium took out their frustrations by winning 8-0. Unfortunately for Vincent, it was not the cathartic game he might have wanted it to be as, after just twelve minutes, the pain in his back saw him taken off by Anthuenis and replaced by Koen Daerden, who went on to score two goals. It wasn't the best time for Vincent to miss out, as the Belgians were now beginning to find a little bit of form and consistency, having lost just one of their previous six matches.

But, without him, that renewed hope was lost again as the Red Devils then lost 2-0 to Spain and, for the second time, drew 1-1 with Lithuania. That meant that, to many people's surprise, Serbia and Montenegro clinched the overall win in Group Seven, with 22 points, with Spain finishing as runners-up on 20 points, whilst Belgium ended up a distant fourth with just twelve points from their ten matches.

Now, nearly two decades later, how does Anthuenis look back on that time and Vincent Kompany?

'You already felt he was a charismatic personality who stood up for his teammates. He spoke his mind in group discussions and made a positive impression with a lot of what he said. The players saw that, too, and accepted it. I liked to have someone who spoke his mind'.

'And you have the right to speak, regardless of your age.'

'As a coach, you see very well which player might become a coach later on in their career; players who have that certain something in them. They think in the same way that they would act on the pitch. I wasn't too surprised to see Kompany become a coach. Did I talk to him about tactics? No, he was too young for that. I discussed tactics in the players' group: the overall tactics, then individual responsibilities'.

'You can't exaggerate Vincent's role at the time. You don't do players a favour by just giving them too much responsibility. The natural responsibility has to be there in the first place. You are born with it and enforce it with your performances, not just by your words. If you don't show on the pitch that you have more than someone else, it won't work. Vincent showed that from the start, but the experience and maturity were still lacking for him to be the leader par excellence right away.'

'Vincent was so talented that in his creativity as a defender, he sometimes took risks and experimented, but he was still so young and then as a coach, you sometimes have to accept that. Leaders are stubborn and are sometimes so good at it precisely because they dare to think and do what nobody else does, but it was too early for that for Vincent. But it was a good step in his development, and he learned from it. When you are that capable, you show it. And that is good. No, he was not too self-conscious. He is natural and not artificial.'

Anthuenis quit as the Belgium coach at the end of 2005 and, after spells back in club management with Lokeren, Germinal Beerschot and Lierse S.K, he retired from the game that he served, both as a player and coach, for over five decades. He remains the only man to have won the Belgian Manager of the Year award on three occasions.

For the national team, things couldn't possibly be any worse than they were at that point in time – fourth-place finishers in a not-too-demanding World Cup qualifying group and eight points shy of even having a chance in a play-off match.

But for a while, it did get worse.

In their qualifying group for the 2008 European Championships, Belgium finished fifth out of eight countries, winning only five of their fourteen matches, two of which were against Azerbaijan, who finished bottom of the group. That was followed up by a fourth-place finish in their qualifying group for the 2010 World Cup, nine points shy of old foes Bosnia & Herzegovina, who'd thrashed them 4-2 in Genk before, in the qualifying rounds for the 2012 European Championships, they missed out again, finishing third out of six. Clearly, the failure to qualify in 2006 had not been the fault of Anthuenis as his successors, René Vandereycken, Frankie Vercauteren, Georges Leekens and Dick Advocaat, could not turn the tide that continued to push against them.

186

Things only started to get better under Marc Wilmots. Under his leadership, Belgium easily won their qualifying group for the 2014 World Cup, finishing nine points clear of second-placed Croatia. Moreover, they didn't lose one game, scoring eighteen goals and conceding only four.

Around that time, Anthuenis told me, 'Without Kompany, you have a team playing at sixty or seventy per cent of its capabilities. The defence alone is fifty per cent weaker without him because he is the stand-out player, and defensively, we don't have much surplus. At the top level, you need Kompany to be physically in shape, mentally fresh and not injured. He still brings a combination of speed of speed and agility to the defence. He is powerful with his head. He also takes less risks in his game. He has the confidence to show his class: coming out of the defence from the backline and attempting to beat one or two opponents. His influence as captain is invaluable.'

By May 2023, Vincent Kompany had played 89 games for the Belgian Red Devils, the first of which was in February 2004 and the last in June 2019. His overall record was respectable. Fifty wins, nineteen draws and twenty defeats. In those 89 matches, he had scored four goals, made six assists and played 66 full matches. He received sixteen yellow and two red cards in that time.

Kompany was appointed as the national team's captain in 2010 and, to this day, remains a symbol of the nation's 'golden generation' of players who made the Belgian national team such a formidable and feared footballing nation – one transformed from the modest underdogs they had been for so many years.

As of May 31st 2024, Vincent Kompany occupies eleventh place in the all-time appearances table for Belgium, which is topped by Jan Vertonghen and Axel Witsel. Many former or current English Premier League players are in the top ten, including Toby Alderweireld, Eden Hazard, Romelu Lukaku and Kevin De Bruyne.

The website *Transfermarkt.co.uk* lists 31 injuries during Vincent's career, with him missing at least 34 internationals due to injury and, in total, he missed 188 games during his club career for the same reason. According to their data, Kompany had been unavailable for selection for a total of 1,150 days, which equates to more than three calendar years.

Belgium first led the FIFA world rankings in November 2015, where they remained until April 2016 before regaining the mantle from September 2018 to March 2022.

Vincent Kompany also competed with Belgium in the Olympics (4th in 2008) and participated in two World Cup final tournaments (2014 and 2018) as a Red Devil. At his last World Cup, the Belgians beat England to win the bronze medal, whilst in his first World Cup, Belgium reached the quarter-finals.

CHAPTER NINE
MANCHESTER
CALLING

As we have learned, Vincent's choice of new club had surprised many in the game, who had long tipped him for bigger and better things than either Hamburg or even the Bundesliga were perceived to have offered him.

What they did offer – and what many of the self-appointed critics of the game had missed – was the one thing that Vincent Kompany relished above anything else in football or, for that matter, in life itself.

A challenge.

In an interview he gave to the club's official website on the day he'd signed, Vincent was unequivocal in his enthusiasm for the move he'd made.

'I am very glad that I am here. I am sure that I've made the correct decision at the correct time. Thomas Doll impressed me. I hope we have success and get the title which we've not won for more than twenty years.'

There was the reason for his unexpected move to Germany. He wanted to win a title and one that, unlike what was expected at Anderlecht, would be challenging to win.

Challenging? It would be exceedingly difficult.

But Vincent's ambitions and expectations at Hamburg matched those of the club, who were determined to recreate something of the glory years they'd experienced in the Seventies and Eighties when they were one of the most successful club sides in Europe. Three Bundesliga titles (1979, 1982 and 1983); two DFB-Pokal (the German equivalent to England's FA Cup) successes in 1976 and 1987 as well as, most significantly of all, a European Cup (now the Champions League) win in 1983.

Now, HSV wanted to taste some of that glory again.

Of their ambitions, at least, it seemed questionable that they'd sold their most high-profile player to one of their biggest rivals. Daniel Van Buyten had left for Bayern Munich and, at least for him, the genuine expectation that he was now in a place to win things that he may not have done at Hamburg. But Vincent, his international teammate and the man who'd been brought in to replace Van Buyten, clearly thought differently.

Thomas Doll certainly did, saying of his new acquisition, 'He appears unbelievably mature for his age, and I'm sure we'll have a lot of fun with him. I desperately wanted him.'

That public admittance of just how much Doll wanted Vincent at the club was another reason the now twenty-year-old Kompany chose Hamburg over his numerous other suitors.

'There are clubs that are interested in you. And there are clubs that *really* want to sign you. This was the reason for coming to Hamburg. The future seems bright'.

'The club has drive. The infrastructure is almost futuristic, and look at the players. They are young and quick. Raphaël Wicky. Khalid Boulahrouz. Mehdi Mahdavikia. This team is young and ambitious. I don't want to sound arrogant, but for a footballer, it's natural to aim for the best. I want to be successful and get the title that the club have been waiting for more than twenty years for. The German Championship.'

Yet, in much the same way as his final season with Anderlecht had been, Vincent's time at Hamburg was disappointing and marked by unfulfilled dreams. In his debut (2006/07) season, he only made six starts in the Bundesliga before suffering an achilles injury that ruled him out for the rest of that campaign. It was one that saw Hamburg struggle in their Champions League campaign, finishing bottom of Group G with only a 3-2 win over CSKA Sofia in those group games providing any reason for excitement.

An eventual finishing place of seventh in the Bundesliga, which at least granted them qualification for the following season's Intertoto Cup, wasn't much cause for celebration either, with the one bright spot for Vincent in what had turned out to be, quite possibly, the most disappointing season of his career to date, being his selection in Belgium's provisional squad for the 2007 UEFA European U-21 Championships. He also made an impression in his new club's, Intertoto Cup campaign, scoring in their 4-0 win over FC Dacia Chisinau of Moldova. This result was part of a successful run in UEFA's runt tournament as they eventually progressed far enough to qualify for the more respectable UEFA Cup, where Hamburg's campaign saw them finish top of Group D in what was, admittedly, a rather uninspiring selection of group stage opponents – namely Basel, Brann, Dinamo Zagreb and Rennes – with Vincent marking his first appearance in the competition by scoring the only goal in Hamburg's win in Norway.

Yet, whilst he might have been satisfied with his performance and the result, Vincent had undoubtedly not moved to Germany to advance his career in front of barely 13,000 spectators at a ground in desperate need of rebuilding, so antiquated and unfit for purpose had it become.

Hamburg eventually spluttered their way through to the round of sixteen in the tournament before being eliminated by fellow Bundesliga side Bayern Leverkusen.

A fourth-place finish in that season's Bundesliga followed, an improvement on the previous campaign maybe, but, in terms of points won, Hamburg still finished that season a massive twenty-two points adrift of eventual winners Bayern Munich.

Vincent's bravado upon signing for the club and his claim that he wanted to win the title with HSV now looking rather fanciful. It was beginning to seem as if, much like the archaic surrounds of the Brann Stadion, the location for one of his rare highlights that season, that Hamburg SV were also now unfit for purpose as far as Vincent Kompany was concerned.

His move to Germany had turned out to be something of a disappointment for all concerned. Hamburg had, for all their efforts to reassert themselves as one of the elite clubs in both the Bundesliga and in European football as a whole, struggled to make any impression at even national level as the rise and rise of Bayern Munich, together with the surprise Bundesliga triumphs for VfB Stuttgart (2006/07) and VfL Wolfsburg (2008/09), left them as the perpetual also-rans of German football. where they have, clearly, remained. Forty years of hurt. And counting.

One consolation for Hamburg was that, in Vincent, they had a very sellable asset on their hands, a player who, like Daniel Van Buyten before him, could be traded to provide funds for yet another squad rebuild.

And interest in Kompany was considerable. It mattered not that Vincent's career had, to all extents and purposes, been put 'on hold' during his time in Germany's second-largest city. He was, by the time the 2008/09 Bundesliga season began, still only 22 and an established Belgian international, a player whose confidence was matched by that of all the clubs who were now reported to be once again interested in signing him – many of them familiar names who hadn't been put off by his snubbing of their advances two years earlier.

There was, however, one new arrival on the scene, a club soon to be adorned with the sort of financial riches that very much suggested that, whilst their recent footballing history, especially in European competition, was, to say the least, extremely modest, they now had the means to put an end to that. One that didn't care whose establishment noses they bloodied in the process.

Manchester City.

It wasn't the first time that Manchester had courted Vincent Kompany.

In an interview given to *TalkSPORT* in the summer of 2023, Vincent revealed that he had been one of four players identified by then Manchester United manager Sir Alex Ferguson ahead of the 2004/05 season, the other three being Gabriel Heinze, Philippe Mexès and Gerard Piqué.

Was he flattered by their interest at the time?

Yes.

So, did United have any chance of signing him from Anderlecht?

No.

'United asked about me, but I had other priorities at the time. I was studying for my A-levels, and my mother made me finish my education before I could concentrate on football'.

So that was that.

Mark Hughes was the manager who signed Kompany for Manchester City in August 2008, but in an interview given to the *Coaches Voice* website in March 2020, he admitted that he'd had his eye on Kompany for quite some time.

'Vinnie impressed me from the first time I saw him – he was playing for Hamburg and I was with Blackburn on a pre-season tour of Germany. He was playing in midfield and clearly a big presence; he was directing people, telling them where to go and what to do and was obviously a leader of the men around him. I thought that if I ever got a chance of getting in a room with him, he'd be one that I would want to sign.'

Hughes now had the chance to do just that.

'City weren't viewed as a top club in Europe when we were flying out to try and buy all these top players and getting laughed out of town if we're honest. But I sat down in front of Vinnie and just explained what I felt the club's direction would be. Very quickly, he understood. I was trying to tell him this club's going places; we were going to do this; we're going to do that'.

'I needed players that were leaders.'

'I needed players to manage the dressing room, and I'd seen him before – he acknowledged that I wasn't just picking names out of a hat – that I actually wanted him personally. That was the start of a relationship that's continued. He's an outstanding individual, notwithstanding his ability as a football player. So his manner, and his behaviour and his standards, those are the ones that I wanted at the club.'

Hughes had made it quite clear to Vincent how much he wanted to sign him and what sort of role he envisaged him playing at City. The sort of words and ambition that we already know appealed to his character more than money or the chance to cover himself in personal glory. There was a big project going on in Manchester, one that wasn't connected with the City's more illustrious team. And their manager, a man who had played for not only City's biggest rivals but also Barcelona and Bayern Munich, wanted him to be a part of it.

Sold!

Vincent was, naturally, asked about how he felt after he'd put pen to paper at his third club – his words, again, reflecting his hopes for the future in much the same way they had when he'd signed for Hamburg.

'The chance came at the right moment – this is a club with a lot of ambition. I just had a good feeling about this move. They are dynamic people at City, who know a lot about football, you realise you are in a good environment to improve your game.'

His time in Hamburg had come to a sudden but not at all unexpected end. He'd even, much to a lot of people's surprise, lined up for them against Bayern Munich in their opening match of the season, one that might have offered their fans some hope for the future. The game ended in a 2-2 draw with Vincent prevalent throughout, with his place back in the side having been secured after a fall-out with Martin Jol, the club's new coach, had been smoothed over.

Yet, a week later, he was gone, with Mark Hughes again waxing lyrical about his latest acquisition, this time in talking to the *BBC*.

'The thing I like about him is his flexibility to play exceptionally well in a number of positions. That will help the team as the Premier League is a long, hard season, and there will be injuries, unfortunately. We will need players who are adaptable, and Vincent will bring us that quality.'

It seemed the proverbial match made in heaven. A fiendishly ambitious football club, paired with an equally ambitious young footballer who wanted to go the extra mile to not only prove himself in the football world's most talked-about league but also to make up for the disappointments he had experienced with Hamburg.

The success that the move brought both player and club is well-documented, and it would be somewhat trite to list them all verbatim here. What may be of more value is to look back at Vincent's time with Manchester City through the eyes of one of their supporters, in this instance, author and long-time fan Ryan Foley, who, when I asked him to list five personal highlights relating to 'Vinnie' and his eleven years with the Sky Blues had no hesitation in picking the following moments out.

Vincent's goal in Manchester City's crucial 1-0 win over Leicester City on May 6th 2019.

Described at the time by Simon Burnton at *The Guardian* thus; 'Nobody closed him down because, well, he's Vincent Kompany. Big mistake. That was an absolute cracker of a shot! Brilliant!'

How important a goal was it? Important enough to mean that City now 'only' needed to win their last game of the season to be confirmed as Premier League champions. Had, as seemed likely, the match ended goalless, City would have gone into their last fixture a point behind Liverpool and needing Wolves to do them a favour at Anfield, even if they did win their own final game at Brighton.

So yes, in terms of important goals, Vincent's long-range strike against Leicester was about as crucial as they get.

A typical sign of leadership and responsibility shown by their captain.

Talking to *The Guardian* after the match, Vincent admitted, 'I always feel in big moments, I'm going to do something. Today was a little bit of frustration because everyone was saying, "Don't shoot, don't shoot". I could really hear it. And it was annoying me. And I said, "Hold on a second, I've not come this far in my career for young players to tell me whether I can take a shot or not". And I just took it. I've scored goals like that in training. You know what, it's a funny story. It's fifteen years of having midfielders tell me, "Don't shoot! Play the ball wide!". For fifteen years, I've said, "One day, I'm going to have a shot from outside the box, and it's going to go in, and you're going to be happy with that one". And today, it happened'.

His goal and Man of the Match performance in the 2018 League Cup Final win against Arsenal.

City's 3-0 win secured Pep Guardiola's first trophy at the club in a game they dominated throughout, with Guardiola's faith in Vincent being fully justified for that match and throughout the season.

His place in the starting line-up, ahead of £47.5 million signing John Stones, surprised more than a few observers. Still, Guardiola knew just how much of a figurehead and leader Vincent had been in the Manchester City teams that had won Premier League titles under Roberto Mancini and Manuel Pellegrini. Again, his 2017/18 season had been plagued by injury concerns, absences that had seen him play in just 22 of the club's 59 games during the 2015/16 season and only 15 out of their 56 games played in the 2016/17 season.

He'd struggled for much of this campaign as well, appearing in just 13 of Manchester City's 43 games leading up to the match against Arsenal, but demonstrated, as capably as ever, just what an asset he was to the club at Wembley, rendering the presence of Arsenal's Patrick Aubameyang as largely irrelevant throughout, as well as scoring the crucial second goal of the game in the 58th minute.

An indispensable squad member then and for a while to come yet.

His Man of the Match performance in City's win over Liverpool in the 2016 League Cup Final.

Another triumphant return to the Manchester City side for Vincent in a game that was only his third start after recovering from a calf injury that had kept him out of the side for three months prior to that new run in the team. He'd spoken to the *Manchester Evening News* before the game, explaining how much the club still meant to him.

'When I came here, I wanted to learn about the club and its past. And I learned that some people mistake trophies for history.'

'Globally, it is obvious that people only see the Manchester City of the last six or seven years. They mistakenly see us as a new club. Our fans, the people of Manchester, know that our club has an unbelievably rich history.'

'For me, football isn't just about celebrating success. It is about handling disappointments as well – and I don't think there are many clubs out there who have had such a varied past. That's why I love City and why I love being the captain. I don't need other people to tell me what Manchester City means because I feel a part of it.'

His goal on the final day of the 2013/14 season that helped Manchester City win the Premier League title.

A routine 2-0 win over West Ham that confirmed City as the 2013/14 Premier League champions and a second goal that was almost as routine as the result itself, claimed by Vincent when he turned and scored from close range in the 49th minute after a corner had initially rebounded off the back of Edin Dzeko.

During the post-match celebrations, Vincent had ensured that some of the club's fringe players took their place on the podium, determined that both the club and its supporters should acknowledge the role that they had played, on and off the pitch, during the season and the importance of having a squad that was as united as the team on the pitch was.

But with Vincent Kompany as captain and leader, there was little danger that the youngsters and squad members would be anything other than that.

His headed goal against Manchester United in the final weeks of the 2011/12 season.

The game that put City back in control of the Premier League title race as that memorable season approached its unforgettable climax and that never to be forgotten 'Aguerrroooo!' moment, courtesy of *Sky's* Martin Tyler.

Yet, as iconic a moment and match that was, the importance of Vincent's headed goal in first-half stoppage time in the United game should always be seen as a defining moment of that season. It had given Manchester City a win and the three points that put them ahead of their biggest rivals at the top of the Premier League table on goal difference just three weeks after they had trailed Manchester United by eight points, the race seemingly won, done and dusted in favour of Sir Alex Ferguson's team.

Agüero's goal may have won the Premier League for Manchester City. But there is little doubt that it was Vincent Kompany's winner against United a little less than a fortnight earlier that gave them the platform to go on and win the title. For that reason alone, it might be the most important goal scored by a Manchester City player in the club's history.

Yet, as far as quotes go, the one that Vincent gave to *Sky* television after that title-winning match against QPR back in May 2012 might go down as the most memorable that he ever gave when he was at the club. Sought out by a reporter after the match and in the midst of the celebrations, the question asked was, 'Vincent, are you still in a state of shock?'

Manchester City fans will never forget his reply.

'I don't know, erm, you know you want to say it's the best moment of your life but, if I'm honest, please never again this way... *(pause)*... please never again'.

Some things were too much for even Vincent Kompany to bear.

He went on to enjoy further successes whilst he was at Manchester City, winning four Premier League title winners' medals, an additional two in the FA Cup, four more in the League Cup, as well as two in the Community Shield. There were also a plethora of individually earnt honours that were topped off with him being inducted into the Premier League Hall of Fame in 2022, one of only (at the time of writing) ten non-English players to have been awarded the accolade.

Yet, for all of that, success in European competition continued to elude him as a player. If Vincent was ever to win the Champions League, it would have to be as a coach rather than a player.

His first steps into coaching came in 2019 when he left Manchester City to take up the position of player-coach back at Anderlecht, his first club, before, a year later, retiring as a player to become the full-time coach of the club, announcing his ambitions at a news conference.

"If I hadn't been injured, I would have continued playing. I don't want to set the bar lower than winning the title. I'm here to win. I want to fully commit to my role as a coach and need 100% of my time and focus for it. That's why I'm quitting as a football player'.

'Our ambition and our hunger remain the same. I want to stay with the club for at least four seasons and prove that Anderlecht can play a modern style of football with results.'

Typical Vincent. Nothing had changed. But his appointment had been very poorly managed by Anderlecht, who ended up being fined €5,000 for appointing him as a coach without Vincent having gained the required diploma demanded by the Belgian FA, who, via a statement, said, 'The club violated the regulations for a long time and despite that being against the rules, did not hesitate to publicly unveil a new coach without the appropriate diploma having been won.'

The diploma in question was the UEFA Pro licence.

Anderlecht argued against the fine, claiming that the former Manchester City Academy chief, Simon Davies, who'd left Manchester City to join Anderlecht with Vincent, *did* hold the UEFA Pro licence and that *he* was, in reality, the club's head coach. They then turned to evergreen club favourite Frankie Vercauteren, who also held the required diploma, claiming he'd been appointed head coach, with Davies stepping down to work as his assistant.

But the Belgian FA were having none of it, and the fine stood.

In amongst all of that confusion, Vincent didn't enjoy the best of starts to his time as (or not as) coach, with Anderlecht only winning two of their opening ten league games and slipping, at one point, to thirteenth place in the Belgian league.

It hadn't, for myriad reasons, been the fairy tale return to his footballing roots that everyone had expected. And, from that moment on, it seemed only a matter of time before Vincent Kompany moved onto a bigger and more substantial challenge.

The fact that he did just that in May 2022, therefore, came as a surprise to nobody.

But the identity of his next club certainly was.

Never predict the predictable where Vincent Kompany is concerned.

CHAPTER TEN
EXPECT THE
UNEXPECTED

Vincent Kompany has turned doing the unexpected into an art form.

If that skill could be visually depicted, we'd go and see it hanging in The Louvre.

Nobody expected him to stay on at school and pass his examinations. He did.

Nobody expected him to stay for very long at Anderlecht, either, given the high-profile interest that was shown the moment he started to blossom.

But he stayed at the club for three full seasons as a first-team player and would, doubtless, have made many more appearances and even more of an impression if his formative years in the game hadn't been affected by injury.

When he did finally leave Anderlecht, it was to go to Hamburg SV in the German Bundesliga. Nobody saw that coming, either.

He likes to keep people guessing. He likes to avoid the obvious.

When Vincent joined Manchester City in 2008, it was, again, despite interest being shown in him by bigger and far more established elite-level clubs than Manchester City were at that time.

But, as with the reasons he gave for his move to Germany, Kompany cited a club's ambition as the reason he chose them above anyone else. He'd also impressed the club's then assistant manager Mark Bowen, who, in an interview with the *Daily Mirror* some years later, said of Vincent, 'Straight away you could see he was a leader, a fantastic professional. He was a man's man, and although he was a Belgian who'd arrived from Germany, he spoke fluent English. He came across as a level-headed person who would immediately improve the club'.

For Vincent, it was about improving his game and honing the exceptional skills that had been evident since he first kicked a football.

Nothing much, it would seem, has changed since then.

Kompany left Manchester City at the end of the 2018/19 Premier League season when he was 33. It's fair to say that, even then, he could still have had his choice of elite clubs around Europe to join, or perhaps he could have chased the money in the MLS.

Yet he returned to Anderlecht as player-coach, telling Manchester City fans upon his departure that it was 'the most passionate, yet rational decision I've ever made'.

It wasn't an easy time for him. Anderlecht suffered from serious injuries to key players and endured a terrible start to their 2019/20 season — their worst for two decades. It was bad enough to prompt Kompany to step aside from his managerial duties, to focus more on utilising his playing skillset, and to take responsibility on the pitch where he felt he could still be most effective. The mark of a natural leader, you could say.

Kompany remained at the club for three full seasons before, in June 2022, he surprised everyone in the game yet again by being appointed as head coach of English Championship side Burnley, fresh from relegation from the Premier League and with a reputation for playing a style of football that was, at best, described as prosaic.

Why Burnley?

Speaking to *burnleyfootballclub.com*, Kompany gave his reasons.

'I did have other offers. But when I laid out all of the offers on the table, some were perhaps more appealing in terms of name and what they would represent to the wider public, but I had a chance to look in great depth into everything that Burnley is.'

'I looked at what Burnley wanted to achieve, and I'm not saying it's easy, but I saw a path that was different from that in other places. I saw a plan, and I saw good people. I want to work with people that are already at Burnley. I'm allowed to bring good people with me as well, and together, we don't have to change everything. To make a long answer short, I've chosen this project because I know that after a difficult start will come an incredible future.'

Typical Vincent Kompany. To paraphrase what the late President John F. Kennedy had said about landing a man on the moon during his famous 1962 speech, he'd chosen to go to Burnley, not because it would be easy but because it would be hard.

However, it didn't look like it had been particularly difficult when Kompany's Burnley won the English League Championship title by a margin of ten points, having suffered just three defeats in 46 league games and scoring 87 goals in the process.

The Premier League is, of course, a different proposition. And, after a difficult start to life in the top flight, the Clarets eventually won their first match of the 2023/24 season, at the seventh attempt, in October's hard-fought 2-1 victory at Luton Town, who had come up from the Championship with them at the end of the previous campaign.

At one point, it hadn't looked as if Burnley would claim all three points as, after going ahead in first-half stoppage time thanks to a good finish from Lyle Foster, they let Luton back into the game with many of the club's travelling fans fearing their team would be fortunate to head back north with even a point to their name after Elijah Adebayo equalised with five minutes to go.

They'd seen precious points snatched away cruelly once too often at the death; would Luton's renewed belief see them go on and win?

But Burnley were resolute, regaining the lead a minute later when Jacob Bruun Larsen, a Denmark international who'd previously played for Kompany at Anderlecht, scored a winner that meant so much to the club's fans, the players and their coach. Those moments were all too infrequent, however. Vincent was more than happy to talk to *Sky Sports* after the game.

'I'm happy for the group, happy for the fans and already substituting it for preparing for the next game and moving on. We know this team can get results, so it's a nice reward today.'

'Performances have been good. If I have to summarise what we showed today, the first half has some really good bits and some good chances. I thought we showed a lot of quality in phases in the second half, but I don't think we looked after the ball well enough.'

'Many people in the Premier League don't know our team's history in the Championship. We didn't get given anything – we struggled, we had moments where we'd concede a goal late on'.

'We've got to show character and grit. Our fans know we have it, and today, we just showed the Premier League what we're used to, but this game is done now. We have to move on.'

'It's nice to win as a manager. I've had the experience of winning in the Premier League, so I'm alright. I'm just ready to go for the next game. I'm ready to try and bring the first win at Turf Moor as well. That's important for us.'

Sadly, thoughts of that victory becoming a turning point would be premature. Six consecutive Premier League defeats followed, 16 more goals were conceded, with only four scored, one of which was a penalty in a 2-1 defeat to West Ham at Turf Moor, with the Hammers' winner coming deep into stoppage time.

After the game, Kompany looked a little downhearted when talking to a reporter from the BBC's *Match Of The Day* programme, but he opted to sound both positive and realistic.

'There's nothing more cruel than a game like today. I'd be a hypocrite if I started laying into my players, who were outstanding for 86 minutes, but they're facing the margins of this league, the importance of every detail. That's painful for us, but if anyone knows anything about me... I feel like going again'.

He wouldn't give up, but it was often a hard watch for their fans.

After the Luton game, Burnley only enjoyed four more victories that season, the highlight of which was a 5-0 win at Sheffield United. The result seemed to vindicate Kompany and how he wanted to lead and coach his team, yet the safety zone remained out of reach. After that game, Vincent told *The Guardian* newspaper, 'I feel really happy. The main thing I care about is that we keep playing without fear and focus on improving. Hopefully, we can keep the momentum building and take things to the end'.

When the end did come, a 2-1 defeat at Tottenham Hotspur on May 11th 2024 confirmed Burnley's relegation, Kompany was typically philosophical post-match as he talked to the BBC's Jonathan Pearce about the ever-widening gap between the Championship and Premier League in England – one that, regardless of the achievements of the previous season, his team had found impossible to bridge.

'In my mind, Burnley will be in the Premier League again. The Championship is tough, but it's an exciting league, and you must keep trying until you bridge that gap. And we have ideas about how to do it.'

He was, it seemed, already making preparations for another arduous season of Championship football as the head coach at Turf Moor, with the club's hierarchy continuing to stand fully behind Kompany, where they had remained even during the season's most trying moments.

As he talked to Pearce, there can be little doubt that working hard to return Burnley to the Premier League was at the forefront of his mind at that moment, and nobody at the club had reason to think differently. But as he'd also said, you can never take anything for granted in football.

I asked Burnley fan and the author of many excellent books on the club, Dave Thomas, for his thoughts on Vincent's arrival and time as the Clarets' head coach.

'When Vincent Kompany became manager of Burnley in the summer of 2022, he joined a club that had just been relegated, where morale and spirits were at a low ebb. He inherited an ageing squad, players were jaded, with a style of football that, although it had brought success under Sean Dyche, had become stilted and tired. Dyche had worked miracles at this small club and had even taken us into Europe, but most people agreed it was time for change and new ideas.'

'Nor was there a great deal of money, so players were sold, and other key players on high wages were allowed to leave as their contracts had expired. In short, this was a low-ebb club with diverse problems.'

'In stepped Vincent Kompany and transformed the place'.

'Supporters already knew of him as a player who had visited Turf Moor several times, almost always on the winning side, but few knew anything about him as a manager, although he had gained some success in Belgium. By and large, Burnley supporters are a hard lot to please, but chairman Alan Pace saw in Kompany someone with leadership qualities and beliefs that could take the club forward'.

'To say "take the club forward" is, in fact, an understatement. He took us on a journey that was quite simply sensational. Players left, and new players arrived with almost bewildering rapidity. The players that arrived came from Europe or on loan from the UK, some of whom he already knew. To us Burnley fans, they were unknowns, but they gelled with members of the old guard that had remained'.

'The first game, a 1-0 win at Huddersfield, was televised. The transformation in style of play had us open-mouthed. We had not seen this passing game for many years, perhaps not since the Jimmy Adamson team of 1972/73, fifty years earlier. The next few results were mixed, with several draws when goals were conceded in the dying minutes, but slowly and surely, the defects were ironed out so that it became a promotion season to remember'.

'The word astonishing can be overused, but no better word describes what was taking place'.

'His accomplishment is well documented in my book of the season, *Burnley – Champions Again!* For me, certain games stood out. A 2-1 win at home against a rugged West Bromwich Albion side after being 1-0 down, a stunning 3-0 win against the old enemy Blackburn Rovers and a marvellous away win at Middlesbrough that clinched promotion. The thunderclap at the end will live in our memories for a long time. Kompany stood back and gently smiled. And then, the icing on the cake, clinching the title away at Blackburn Rovers with a stunning Benson goal. You could not write a better script'.

'Imagine taking on a new house that is old and shabby and needing renovation and transforming it to how you want using vibrant colours and materials at minimal cost. This is what Vincent Kompany did with a football club. It was a season to remember, one that sparkled and entertained and had the pundits purring at the style and elegance, the possession, the pace, intricacy, marvellous goals and only three defeats'.

'Nobody expected the same kind of success as the promotion season; that would be fantasy. Supporters were realistic. Results from the early part of the 2023/24 season saw just four points gained from a possible 24, with Kompany clearly needing to find ways of competing better in the Premier League. But there was a mini-league at the bottom in which Burnley should have won more points'.

'Initially, relegation didn't seem an obvious conclusion; however, by the end of October, it was clear there were serious failings, including the absence of Nathan

Tella, a proven goalscorer when on loan during the promotion season. Burnley would not meet the reported £20 million price tag and the Nigerian winger signed for Bayer Leverkusen instead. Despite missing out on Tella, it was a summer of spending, with £100 million paid out on what many fans considered average players. Only Sander Berge looked the part, and our strikers were ineffective. With so many inadequate players signed, relegation was a clear possibility by Christmas. It was a business model based on signing and developing young players who'd later be sold on for profit.'

'However, Kompany's own inexperience in managing at this level was also critical. Naïve is a word that has been used many times. A failure to adjust formations or adopt a more defensive style. Playing James Trafford in goal for so long was almost inept management in some fans' eyes. Despite everything, even as March arrived, relegation was still not nailed on, largely because of the points deductions incurred by Nottingham Forest and Everton as punishment for breaking Premier League financial sustainability rules. But just six wins all season is a damming statistic.'

'Kompany said several times during the season that, even if we lost game after game, he would not change. Critics have lambasted him for this. Obviously, these complaints were aired during our promotion season because we won almost every game. They only became an issue last season. Was it because he was limited and had no plan B? We will never know. It was Plan A every time. I felt it was an easy cop-out to justify all the defeats and a way of preserving dignity and principles. If he had changed his philosophy but continued to lose, he would have perhaps shown the full range of his limitations. By insisting on not changing meant, in his own mind at least, he could hold his head high even after a disastrous season.'

'But nobody imagined he would walk away. There was a 'five-year plan project' that the owner, Alan Pace, bought into with a business model built around developing young players and profiting from their sales. Sacking Kompany would have been a no-no anyway, with the huge compensation payable for his five-year contract, plus those of all his staff.'

'None of us begrudge his move to Bayern Munich, but failing to deliver on the 'five-year plan' and 'project' leaves an aftertaste, and I understand that many people at the club feel betrayed. In the coming season, perhaps he would have been sacked by Christmas with more poor results, but again, we shall never know. As it is, the club has dodged a bullet and gained millions in compensation. Chairman Pace, we can presume, was initially shell-shocked, and maybe he, too, has been naïve. But he has come out of it well.

Vincent had always respected the fans and the club's history, although one sad aspect was the cessation of the annual supporters' group presentation awards to players, which previous managers always attended and were seen as key annual events. Fans' groups were left disappointed and angered by this; although he attended a glitzy club-led fundraiser event in Manchester with the players, leaving many rank-and-file fans feeling excluded.'

'Kompany certainly leaves a legacy, both positively and negatively. There is a lasting memory of the wonderful promotion season with dazzling football from a team seen as one of the best Championship sides ever. He transformed a dispirited and weary club. He changed the culture and style. Brought glamour even. Raised morale. Brought real joy to the club. Fans truly bought into Vincent and revelled in the wins. But then there is a huge body of fans who will always say he blew it all. Didn't extend key loans. Failed to sign Tella. Spent over £100 million on players who were mostly not up to the job. He produced a new side that was ill-equipped to cope with Premier League football. Now the club is left with a bloated playing staff and players returning from loans that he signed but decided he did not need. The new Burnley manager has a mammoth task sorting things out.'

'At first, the news of the Bayern offer caused a wide-eyed reaction following such an embarrassing season. As the rumours became ever more serious, there was disbelief that such a prestigious club would approach a manager who had just overseen relegation. Some fans were shocked. Once his leaving was confirmed, it seemed almost hilarious, such was the improbability scale. How could failure be rewarded with such a job offer? No one begrudged him the move. Nobody in any walk of life would refuse such an offer. How could anyone turn Bayern down? Finally, when the deal was done, there was a feeling of relief. Now, the club can move on. Of course, we will wish him good luck, but with the caveats I've explained.'

'Of course, Kompany will play a key part in Burnley's history, but my abiding feeling is, '…was he really here?''

Natalie Bromley, editor of the Burnley fans' independent podcast *No Nay Never*, is equally honest in her thoughts about the rise and fall of Vincent Kompany's reign at Turf Moor. Her words underpin what most of the club's fans feel at the loss of such a high-profile head coach and offer a genuine, measured appraisal of a contrasting era.

'As soon as the news broke that he was in the frame, I was excited as it felt completely different to anything else we'd seen from a manager, Kompany would deliver the image change I was looking for at the club. I was a little worried at his lack of experience in the Championship, but clearly that wasn't an issue.'

'I thought relegation under Sean Dyche would have ruined our chances of landing Kompany; that he'd only come to us if we were a Premier League side. As it turned out, the opposite was true, and he relished the challenge.'

When Kompany arrived, he struck me as both humble and ambitious. In the media, he admitted that he wasn't yet a proven manager and clever about managing expectations while pushing his ambition for the club. He felt like he understood us and wanted to grow with us. His understanding of the local area and the way of life in the North West was really clear.'

'That didn't change in the Championship either, and we developed a good connection with him during the title-winning season. By the time we won the title at Ewood Park, it felt like we had a real bond.'

'Kompany also brought diversity to a town with many challenges, such as overcoming prejudice. He was our first foreign manager. Our first manager of colour. With a team of multicultural, multi-faith players from all across Europe and the World. That was an important step for Burnley and its community.'

'But something changed in the Premier League season. Reinventing the team so much during the summer felt inconsistent with the strong dressing spirit he had portrayed to the outside world. Without explanation, fan favourites had been alienated from the side, and a new class of players were introduced. Then the poor results started.'

'The perception, which is caveated with the acknowledgement that we are not privy to what goes on behind the scenes, was that he was growing distant from us. The connection to supporters and some of his players seemed to have gone. In games, you'd see him slumped in his seat in the dugout and not managing from the sideline.'

'Is that inevitable when you have an ambitious winner as your manager? Yes, I think so. But we needed him to be our leader during those tough times. I didn't feel that from him.'

'I was realistic about our survival chances and never believed the hype some bestowed on us. We were never going to finish in the top half, but I genuinely believed that we would do better than we did. The bad of last season equalled the great of the season before. We made so many mistakes right from day one and didn't appear to be learning from them either. Perhaps we underestimated the gulf in class between the Championship and the Premier League. However, Burnley were nowhere near as competitive as Kompany told us he wanted us to be.'

'Football today is style over substance. Owners and chairman look for the manager's style of play, not always what they've achieved. I think it is important to remember that Kompany was not Bayern's first choice, or even second or third, but he's done well to be on that radar nonetheless. He wants to play a style of football that gets coverage. He's also a manager who speaks five different languages fluently. That's a very powerful skill to have if you want to manage a European side with multi-national players.'

'But despite the sour end to his reign, that season in the Championship will forever stay with me. Thanks for Ewood, Vincent.'

Vincent Kompany's presence at Burnley was undoubtedly pivotal in persuading former NFL star JJ Watt to invest in the Clarets in 2023. During an insightful interview on the *Stick To Football* podcast, Watt outlined the main reasons he took a stake in the East Lancashire club – telling Gary Neville, Jamie Carragher, Roy Keane, Ian Wright and Jill Scott that; 'I knew that I wanted to get involved with ownership after my career, so I started to look for opportunities, both in America and in the UK. I love football, I really do. I've watched the Premier League since 2010/11, looked at a few clubs, and somebody said you should talk to Burnley. I went up and visited, met with everybody, with Vincent, saw the town and it just felt right.'

Despite the Premier League campaign proving to be a struggle from start to finish, Watt and the Burnley board were clearly in no mood to recruit an alternative head coach, as is so often the case at other football clubs desperate to survive at any cost in the richest league in the world.

'Vincent Kompany is a great leader', Watt stated. 'I think the way he commands the respect of the players is because of his knowledge. Also, he's a brilliant man; he speaks six or seven languages, so to watch him coming out to practice and he's speaking to [David] Fofana in one language, and he's speaking to [Lorenz] Assignon in another language – he's just seamlessly moving between these guys, and it's incredible. And then he also keeps level-headed. All season long, even when things haven't been going how we have wanted them to, just the mindset and the ability to keep the players moving – it's been enjoyable!'

Solid backing from a major investor, then. Plus, a colourful homage from Burnley Chairman Alan Pace, a man who you suspected would never have even considered firing Kompany after their less than auspicious Premier League campaign, once you read what he memorably said about his soon-to-be ex-manager.

'My worry is, as I've tried to explain, it's like dating the most beautiful girl in town and knowing there's probably no chance she'll ever marry you,' was how Pace summed up what always looked like a dreadfully imbalanced relationship between a football club and it's manager. 'But, everybody else wants to marry her. So it's like, how long can you date, how long can you stay together, how long can you stay a couple? I hope it's for a very, very, very long time. But it's up to 'her'.'

And continuing that metaphor, Pace seemingly knew deep down that one day he'd be left sobbing at the alter as his bride ran off into the sunset with a richer, more attractive partner.

But he couldn't have suspected 'the split' would have happened so quickly after the end of the season. Kompany had said, 'We stick together, and we will have the good times again' after Burnley's relegation. Yet, despite the season ending in failure, covetous glances were again directed Vincent's way.

And from a most unexpected source.

CHAPTER ELEVEN
BAYERN MUNICH
AND THE KING
OF THE DRIBBLES

While coaching at Anderlecht, Kompany gave the then sixteen-year-old Jérémy Doku his league debut.

Amongst Doku's nicknames at the time were 'The King of the Dribbles' and, interestingly, 'The Arrogant One'.

'Arrogant'? At sixteen. When might Vincent Kompany have heard that accusation before?

According to an article written by Paul Hirst in *The Times*, Doku occasionally annoyed Kompany by failing to track back during matches.

That didn't stop Kompany from taking Doku under his protective wing, with the young winger praising his mentor's influence.

'He was everything to me – a coach, a friend. It was fun and strange at the same time to play with him. He was a legend at Manchester City and gave me my start at Anderlecht. Sometimes we would argue about stupid things, but that happens'.

It does indeed. As the sixteen-year-old Vincent Kompany would be among the first to agree.

Given Doku's move to Manchester City and the rumours that Pep Guardiola may possibly be leaving the club when his contract expires in 2025, maybe Vincent Kompany will end up being Doku's manager again one day?

That is a big assumption, but it is a gaze into the crystal ball that many observers have predicted. This is Vincent Kompany we're talking about, remember?

He never does what people expect him to do and seems to lead a charmed life at times.

This was again underlined in the Spring of 2024 when Vincent abruptly bid farewell to Burnley to accept another irresistible offer from the Bundesliga.

Nobody had expected Kompany to move to Germany when he left Anderlecht in 2006, not when La Liga, Serie A, the Premier League, and Ligue One were all calling. But this wasn't history repeating itself, this news was off the Richter scale in comparison.

Bayern Munich, one of European football's most famous and respected clubs, wanted him as their next head coach, much to the surprise of journalists and pundits alike, with social media going into meltdown as the negotiations progressed towards their conclusion and financial compensation was finally agreed with Burnley.

Kompany was confirmed as the mighty Bavarian club's new head coach on May 29th 2024, and, true to form, wearing a crisp white t-shirt, he said all the right things about his new role and club.

'My mentality is that I never haven't ever worked for a top club in my head. A top club is the environment you create. It's the mentality you have towards your job in good and bad times, that's what defines working at the top level'.

'It already feels like home'.

As usual, a masterful use of positive superlatives and humble ambition from the new man at the Allianz Arena.

But you couldn't help but wonder how those words might have gone down with Burnley fans, who had to make do with an extremely brief farewell video message, which the club's website ran more than a week after the departure had been rubber-stamped. The following message lasted less than a minute.

'It starts with a message of thanks, of course.'

'I was very lucky. I was surrounded by hard-working people and players who gave everything; I think that I felt privileged and honoured to be welcomed and to be able to be part of such a good environment. So, for that, thank you.'

'The best way for me to describe how I lived it is that I gave everything back.'

'The best memory I have is beating Blackburn at home three nil and going on to beat them at their home and winning the league there.'

'It's been a very, very important part of my life.'

The Burnley door had now been firmly shut.

Speaking at the press conference that confirmed his Bayern appointment, Kompany clarified his priorities at his new club.

Winning. And being successful. At levels he knows he would never have reached with Burnley.

'I'm actually excited to start pre-season with them (the players). I make no distinction; I want to see which players are most hungry to represent this club next season, win again, and be successful.

'I'm excited to work with every player, but also, I'm excited to find out how hungry a player is. We're in a situation now where last year we lost (the Bundesliga title after winning it for the previous eleven seasons) and, from having been in this position as a player myself, I know this is when you react, you see real winners come to light'.

He'll need to hit the ground running.

The absolute bare minimum that Bayern Munich fans will expect in the 2024/25 season is for the club to regain the Bundesliga title.

They might also expect him to take them a step further in the Champions League.

That would mean leading his team to the final, which is due to be played on May 31st 2025, almost a year to the day after he joined the club.

At the Allianz Arena.

Is it time to start expecting the unexpected again?

Remember, this is Vincent Kompany we're talking about!

ACKNOWLEDGEMENTS

I sincerely thank everyone who agreed to be interviewed for this book, which gives a real insight into Vincent Kompany's personality. Also, to Leo de Haes for his excellent work on the final edit of the original language version of the book. Many thanks go to Edward Couzens-Lake for writing the excellent additional material and for the intelligent editing work needed by Edward, David Lane and Lewis Coghlin to refine the text for the English-language version of the book.

Frank Van de Winkel

SOURCES

Newspapers: *Bild, The Guardian, De Morgen, Hamburger Morgenpost, Het Laatste Nieuws, Het Nieuwsblad, Le Soir, De Standaard, De Tijd.*

Magazines: *Humo, Knack, Sport-Voetbalmagazine, Story.*

Radio and television: *Congo WWS, Radio 1, VTM, RTL-TVi.*

BIBLIOGRAPHY

Buelens, Frans. *Congo 1885-1960. Een financieel-economische geschiedenis.* EPO, 2007.

Etambala, Zana Eziza. *Congo 55-65: Van koning Boudewijn tot president Mobutu.* Lannoo, 1999.

Etambala, Zana Eziza. *De teloorgang van een modelkolonie: Belgisch-Congo 1958-1960.* Acco, 2008.

Ndaywel è Nziem, Isidore. *Histoire générale du Congo. De l'héritage ancien à la République Démocratique.* De Boeck & Larcier, 1998.

Nzongola-Ntalaja, Georges. *The Congo. From Leopold to Kabila. A People's History.* Zed Books, third edition, 2007.

Rorison, Sean. *Congo: Democratic Republic. The Bradt Travel Guides,* 2012.

Van Reybrouck, David. *Congo: een geschiedenis.* De Bezige Bij, 2010.

Willems, Raf. *Sympathy for the devils: De Belgen in de Premier League.* Lannoo, 2013.

Websites: www.gopress.be, www.rsca.be, www.rbfa.be, www.fifa.com, www.sos-kinderdorpen.be; www.wikipedia.org, www.youtube.com, www.hsv.de, www.nike.com, www.paluche.org, www.mcfc.co.uk/, www.transfermarkt.co.uk, www.bxbrussels.com, www.resc.be

GET UP, STAND UP.
STAND UP FOR YOUR RIGHT.
GET UP, STAND UP.
DON'T GIVE UP THE FIGHT.